New International
A MAGAZINE OF MARXIST POLITICS AND THEORY

NUMBER 3 SPRING–SUMMER 1984

Contents

In this issue *3*

Communism and the fight for a popular revolutionary government: 1848 to today
by Mary-Alice Waters *25*

National liberation and socialism in the Americas
by Manuel Piñeiro *169*

'A nose for power': Preparing the Nicaraguan revolution
by Tomás Borge *217*

Index *253*

EDITORIAL BOARD: Steve Clark, Malik Miah, Joan Newbigging, Steve Penner, José G. Pérez, John Riddell, Larry Seigle, John Steele, Mary-Alice Waters

Many of the articles that appear here in English are also available in French, Spanish, and Swedish. All four publications are available from Pathfinder Press, at www.pathfinderpress.com.

Copyright © 1984 by New International

All rights reserved
ISSN 0737-3724
ISBN 978-0-87348-638-5
Manufactured in Canada
Sixth printing, 2022

IN THIS ISSUE

"In the daily events of the class struggle, one must tenaciously forge the conditions that will help to advance along the road to the conquest of power."

—**Manuel Piñeiro**
April 1982, Havana

"From the beginning, we always had a nose for power, and we went on developing that instinct and transmitting it to our cadres even when we recruited them through struggles around immediate demands."

—**Tomás Borge**
May 1983, Managua

"Those who believe that they are going to win against the imperialists in elections are just plain naive, and those who believe that the day will come when they will take over through elections are even more naive."

—**Fidel Castro**
August 1967, Havana

"Only the workers and peasants will go all the way."

—**Augusto César Sandino**

THIS ISSUE OF *New International* concentrates on what has been the fundamental focus of proletarian strategy and the development of the Marxist program since the founding of the modern communist movement nearly a century and a half ago: the fight by the working class to lead a popular revolution to overthrow the state that defends the exploiters, and to replace it with a state that defends and advances the interests of the toilers. In the last twenty-five years the struggles of the workers and peasants to accomplish this goal have resulted in giant strides in the Americas, with the Cuban, the Nicaraguan, and—until its overthrow in October 1983—the Grenadian revolutions.

These revolutions in Central America and the Caribbean share decisive elements with the October 1917 Russian revolution, the first revolution in the imperialist epoch in which the modern revolutionary classes seized and held state power. All those throughout the world who are part of the movement to defend—and extend—the historic conquests of workers and farmers governments, beginning with the Bolshevik revolution, are trying to learn the lessons of the Central American and Caribbean victories.

In this issue Manuel Piñeiro, a member of the Central Committee of the Communist Party of Cuba, discusses the experiences of revolutionary struggles in Latin America and the Caribbean in the twenty-five years since the victory of the Cuban revolution. His article is a translation of a presentation to an April 1982 conference held in Havana on "The General and Specific Traits of the Revolutionary Processes in Latin America and the Caribbean." The meeting was sponsored jointly by the Communist Party of Cuba and the journal *World Marxist Review: Problems of Peace and Socialism,* published in Prague. It was attended by representatives from thirty-one parties and national liberation movements, mostly from the Americas.[1]

ENDNOTES BEGIN ON PAGE 20

The article by Tomás Borge deals with many of the questions analyzed by Piñeiro, but from the standpoint of the experiences of the Sandinista National Liberation Front (FSLN) in Nicaragua. Borge is a member of the National Directorate of the FSLN and is Nicaragua's minister of the interior. His article is a translation of a talk given to a group of FSLN cadres in Managua in May 1983, at the Second National Seminar of Political Education.

The article by Mary-Alice Waters, national co-chairperson of the Socialist Workers Party of the United States, deals with the same strategic questions, but from a different standpoint. Waters takes up the programmatic continuity between the course and conquests of the Central American and Caribbean revolutions, and the key strategic conclusions about the proletarian-led fight for a workers and farmers republic codified by Marx, Engels, and the Bolshevik leadership. The article also discusses the extension of these conclusions into a worldwide perspective by the Communist International.

THE REVOLUTIONARY EXPERIENCES of the twenty-five years since the triumph of the Cuban revolution, says Piñeiro, "represent today's best school for the revolutionary movement of Our America." It is a period rich in the lessons of revolutionary opportunities, of victories as well as missed chances and disastrous defeats.

For its first quarter-century revolutionary Cuba stood alone, the first country in the Americas with a government to emerge from a successful anticapitalist revolution. Class-collaborationist opponents of revolutionary struggle insisted that the Cuban revolution was an exception, that its victory had been the result of mistakes by the U.S. government and by the imperialist-backed Batista dictatorship that would not be repeated. This line of argument appeared to be strengthened by the defeats suffered by various guerrilla fronts in the 1960s, as many attempted to schematically repeat what they thought—erroneously—to have been the course of the Cuban revolutionaries in the fight to overthrow Batista.

The lives of thousands of courageous and self-sacrificing militants were lost. The reformists argued that these defeats showed that state power cannot be conquered through armed struggle. Instead, they promoted the strategy of electoralism. Political power, they said, can be wrested from the rulers through elections. This strategic orientation left the Chilean revolution defenseless in face of the counterrevolutionary coup by the bourgeois army, encouraged and backed by U.S. imperialism, and led to the imposition of the blood-soaked Pinochet dictatorship.

In March 1979, there occurred the victory in Grenada of the New Jewel Movement, led by Maurice Bishop, bringing to power a workers and farmers government. Then, in July, the FSLN led the Nicaraguan masses in an insurrection that crushed the Somozaist tyranny, installing in its place the revolutionary workers and peasants regime against which Washington is today waging war. "Nicaragua and Grenada, with their victorious revolutions," says Piñeiro, "have reaffirmed the validity of the road to power opened by Cuba. . . ."

WHAT ARE THE LESSONS to be learned from the "road to power" opened by Cuba and followed by the Grenadian and Nicaraguan revolutionists? Piñeiro spotlights a number of them.

First, "the central problem of the revolution is the seizure of power." This involves "the destruction of the bourgeois state apparatus and its replacement by a revolutionary state based on the hegemony of the proletariat in close alliance with other popular classes and sectors." There can be "no substitute for this historic break," the Cuban leader emphasizes. Moreover, this goal can not be separated from the daily struggles of the toiling people by an artificial wall built between immediate demands and the strategic goal. In the "daily events of the class struggle," Piñeiro says, "one must tenaciously forge the conditions that will help to advance along the road to the conquest of power."

Second, there is an inseparable connection between the resolution of the anti-imperialist, democratic tasks facing the workers and farmers governments that genuine revolutions will bring to power, and the proletarian socialist tasks they will face. The revolution in Latin America and the Caribbean is, in Piñeiro's words, "an original combination of democratic and popular tasks on the one hand, and economic, political, and social demands on the other—all of which contribute to the historic socialist course of the revolution. It is a combination of anti-imperialist, national liberation tasks, alongside the consolidation of power by workers, peasants, and other toiling layers against latifundist and capitalist exploitation."

Third, Piñeiro outlines the strategic course of the proletariat in the revolution in relation to class alliances. "In Our America the proletariat—the main historical agent of the new society—is the most important social force." Essential to the victorious mobilizations of the masses in the fight for power is the alliance between the working class and the other exploited producing classes, first and foremost the poor peasants.

Fourth, given the necessary combination of democratic, anti-imperialist, and socialist tasks, "the proletarian revolution in Latin America and the Caribbean is at the same time eminently a people's revolution. To take power and keep it, the working class needs to weave close political, ideological, and military ties with the rest of the masses."

Fifth, the broadest possible anti-imperialist united front is indispensable in advancing the fight for political power—involving not only professionals, civil servants, and other components of the "middle layers," but even sectors of the capitalist class if and when they take action to fight against a tyranny in an effort to advance their own interests. Such an alliance can lead to triumph, however, only "on the condition that the revolutionary parties and organizations succeed in previously consolidating the leadership nucleus in such fronts."

Sixth, the working class must develop its own vanguard organization, its revolutionary party, capable of clearly projecting the road forward to the state power it seeks to conquer, while leading the day-to-day struggle of the toilers in a direction that can advance toward that objective.

The 1982 Havana conference brought to the revolutionary capital delegates from organizations with differing opinions of these fundamental issues, on which Piñeiro presented the stand of the Communist Party of Cuba.

The Cubans set an example of how to participate in the debates that go on among revolutionaries and those claiming to be revolutionary. They rely on the weight of their arguments and the class-struggle experiences of the vanguard to advance a revolutionary working-class line. They scrupulously avoid substituting organizational muscle for this process. They do what they can to involve in the discussion all those who proclaim their allegiance to Marxism, even those who strongly disagree with the course being followed by the Cuban CP and others who share its outlook.

The Havana conference Piñeiro addressed included representatives of Communist parties in the Americas that follow the reformist course that became dominant in the CPs of Latin America in the years following the Seventh Congress of the Comintern in 1935. Also represented were national liberation groups of varying ideologies and strengths, including some engaged in guerrilla warfare, as well as the FSLN of Nicaragua, which led the toilers to power, and the Farabundo Martí National Liberation Front (FMLN) of El Salvador, which is advancing toward that goal. Gathering these forces together for a discussion of this kind was a significant accomplishment.

FIFTEEN YEARS EARLIER, another conference was organized in Havana, which also provided a forum for discussion and debate. That occasion, in the summer of 1967, was the conference of the Organization of Latin American Solidarity—OLAS. (The English- and French-speaking Caribbean was not yet incorporated into the regional framework.) The contrasts and similarities between the two conferences show the continuity of the revolutionary proletarian line of the Cuban leadership, as well as the growth since the OLAS conference of the revolutionary wing within the Latin American and Caribbean left as a result of the victories in Grenada and Nicaragua, and the emergence of the FMLN in El Salvador.

The OLAS conference was held during a period of widespread rural guerrilla struggles in Latin America, many waged by fighters inspired by the Cuban victory and seeking to repeat it in new countries. Most of these efforts, however, suffered defeats because of their isolation from the peasants and workers. In some cases they suffered from political adaptations to bourgeois nationalist forces or reformist formations, in others from ultraleft schemas, such as calling on the peasants to fight for socialist revolution, downplaying or ignoring democratic, anti-imperialist demands.

By the time of the OLAS conference, a series of devastating defeats suffered by the guerrillaist groups had already been registered. As a result these movements were on the decline. Less than three months after the conference, the capture and assassination of Che Guevara in Bolivia, where he had gone to lead a guerrilla struggle, brought home this reality to revolutionaries throughout the world.

The leaderships of several Communist parties in Latin America opposed and even sabotaged the guerrilla fronts. Taking advantage of the guerrillas' isolation from the mass movement, they began to openly repudiate armed struggle, arguing instead that the "peaceful road"—by which they meant a legalistic and electoralist strategy—was the only way forward. With the defeats suffered by the guerrilla fighters, these attacks became more public.

Some Communist parties went so far as to launch public attacks on the Cuban leadership because of the solidarity, aid, and political backing Cuba had extended to the guerrilla fighters in several countries. The imperialist press gave big play to these factional attacks, hoping to politically isolate Cuba. The anti-Cuba campaign reached its height with public charges leveled by the leadership of the Venezuelan Communist Party, which had betrayed the guerrilla movement in that country. The Venezuelan CP announced that it was giving up armed struggle and would campaign instead for a "democratic peace," by supporting a candidate of "national unification" in the upcoming presidential elections. ("Giving up armed struggle," said the CP, "will open up channels for reincorporating all our cadres in legal activities with a single basic objective: the participation of the Communist Party in the next presidential election.")[2] The Venezuelan CP leaders even accused the guerrilla fighters there of being Cuban agents, and accused the Cubans of intervening in the internal affairs not only of the CP but of Venezuela itself! The public slanders against the Cubans leading up to the OLAS conference left them with no alternative but to respond in public, which they did, including at the conference itself.

AT OLAS, THE CUBANS SOUGHT to draw some initial lessons from the defeats that the guerrilla fronts had suffered. But these efforts were secondary to the political battles to defend a revolutionary perspective against the attempts being made to justify rejection of armed struggle in favor of an electoral strategy. The Cubans argued that the rejection of armed struggle as a necessary component of the struggle of the toilers to take power into their own hands amounted to a rejection of revolution in favor of class collaboration.

A movement built on a strategy of *electoralism* can only be an obstacle to the mobilization of working people toward taking political power. A would-be vanguard whose activities revolve around electoral considerations will mislead struggles even for the most immediate and limited goals of working people. Its cadres will be miseducated in the practice of accommodation to the ruling-class definition of politics as consisting of elections and the construction of vote-catching machines. Such a party can often make big strides in size and political influence in certain periods, but it will never be able to switch gears when the objective conditions change. A party that over time drifts into an electoralist strategy, despite the stated adherence to long-term revolutionary goals by its leaders, will never lead a struggle for power.

Breaking the hold of electoralist illusions promoted by the ruling class and reformist currents within the working-class movement is an essential task of the revolutionary vanguard. Tomás Borge describes how this was accomplished in Nicaragua.

The bourgeois opposition to Somoza insisted on confining the struggle against the dictatorship to electoral campaigns and civic protests. In January 1967, when the bourgeois opposition forces concluded that Somoza's control of the ballot box meant they could never win an election, they called on the people to demonstrate against the tyranny. On January 22, 1967, some 60,000 people turned out in Managua, some of them armed. The capitalist politicians had spread the rumor that they would hand out arms to the demonstrators to overthrow Somoza. But they didn't, and Somoza's National Guard massacred hundreds of the protesters.

As Borge puts it, "That opened the final chapter in the bourgeoisie's hegemony as the social sector guiding the anti-Somozaist struggle in our country. Along with the peasants who died that day, the possibility that the Nicaraguan bourgeoisie would lead the anti-Somozaist struggle was also buried."

But the actions of the FSLN showed the toilers that there was another leadership, and another strategy.

"The armed struggle was reaffirmed," Borge explains, "while the impossibility of overthrowing the military dictatorship through peaceful methods was demonstrated. When I say this, I mean that the Nicaraguan people became conscious that only armed struggle was capable of defeating the Somozaist dictatorship. This involved a total discrediting of the so-called civic methods of struggle."

This point should be kept in mind not only by revolutionaries in Latin America and the Caribbean, but also—and especially—by those in the imperialist democracies. It is in these countries that working people suffer the deepest illusions that the exploited and oppressed can advance their struggles within the political framework established by the ruling class.

Nowhere is there greater pressure to succumb to "parliamentary cretinism" than in the United States, the mightiest and richest imperialist country. The overwhelming majority of those who consider themselves socialists and communists in the United States have long since given up the conviction that the strategic goal of the conquest of state power by the workers and farmers is both possible and necessary. Although for some the goal remains on paper, it has become so distant in their minds, and so remote from "politics" of the day, that it no longer has any connection to their political perspective. They can see no way in practice to bridge the gap between now and then. They have, as a result, turned their backs on the fight for working-class political action that is *independent* of the capitalist political framework and the capitalist vote-catching alliances themselves.

Tactics of reforming the Democratic Party, one of the twin parties of U.S. imperialism, and of electing the Democrats in order to "defeat Reagan at all costs" have swept virtually the entire socialist and communist left in

1984. They either can not or will not recognize that this course will not only fail to stop "Reaganism" and the bipartisan drive toward war and austerity, but will guarantee much worse ruling-class attacks on working people and the oppressed in the future.

A striking exception is the Socialist Workers Party of the United States, which is taking advantage of the presidential campaign to present a class-struggle strategy, and whose candidates—Mel Mason for president and Andrea González for vice-president—are explaining the program of revolutionary Marxism to those who are looking for ways to fight back against the ruling-class offensive at home and abroad.

Thus, North American working people have much to learn from the revolutionary alternative to electoralism presented at the 1967 OLAS conference by Fidel Castro. Speaking specifically of Latin America, he explained:

"The first thing that a revolutionary has to understand is that the ruling classes have organized the State so as to dedicate every possible means to maintaining themselves in power. And they use not only arms, not only physical instruments, not only guns, but all possible instruments to influence, to deceive, to confuse.

"And those who believe that they are going to win against the imperialists in elections are just plain naive, and those who believe that the day will come when they will take over through elections are even more naive. It is necessary to have lived in a revolutionary process and to know just what the repressive apparatus is by which the ruling classes maintain the status quo, just how much one has to struggle, how difficult it is.

"This does not imply the negation of forms of struggle," he added. "When someone writes a manifesto in a newspaper, attends a demonstration, holds a rally or propagates an idea, he may be using so-called famous legal and illegal means; methods should be classified as revolutionary or non-revolutionary."

In a speech presented fifteen years later, Piñeiro too warns against allowing democratic illusions to disorient vanguard fighters into thinking that the fight for power can be resolved by peaceful methods. Even in those countries where "democratic norms of life predominate and the vanguards have constitutional channels adequate for carrying out their activity, the role of arms will be shaped not by their inopportune use but rather by psychological preparation and the creation of the consciousness in all militants that—at some point, in some form—military confrontation will be indispensable, even though it would not be valid under existing circumstances."

He goes on then to refer to previous debates over armed struggle in Latin America, in which "false dichotomies have been put forward that counterpose armed and nonarmed forms of struggle." And he stresses that "a struggle is not reformist simply because it is legal or because it seeks to open a democratic space; nor can a struggle be called revolutionary simply because it has an armed character. In our opinion, the revolutionary content of any form of struggle is measured by its results, that is, by the advance or retreat it implies for the final objective of the popular masses." That final objective is the conquest and consolidation of political power by the working class and its allies, the "historic leap" that opens the door to the construction of socialism.

Tomás Borge also discusses the process by which the Nicaraguan vanguard, the FSLN, learned the lessons of the "errors committed by enthusiastic Latin American revolutionaries who had mechanical conceptions about the victory of the Cuban revolution." In Nicaragua, there was no lack of armed actions undertaken, but they didn't all grow out of the class struggle. The FSLN itself had to learn, including from its own mistakes, how to transform itself from simply a guerrilla group into a vanguard party, with deep roots in the mass movement. Essential to this was the development of a structure and political functioning in the urban areas.

As Borge puts it, the FSLN "had organized in a way that went beyond guerrilla characteristics. This made it different from other, exclusively guerrilla, organizations that had disappeared completely once guerrilla warfare came to an end. We expanded beyond a guerrilla conception. We overcame that limitation, and when the guerrilla movement temporarily disappeared [in the mid-1960s], the Sandinista National Liberation Front continued to exist."

In making this turn, the FSLN deepened its involvement in the daily struggles of the working people, recruiting from these struggles the most determined fighters, and transforming the FSLN in the process. It did so by keeping clear the relationship between the daily struggles in which it was involved and increasingly providing leadership to, and the strategic line of march toward political power.

The immediate aim of this work in the urban areas, Borge says, "was to organize the barrios to struggle for better living conditions, raising immediate demands such as potable water, electricity, medical services, and so on, but without falling into making these demands ends in themselves. We differed from other groups that made immediate demands their final aims. For us, they were instead a means for seeking out the best individuals among the people and instilling in them the notion that they must organize for the taking of power."

THIS GOES TO THE HEART of revolutionary proletarian strategy. In the prolonged periods prior to the emergence of a revolutionary situation, the level of the class struggle can seem to make the fight for political power irrelevant or utopian as a strategic framework. Even if it is kept in the program, and speeches are given about it on ceremonial occasions, the orientation toward the fight for political power can become so removed from the activity of the vanguard that it loses all meaning. Under these conditions, pressure is felt to put aside the strategic goal altogether, and replace it with ultraleft or reformist schemes.

Ultraleft groups that have recently split from the FMLN in El Salvador, and that identify themselves as continuators of the line of Salvador Cayetano Carpio, argue against "premature" attempts to take power, advocating instead the perspective of decades of guerrilla war, without which the masses will not be prepared to run the country even if they should come to power. These ultraleft, semi-anarchist groups counterpose this conception, which they call "prolonged people's war," to the FMLN's orientation toward the fight to bring to power a workers and peasants government through an armed insurrection of the Salvadoran people. The ultraleft line is also reflected in warnings about the importance of avoiding the "error" of the Nicaraguans who, it is said, seized power too fast and are now experiencing the consequences of a revolution for which the masses weren't prepared.

Another strategic orientation has been followed by many Communist parties of Latin America. This outlook was described by Schafik Jorge Handal, a leader of the Salvadoran FMLN and general secretary since 1973 of the Salvadoran CP. In an article written around the time of the 1982 Havana conference, Handal pointed out that while "two great true revolutions have taken place" in the Spanish-speaking Americas, in Cuba and Nicaragua, "In neither of these two cases was the Communist Party at the head."[3] Why? Because, said the CP leader, these parties, established in the 1920s and 1930s, had "stopped having the struggle for power central to their activity." Instead, they cast themselves "in the role of just being a supportive force," relying on liberal bourgeois and middle-class sectors to lead the struggle for democracy, economic development, and freedom from imperialist domination. They viewed the democratic tasks as being completely separated from the tasks of a specifically proletarian, socialist character in Latin America. As a result, Handal said, the Salvadoran and most other Latin American CPs had "worked for decades with the idea of two revolutions."

"We convinced ourselves," he continued, "that the democratic revolution is not necessarily to be organized and promoted principally by us, but that we could limit ourselves to supporting it, and conform to this support role, in order to assure the range and breadth of the participating democratic forces." In other words, the Communist parties rejected the strategic orientation toward the fight for power.

Handal explained that, from this standpoint, the Cuban revolution appeared to the CPs to be a "peculiar exception." However, in light of the experiences in Nicaragua and in El Salvador since 1979, he has come to the opposite conclusion. "One can't go to socialism except by the democratic anti-imperialist path, but neither can the democratic anti-imperialist revolution be consummated without going on to socialism. To the extent that between these two there is an essential and indissoluble connection, they are facets of one revolution and not two revolutions."

Handal explained that he is convinced that "in the Latin American communist movement there has to be a tremendous ideological struggle to free ourselves from all that reformist ballast."

THE LESSONS BEING DRAWN by proletarian revolutionists in El Salvador, Nicaragua, Cuba, and elsewhere are based on the experiences of the revolutionary movements in which they have participated, combined with a study of the lessons taught by Marx, Engels, and Lenin. These lessons have great value for revolutionary fighters on a world scale, including in the imperialist countries.

In order to orient themselves strategically, and to see the line of march that links the daily struggles of working people with the strategic goal of leading a revolution to bring a workers and farmers government to power, revolutionists have to base themselves on the experiences of the class struggle in their own country. At the same time, they have to see these experiences as a concrete manifestation of the world revolution, and in the framework of the historical advance toward a worldwide proletarian internationalist party. They must anchor this perspective in the accumulated lessons learned by the modern working-class movement.

The article by Mary-Alice Waters traces the political continuity of the fight for a popular revolutionary dictatorship over the last 150 years. It begins with the lessons incorporated in the 1848 *Manifesto of the Communist Party*, written by Marx and Engels, and the new experiences later that year as revolution broke out over much of Europe. It looks at the Paris Commune of 1871, the first, brief experience with a government of the exploited producers. It reviews the further political and strategic conquests from the Russian revolutions of 1905 and 1917 and the Soviet workers and peasants republic during its first years. And it traces the efforts of the Bolshevik leaders of the Communist International between 1919 and 1923 to develop this continuity into a worldwide perspective, corresponding to the epoch of anticapitalist revolutions, giving rise to workers and farmers governments, that have been opened by the historic conquest of October 1917.

NOTES

1. The speech by Piñeiro was published in issue no. 4 of the journal *Cuba Socialista,* and subsequently also in the July–August 1983 issue of *Casa de las Américas,* both published in Havana. An English translation of an excerpt from the concluding part of Piñeiro's speech was published in the January 31, 1983, issue of *Intercontinental Press,* published in New York. The points made by Piñeiro in the section of the speech that was published in *Intercontinental Press* were discussed at some length in the article "Their Trotsky and Ours," by Jack Barnes, national secretary of the Socialist Workers Party of the United States, in the inaugural issue of *New International.*

2. Quoted in *World Outlook,* May 5, 1967, p. 470.

3. This article was published in English in *Intercontinental Press,* November 15, 1982, p. 819.

THE WORKING CLASS FIGHT FOR POWER

The Fight for a Workers and Farmers Government in the United States
JACK BARNES

The shared exploitation of workers and working farmers by banking, industrial, and commercial capital lays the basis for their alliance in a revolutionary fight for a government of the producers. In *New International* no. 4. $14

The Workers and Farmers Government
JOSEPH HANSEN

How experiences in post–World War II revolutions in Yugoslavia, China, Algeria, and Cuba enriched communists' theoretical and practical understanding of revolutionary governments of the workers and farmers. "What is involved is governmental power," writes Hansen, "the possibility of smashing the old structure and overturning capitalism." $5

The Transitional Program for Socialist Revolution
LEON TROTSKY

The Socialist Workers Party program, drafted by Trotsky in 1938, still guides the SWP and communists the world over. The party "uncompromisingly gives battle to all political groupings tied to the apron strings of the bourgeoisie. Its task—the abolition of capitalism's domination. Its aim—socialism. Its method—the proletarian revolution." $17. Also in Farsi.

For a Workers and Farmers Government in the United States
JACK BARNES

$6

WWW.PATHFINDERPRESS.COM

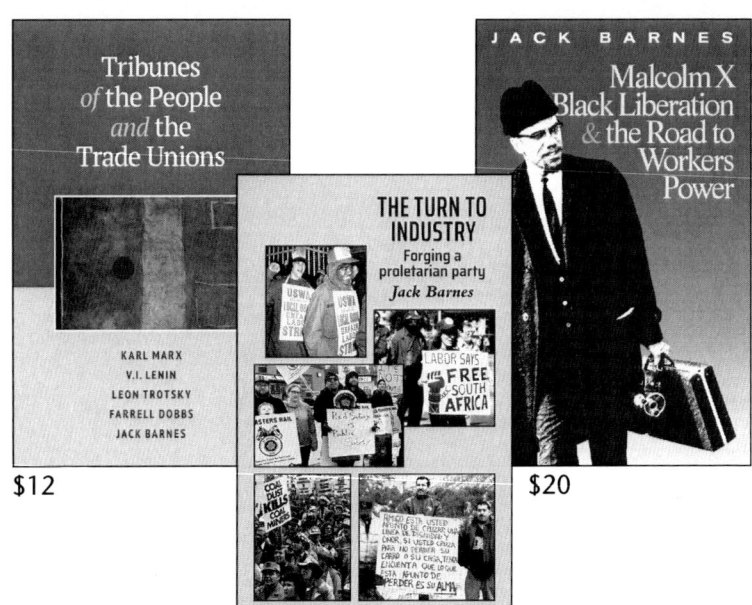

$12 $20

$15

Three books to be read as one...

about building a party that's working class in program, composition, and action. One that recognizes, in word and deed, the most revolutionary fact of our time...

... that working people have the power to create a different world as we act together to defend our own class interests—not those of the privileged classes who exploit our labor, not of those who fear us as "deplorables," or just plain "trash."

As we advance along a revolutionary course toward workers power, we will transform ourselves and awaken to our own worth. Also in Spanish and French.

Special Offer!
All three $30

The Turn to Industry and *Tribunes of the People and the Trade Unions* $20

Either book plus *Malcolm X, Black Liberation, and the Road to Workers Power* $25

'THE HISTORY OF EXISTING SOCIETY IS THE HISTORY OF CLASS STRUGGLES'

Labor, Nature, and the Evolution of Humanity
The Long View of History

FREDERICK ENGELS, KARL MARX, GEORGE NOVACK, MARY-ALICE WATERS

Why is it important to know that social labor, transforming nature, has been the motor force of humanity's evolution for millions of years? Because without that knowledge, working people are unable to see beyond the capitalist epoch, beyond the class exploitation that warps all human relations, ideas, and values. The dictatorship of capital had a beginning ... and it will have an end. But only the revolutionary conquest of state power by the working class can open the door to a world free of capitalism's dog-eat-dog social reality. A world built on human solidarity. A socialist world. $12. Also in Spanish and French.

We Are Heirs of the World's Revolutions
Speeches from the Burkina Faso Revolution, 1983–87

THOMAS SANKARA

How peasants and workers in this West African country established a popular revolutionary government and began to fight hunger, illiteracy, and economic backwardness imposed by imperialist domination. They set an example not only for workers and small farmers in Africa, but their class brothers and sisters the world over. $10. Also in Spanish, French, and Farsi.

Understanding History

GEORGE NOVACK

How did capitalism arise? Why and when did this exploitative system exhaust its once revolutionary role? Why is revolutionary change fundamental to human progress? $15

WWW.PATHFINDERPRESS.COM

COMMUNISM AND THE FIGHT FOR A POPULAR REVOLUTIONARY GOVERNMENT: 1848 TO TODAY

by Mary-Alice Waters

THE HISTORIC TASK facing the working-class movement is to wrest political power from the small minority of wealthy property owners, whose class dictatorship is predicated on war and on the misery, hunger, and disease of the great majority of humanity. The task is to establish a new kind of state power—a popular revolutionary dictatorship—supported by the vast majority, the exploited producers, who are organized and mobilized to fight for their interests. The challenge before the vanguard of the working class is then to wield the powerful weapon thus created, a government of the workers and farmers, in order to defend the initial revolutionary conquests and to begin the process of transforming the economic foundations of class society, as well as the social relations that flow from the division of humanity into the classes that own land, factories, and machinery, and those who do not. Accomplishing this is intertwined with using the new state power to aid and advance the world revolution.

Every revolutionary struggle since 1848, whether ending in victory or defeat, has enriched our understanding of how the working class can move more surely and rapidly along this strategic line of march outlined in the 1848 *Manifesto of the Communist Party*. The popular revolutionary victories in Grenada and Nicaragua in 1979 were no exception. Years of struggle by increasingly broad layers of the Nicaraguan and Grenadian people culminated in 1979 in armed insurrections that smashed the imperialist-backed tyrannies. In both countries the scope of the revolutionary mobilizations and the capacities of the vanguard organizations that had been forged in the course of these struggles resulted in the formation of workers and farmers governments—popular revolutionary regimes based on the exploited producers. The hated police-state regimes of Gairy and Somoza, the protectors of imperialist superexploitation, had been overthrown, their repressive forces shattered.

The lands, factories, shipping lines, and holding companies of the hated tyrants were expropriated, placing control over important sectors of the economies in the hands of new revolutionary governments. The foundations of landlord-capitalist power had been cracked. But the task of uprooting the capitalist economic and social relations that had produced Gairyism and Somozaism still lay ahead. The challenge before the new regimes was to secure and defend the positions won, to organize and educate the working people, to institutionalize the new workers and farmers republic, and to move forward with the transition to a new social and economic order.

Revolutionists around the world greeted these historic victories with deep appreciation of the capacities, courage, and determination of the women and men who had made them possible. As Cuban President Fidel Castro expressed it, speaking to the Federation of Cuban Women in March 1980, "one must have a sense of history to know . . . what revolution means here, next to the imperialist monster."[1]

The Grenadian revolution subsequently went down to defeat. First betrayed from within by the faction led by Bernard Coard that overthrew and then murdered Prime Minister Maurice Bishop in October 1983, Grenada was then invaded and occupied by the armed forces of U.S. imperialism. The Nicaraguan workers and farmers continue to move forward, however, despite the escalating efforts of Yankee imperialism to prevent them from taking their own destinies in hand.

In the United States, the Socialist Workers Party threw itself into the tasks of spreading the truth about the advances of the working people of Nicaragua and Grenada, and of organizing opposition to Washington's military, economic, and political aggression.

WE HAVE ALSO HAD another task: to study and learn from these unfolding revolutions. We have had the opportunity to examine our party's program and theoretical foundations in light of the course being taken by actual revolutions, and to make whatever adjustments are dictated by the facts, by the new conquests of our class on a world scale. Any program, any revolutionary theory that ceases to develop, that ceases to incorporate new lessons as the class struggle itself advances, is no longer a guide to revolutionary action by the working class. It becomes dogma, a sectarian doctrine. Its truth and effectiveness cannot be tested by living reality.

In 1847, in the first years of the modern revolutionary

workers movement, Frederick Engels wrote that communism is not a doctrine "but a *movement;* it proceeds, not from principles but from *facts.*" Its point of departure is not some philosophy or ethical goal, but "the whole course of previous history." Insofar as it is expressed in a political program, Engels wrote, communism is simply "the theoretical expression of the position of the proletariat in this [class] struggle and the theoretical summation of the conditions for the liberation of the proletariat."[2]

Every historic victory—or defeat—for working people affects the position of the proletariat in the class struggle and alters the conditions for its liberation. Thus we must be constantly adjusting our program—our guide to action—to this changing social reality. New experiences enable us to view previous struggles more clearly, as well. We understand things we did not comprehend before. We advance with the experience of our class.

Throughout the 1960s and 1970s, for example, as we deepened our understanding of the dynamics of the Cuban revolution, we were able to appreciate much more fully the necessary and irreplaceable role played by transitional revolutionary regimes such as the workers and farmers government that came into being in Cuba in the second half of 1959. That revolutionary government was a more powerful weapon than any political party, trade union, or other mass organization alone could ever be. It was used by the Cuban vanguard to organize the toilers to bridge the chasm separating the society they had inherited, based on capitalist property relations, from the new social order they were inaugurating, which would have to be based on social ownership of the means of production and a planned economy. Under the accelerating attacks from U.S. imperialism, that process moved exceptionally fast, to the expropriations of imperialist-

and Cuban-owned capitalist property in the summer and fall of 1960.

The Cuban revolution demonstrated how such a popular revolutionary government—made possible by a mass upheaval that smashes the repressive instruments of the old state power, and drawing its legitimacy from the direct intervention of the workers and peasants into political action—leads the exploited and oppressed to meet their most pressing social and economic needs. This can be achieved only by deeper and deeper inroads into the prerogatives and property of the capitalist class.

THROUGH WHAT WE LEARNED from the experience of the Cuban revolution we were able to more richly appreciate our political and theoretical continuity with the early Communist International (Comintern). The resolutions on the agrarian question, on the national and colonial questions, on soviet power, and on the fight for a transitional workers and peasants government were especially useful. The conclusions reached by the Comintern, with the help and guidance of Soviet Russia's Bolshevik leadership, incorporated the lessons of the Russian revolution and those drawn from the entire post–World War I revolutionary upsurge. They also incorporated the cardinal fact that the existence of the workers and peasants regime in Soviet Russia qualitatively changed what was possible on a world scale.

In light of the Cuban experience, we have also been able to better understand the Chinese and Vietnamese revolutions and the establishment of the Eastern European workers states following World War II, as well as the role played by transitional workers and farmers regimes in securing those revolutionary victories.

Now with the lessons of Nicaragua and Grenada—and the advances being registered in El Salvador—to draw on too, we can look back on Cuba as well, with further insights into aspects of that revolutionary experience.[3]

THE PURPOSE of the current article is to look at the question of the workers and farmers government through a wider historical lens: to go back to the beginning of scientific socialism and trace the evolution of our program on the question of popular revolutionary dictatorships. The intent is to look at the historical situation and class relations confronting our predecessors in the communist movement, and to see how, under those concrete conditions, they sought to chart a course that would lead the working class toward political power. By doing so, we can gain a deeper appreciation of the workers and farmers government *today* as a tool in the hands of the working class and its allies that advances the proletariat—and with it all humanity—along the road to liberation.

Throughout this article we will be looking at several interrelated lessons:

1. Every revolution worthy of the name—and especially every revolution led by the working class—is a genuine *people's* revolution. It unleashes a "revolutionary whirlwind" (to use Lenin's phrase),[4] powered by the direct political activity of the exploited and oppressed. The common people "simply set to work," as Lenin said, "without more ado to smash all the instruments for oppressing the people, seize power and take what was regarded as belonging to all kinds of robbers of the people." The intellect and reason of millions of downtrodden people awakens "not only to read books, but for action, vital human action, to make history."[5]

2. The revolutionary vanguard of the working class strives always to lead the broad masses of working people toward the conquest of power.

Tomás Borge put it well in a speech he made in 1983 discussing some of the lessons of the Nicaraguan struggle (printed elsewhere in this issue). The Sandinista National Liberation Front (FSLN), he said, "differed from other groups that made immediate demands their final aims. For us, they were instead a means for seeking out the best individuals among the people and instilling in them the notion that they must organize for the taking of power.

"This is very important," Borge continued. "From the beginning we had always had a nose for power, and we went on developing that instinct and transmitting it to our cadres even when we recruited them through struggles around immediate demands."

3. History teaches us that during every successful social revolution, whether bourgeois or proletarian, the revolutionary class or classes have forged, in the heat of battle, a popular revolutionary dictatorship to consolidate the conquest of power and defend it against counterrevolution.

Lenin used an analogy to explain this: "If you are storming a fortress, you cannot discontinue the war even after you have taken the fortress," he noted. "Either the one or the other: either we take the fortress to hold it, or we do not storm the fortress and explain that all we want is a little place next to it."[6]

"The history of the doctrine of revolutionary dictatorship in general," Lenin wrote in 1920, "and of the dictatorship of the proletariat in particular, coincides with the history of Marxism." More importantly, he went on, "the history of all revolutions by the oppressed and exploited classes, against the exploiters, provides the basic material and source of our knowledge on the question of dictatorship. "Whoever has failed to understand that dictatorship is essential to the victory of any revolutionary class has no understanding of the history of revolutions, or else does not want to know anything in this field."[7]

For Lenin, of course, as for Marx and Engels, the use of the term class dictatorship did not imply political autocracy or totalitarian rule, as bourgeois and petty-bourgeois opponents of Marxism falsely assert. Every state represents a social dictatorship of one class or another. Even bourgeois republics with the broadest suffrage are social dictatorships—the class dictatorship of the handful of capitalists who own the factories, mines, mills, and banks. Democratic rights prevail only so long as their use does not threaten the dominance of capital.

4. The workers and farmers governments in our own epoch are popular dictatorships of the revolutionary classes that have taken power.

The conquest of political power by these classes opens up a new stage of struggles that marks the transition to a new social order. Throughout this stage, the working class uses the revolutionary government to extend its political influence, to lead the transformation of the economic and social relations it has inherited, and to move toward establishing the socialist property forms of a workers state, that is, toward the establishment of the dictatorship of the proletariat.[8]

5. Workers and farmers governments tackle the fundamental tasks posed during the transition. They take the necessary emergency measures to protect working people against the impact of acute social crisis. They act to defend the initial conquests against the inevitable combined assault of the deposed ruling classes, the imperialists,

and their assorted counterrevolutionary agencies. They strive to win the support of major sectors of the middle classes, and the acquiescence of others, by showing them in practice that their interests lie with the revolutionary advance of the working class, not with the restoration of capitalist power. They institutionalize the revolutionary workers and farmers republic, developing new forms and structures of popular rule and defense of the revolution. They work to develop proletarian consciousness and discipline, which are prerequisites for the reorganization of society on new foundations. And they strengthen the revolutionary proletarian party as a mass political vanguard, through efforts to bring into its ranks the most class-conscious and self-sacrificing workers.

I. FOUNDATIONS OF THE MODERN COMMUNIST MOVEMENT

WHEN THE political foundations of the modern communist movement were laid, the storm clouds of the approaching 1848 revolutions in Europe were already visible to all classes. At a December 1847 congress in London, a small group of working-class revolutionists, mostly German artisans, founded a new international organization, the Communist League. Karl Marx and Frederick Engels were assigned to draft its program, *The Manifesto of the Communist Party*. This document was published as the first of these revolutionary storm clouds burst over France.

The founding of the league was the product of a political battle waged by Marx, Engels, and their allies. For several years they had worked to win the most conscious working-class revolutionists involved in various secret, conspiratorial societies away from what Marx described as "a hodge-podge" of utopian communist doctrines. They fought to place the revolutionary workers movement on a scientific, materialist basis. The fundamental dividing line in that conflict was the insistence by Marx and Engels that "it was not a matter of putting some utopian system into effect, but of conscious participation in the historical process revolutionising society before our very eyes."[9]

The initial battle won, the new organization placed at the center of its program the strategic line of march of the working class toward political power. The change fought for by those who agreed with Marx and Engels was reflected in Article I of the "Rules of the Communist League." The original draft had retained the previous utopian framework. It said: "The League aims at the emancipation of humanity by spreading the theory of the community of property and its speediest possible introduction."[10] The amended version proposed by Marx and Engels and adopted by the congress stated the historic sequence: "The aim of the League is the overthrow of the bourgeoisie, the rule of the proletariat, the abolition of the old bourgeois society which rests on the antagonism of classes, and the foundation of a new society without classes and without private property."[11]

The Manifesto adopted by the league explained that the immediate aim of the communists is the "formation of the proletariat into a class"—that is, the development of the proletariat's consciousness of itself as a hereditary social class whose relationship to capital is one of unalterable antagonism. It is a class with distinct interests, and with the capacity to organize itself not only to further its own collective interests, but also to act as a political force leading in alliance with all other exploited producers, thus advancing the interests of toiling humanity as a whole. The aim of communists, continues the Manifesto, is the "overthrow of the bourgeois supremacy, conquest of political power by the proletariat."[12]

Once the working class has conquered political power, has raised itself to the position of ruling class and won the "battle of democracy," the Manifesto proclaims, it will begin to organize the transition to a new social order. "The proletariat will use its political supremacy to wrest, by degrees, all capital from the bourgeoisie, to centralise all instruments of production in the hands of the State, *i.e.*, of the proletariat organised as the ruling class; and to increase the total of productive forces as rapidly as possible."

Of course, the Manifesto declares, "this cannot be effected except by means of despotic inroads on the rights of property, and on the conditions of bourgeois production." Partial measures, in the course of their development, "outstrip themselves," requiring deeper and deeper inroads upon the old social order "as a means of entirely revolutionising the mode of production."[13]

ONCE THESE TASKS are accomplished, the political power of the proletariat will have served its purpose and will begin withering away. "When, in the course of development, class distinctions have disappeared," the Manifesto explains, "and all production has been concentrated in the hands of a vast association of the whole nation, the public power will lose its political character. Political power, properly so called, is merely the organised power of one class for oppressing another."

"If the proletariat during its contest with the bourgeoisie is compelled, by the force of circumstances, to organise itself as a class, if, by means of a revolution, it makes itself the ruling class, and, as such, sweeps away by force the old conditions of production," says the Manifesto, "then it will, along with these conditions, have swept away the conditions for the existence of class antagonisms and of classes generally, and will thereby have abolished its own supremacy as a class."[14]

"The proletariat alone," explains the Manifesto, "is a really revolutionary class." All preceding ruling classes have been exploiting property-holders, and they have sought to reorganize society so as to protect and enhance their mode of appropriation of society's surplus product, that is, the particular way they exploit the working classes. But the workers have no property. "The proletarians cannot become masters of the productive forces of society, except by abolishing their own previous mode of appropriation, and thereby also every other previous mode of appropriation. They have nothing of their own to secure and fortify...."[15]

This firmly historical view of the present, materialist basis, and revolutionary class perspectives was new to the proletarian vanguard. Yet, until it was conquered, there could be no advance. Only by understanding that class-divided humanity drives forward through the class struggle itself, regardless of humanity's consciousness (or ignorance) of the underlying economic forces at work; only by understanding that these forces lead inevitably to the social rule of the workers, could the fledgling workers movement confidently chart a course toward political supremacy. To those who rejected the new communist movement's scientific understanding of history, in 1848 the perspective proclaimed by its Manifesto seemed preposterous.

"As for myself, I do not claim to have discovered either

the existence of classes in modern society or the struggle between them," Marx explained in an 1852 letter to his friend and comrade, Joseph Wedemeyer. "Long before me, bourgeois historians had described the historical development of this struggle between the classes, as had bourgeois economists the economic anatomy of the classes.

"What I did that was new," Marx emphasized, "was 1. to show that the *existence of classes* is merely bound up with *certain historical phases in the development of production;* 2. that class struggle necessarily leads to the *dictatorship of the proletariat;* 3. that this dictatorship itself only constitutes no more than a transition to the *abolition of all classes* and to a *classless society.*"[16]

THE POLITICAL ORIENTATION hammered out by Marx and Engels during the first few years of the modern revolutionary workers movement contains a surprising number of the basic components of revolutionary strategy that still guide the communist movement today. It is also important to note, however, that much was not yet in place. Marx and Engels knew that in the beginning is not the *word,* but the *deed.* Their point of departure, as Engels said, was the whole course of previous history. Only the actual experience of the class struggle could show the concrete steps forward.

"There is no trace of utopianism in Marx," Lenin noted in *State and Revolution.* Marx did not try to invent a new society. "He studied the *birth* of the new society *out of* the old, and the forms of transition from the latter to the former, as a natural-historical process. He examined the actual experience of a mass proletarian movement and tried to draw practical lessons from it." Marx learned from every battle of the class struggle throughout his lifetime, Lenin said, "just as all the great revolutionary thinkers learned unhesitatingly from the experience of great movements of the oppressed classes."[17]

The 1848 Manifesto drafted by Marx and Engels made no attempt to describe what a popular revolutionary dictatorship would look like, what political forms it would take, through what institutions the great majority of working people would organize themselves to exercise their rule, or how they would defend themselves against the attempts of the dispossessed minority to return to power. History had not yet begun to provide answers to those questions. Almost another quarter-century would pass before the experience of the Paris Commune produced some important clues.

"Marx waited," said Lenin, "for the *experience* of the mass movement to provide the reply to the question as to the specific forms this organisation of the proletariat as the ruling class would assume."[18]

This experience has not come cheaply, however. The working class had to draw many lessons from defeats and setbacks before it achieved its first victorious conquest of power in 1917. Since that time as well, there have been numerous bloody defeats in addition to further conquests. The world revolution has advanced at a slower pace, and by a more circuitous route, than anticipated by the founders of modern communism or even by the leaders of the first workers state. Its unevenness on an international scale and the resulting combinations have produced complex and contradictory forms, including in those countries where the workers have conquered and retain power.

Through these rich experiences, as we shall see, the great revolutionary proletarian leaders of the nineteenth and twentieth centuries applied and developed the communist program. As working-class politicians they worked constantly to improve their tools in order to better get the job done.

II. THE LESSONS OF 1848

RARELY HAS a new program been put to the test of revolutionary action as rapidly as was the *Manifesto of the Communist Party*. First Paris, then Vienna and Berlin, and soon much of Europe was convulsed by revolutionary upheaval in early 1848. Marx and Engels rapidly made their ways to Cologne, an emerging industrial city on Germany's Rhine River, where they threw themselves into revolutionary activity. They began publishing a daily newspaper, the *Neue Rheinische Zeitung* (New Rhineland Gazette).

In Germany, as on much of the European continent, capitalist industrial production was still in its infancy, and the proletariat correspondingly small. Many members of the German bourgeoisie still dreamed of eliminating feudal obstacles to the development of capitalism by leading a popular revolutionary struggle against the landed aristocracy, overthrowing the feudal ruling classes, and unifying the more than thirty separate kingdoms and principalities into a single German republic. Big sections of the urban middle classes, the peasants, and the emerging working class were ready for revolutionary action to defeat the reactionary order as well. The capitalists and many middle-class democrats were above all interested in establishing the political domination of the bourgeoisie. However, the proletariat and peasantry increasingly saw the defeat of the reactionary aristocracy and the establishment of democratic freedoms and national unification as vital to their struggle to combat the exploitation and oppression they were subjected to daily.

Addressing the tasks of the proletarian class in this bourgeois-democratic revolution that was on the agenda in Germany, the final section of the Manifesto had presented the main lines of action for communists in the following way: In Germany communists fight "with the bourgeoisie whenever it acts in a revolutionary way" against the absolute monarchy and the feudal landowners,

> But they never cease, for a single instant, to instil in the working class the clearest possible recognition of the hostile antagonism between bourgeoisie and proletariat, in order that the German workers may straightway use, as so many weapons against the bourgeoisie, the social and political conditions that the bourgeoisie must necessarily introduce along with its supremacy, and in order that, after the fall of the reactionary classes in Germany, the fight against the bourgeoisie itself may immediately begin.
>
> The Communists turn their attention chiefly to Germany, because that country is on the eve of a bourgeois revolution that is bound to be carried out under more advanced conditions of European civilisation, and with a much more developed proletariat, than that of England was in the seventeenth, and of France in the eighteenth century, and because the bourgeois revolution in Germany will be but the prelude to an immediately following proletarian revolution.
>
> In short, the Communists everywhere support every revolutionary movement against the existing social and political order of things.

In all these movements they bring to the front, as the leading question in each, the property question no matter what its degree of development at the time.[19]

As history was soon to show, Marx and Engels were wrong in their projection that the victory of the bourgeois revolution in Germany—with an immediately following proletarian revolution—was on the order of the day. But what is relevant to note here is that the strategic perspective laid out in these closing paragraphs of the Manifesto—that the working-class vanguard must fight for the furthest possible advance of the bourgeois-democratic revolution, and along that road organize the working-class party to move toward leadership of the struggle—served as the guide for communists during the 1848–49 revolution in Germany.

"Never has a tactical programme justified itself as well as this one," Engels commented in 1884. "Put forward on the eve of the 1848 revolution," he said, "it stood the test of this revolution; whenever, since this period, a workers' party has deviated from it, the deviation has met its punishment; and today, after almost forty years, it serves as the guiding line of all resolute and class-conscious workers' parties in Europe, from Madrid to St. Petersburg."[20]

THE GERMAN REVOLUTION of 1848–49 sharply posed many questions of working-class strategy that remain with us today. From their vantage point as participants and leaders, Marx and Engels tirelessly worked to test their line in practice and to clarify every experience that could throw light on the strategy and tactics of the working class. The lessons they pointed to on three questions in particular deserve attention.

1. The *necessity* of a popular dictatorship exercised by the revolutionary classes to assure victory in any revolution.

2. The incapacity of the German bourgeoisie, demonstrated in 1848–49, to lead a genuine "people's revolution," standing at the head of the peasantry, the urban petty bourgeoisie, and the working class.

3. The perspective of orienting the still small and politically inexperienced German proletariat, as the only consistent revolutionary political force, to lead in carrying through the democratic revolution to the end; and, in that process, to advance its own organization and class interests and those of its exploited allies.

FROM THE FIRST DAYS of the revolution, the German bourgeoisie displayed its unwillingness and incapacity as a class to *act* in a revolutionary manner. It feared to proclaim that its right to rule was based not on the laws of the monarchy, but on the fact that it was leading the entire nation. The bourgeoisie was terrified of challenging the "divine right" of the aristocracy to rule, of proclaiming that its own sovereign authority was legitimized by the revolution and rested on the armed power of the popular forces—the majority of all the oppressed classes—arrayed against the feudal order.

Marx and Engels mocked the timidity of the bourgeoisie in confronting the landed aristocracy (the *junkers*, as they were called in Prussia), the monarchy, the officer corps, and the bloated bureaucracy of the feudal state. They exposed the bourgeoisie's fear of uprooting the feudal social relations of the old regime and the property rights on which they rested. They scored the refusal of the capitalist class to establish its own revolutionary dictatorship—a government that would resolutely lead a struggle for the democratic, antifeudal measures that would have mobilized mass popular support; a government that would act decisively to destroy the capacity of the old reactionary classes to restore their social order.

Under Marx's editorship the pages of the *Neue Rheinische Zeitung* burned with scathing ridicule of the political representatives of the big bourgeoisie, whose attempts to appease and reach compromises with the nobility led only to their own defeat.

"Every provisional political set-up following a revolution requires a dictatorship," Marx wrote in the *Neue Rheinische Zeitung* in September 1848. "From the very beginning we blamed Camphausen [the head of the liberal bourgeois government after March 1848] for not having acted in a dictatorial manner, for not having smashed up and removed the remains of the old institutions." Camphausen had "indulged in constitutional dreaming," while the forces of reaction strengthened their "positions within the bureaucracy and in the army, and occasionally even risked an open fight."

While the government of the liberal bourgeoisie "never hesitated to employ . . . dictatorial measures against the democratic forces" in the name of law and order, Marx pointed out, it "carefully refrained" from using such measures against the counterrevolution.[21]

Marx ridiculed the Frankfurt Assembly, a short-lived constituent national assembly that was made possible by the revolution, as a cowardly body that busied itself "in parliamentary school exercises." What is the use "in framing the best of agendas and the best of constitutions," he asked, if the forces of reaction "meanwhile have placed bayonets on the agenda?"

The Frankfurt Assembly "only needed everywhere to counter dictatorially the reactionary encroachments by obsolete governments [of the various feudal German states and principalities] in order to win over public opinion, a power against which all bayonets and rifle-butts would be ineffective."[22] Its aim should have been "the elimination from the regime actually existing in Germany of everything that contradicted the principle of the sovereignty of the people," and then "to maintain the revolutionary basis on which it depends and to safeguard the sovereignty of the people, won by the revolution, secure against all attacks."[23]

But the Frankfurt Assembly talked on, while the most powerful sectors of the bourgeoisie concluded an alliance with reaction and placed bayonets on the agenda.

THE RECORD OF BETRAYAL by the German bourgeoisie during the first ten months of the revolution, Marx wrote in December 1848, "shows that a purely *bourgeois revolution* and the establishment of *bourgeois rule* in the form of a *constitutional monarchy* is impossible in Germany, and that only a feudal absolutist counter-revolution or a *social republican revolution* is possible."[24]

The alternatives were clear: either a deepgoing people's revolution, a social revolution of the classes oppressed and exploited under the old order, and the establishment of a revolutionary dictatorship of the majority to crush the resistance of the former feudal rulers and expropriate the landed property on which their power was based; or a brutal counterrevolution in which the bourgeoisie itself, and with it the great majority of the people, would be driven back.

The bourgeois-democratic revolution that had begun

in Prussia, Marx wrote in the December 1848 article, should not be confused with those that occurred in France sixty years earlier, or in England 200 years earlier. In both of those earlier revolutions, Marx explained, "the bourgeoisie was the class that *really* headed the movement. The *proletariat* and the *non-bourgeois strata of the middle class* had either not yet any interests separate from those of the bourgeoisie or they did not yet constitute independent classes or class sub-divisions. Therefore, where they opposed the bourgeoisie, as they did in France in 1793 and 1794, they fought only for the attainment of the aims of the bourgeoisie, even if not *in the manner* of the bourgeoisie. . . .

"The bourgeoisie was victorious in these revolutions," Marx wrote, "but the *victory of the bourgeoisie* was at that time *the victory of a new social order,* the victory of bourgeois ownership over feudal ownership" and its primary medieval appendages.

"There has been nothing of all this in *the Prussian March revolution,*" Marx wrote.[25] The German bourgeoisie arrived too late on the historical scene. "The German bourgeoisie developed so sluggishly, timidly and slowly," he explained, "that at the moment when it menacingly confronted feudalism and absolutism, it saw menacingly confronting it the proletariat and all sections of the middle class whose interests and ideas were related to those of the proletariat."

As a result, Marx wrote, from the outset the bourgeoisie "was inclined to betray the people and to compromise with the crowned representative of the old society."[26] They were not equal to the revolutionary tasks accomplished by their English and French (or Dutch and U.S.) class brothers in the previous two centuries. They produced "merely a stunted after-effect of a European revolution in a backward country," Marx said.[27]

Engels later wrote that the German bourgeoisie in 1848 "had only just begun to establish its large-scale industry," and "had neither the strength nor the courage to win for itself unconditional domination in the state. "Terrified not by what the German proletariat was," he noted, "but by what it threatened to become and what the French proletariat already was, the bourgeoisie saw its sole salvation in some compromise, even the most cowardly, with monarchy and nobility."[28]

PERHAPS THE STRONGEST confirmation of this assessment of the German bourgeoisie was its failure to seek to win the peasantry as an ally. The bourgeois liberals refused to mobilize the power of the peasantry in the struggle to eradicate feudal obligations and taxes, which were an obstacle to capitalist development.

"A most wretched botchwork," Marx called a timid bill being debated in the Prussian National Assembly, a half-hearted gesture to meekly adjust the feudal chains oppressing the peasantry. Despite the capitalists' "desire to abolish feudal privileges," Marx noted, they were paralyzed in doing anything effective by their "fear of revolutionarily attacking any kind of property whatever."

Unlike the French bourgeoisie of the previous century, Marx wrote, who "began by emancipating the peasants" and "together with the peasants . . . conquered Europe," the German bourgeoisie "was so preoccupied with its *most narrow*, immediate interests that it foolishly threw away even this ally and turned it into a tool of the feudal counter-revolutionaries."[29]

The ties between landed property and industrial capital were already too strong. The aristocracy had grown too bourgeoisified in Germany. From 1848 on the historical task of marching together with the peasantry against the aristocracy to accomplish the democratic revolution in Europe fell to the proletariat. It was now the only class capable of leading that struggle through to the end, against not only the landlords, but the bulk of the bourgeoisie as well.

The German bourgeoisie preferred sharing power with the monarchy to unleashing the vast social revolution required to bring down the junkerdom and its royal trappings. Thus its representatives merely played at revolution until the energies of the people were spent and the forces of feudal reaction were ready to take the offensive.

From then on it was a settled question for Marx and Engels: the era was gone in which the bourgeoisie in any European country could lead a popular, democratic revolution to a successful conclusion against the decaying feudal order. The strength of the plebeian mass upsurge, which had been the key to victory before, now loomed so powerful, with its still-minority proletarian component sufficiently menacing, that the bourgeoisie dared not try to become sole master of the fort.

Once again the class struggle had confirmed that no new social order can triumph unless a revolutionary class, representing the interests of virtually all but the minority former ruling classes, leads a vast revolutionary movement of the oppressed and exploited to establish a popular revolutionary government, and carries the destruction of the old order through to completion.

The proletariat in Europe had become the only class capable of leading such a genuine people's revolution.

How had Marx and Engels guided the conscious proletarian forces to act as a political force oriented toward establishing a popular revolutionary power, given the relationship of class forces in Germany and Europe at the beginning of 1848? Looking back on these events in 1884, Engels provided a succinct description of the course they had pursued.

The small proletariat in mid-nineteenth century Germany, he pointed out, was very limited in its class-struggle experience, consciousness, and organization. "Grown up in complete intellectual enslavement, unorganised and still not even capable of independent organisation," Engels wrote, the proletariat "possessed only a vague feeling of the deep antagonism between its interests and those of the bourgeoisie."

Since the German working class "was still unacquainted with its own historical role, the bulk of it had, at the start, to take on the role of the forward-pressing, extreme Left wing of the bourgeoisie. The German workers had above all to win those rights which were indispensable to their independent organisation as a class party: freedom of the press, association and assembly—rights which the bourgeoisie, in the interests of its own rule, ought to have fought for, but which it itself in its fear now began to dispute, as far as they concerned the workers.... Thus, the German proletariat at first appeared on the political stage as the extreme democratic party."

Recognizing these factors Marx and Engels had identified the *Neue Rheinische Zeitung* on the front page of each issue as the "Organ of Democracy." The paper's initial battle cry, as Engels explained in 1884, "could only be that of democracy, but that of a democracy which everywhere emphasised in every point the specific proletarian character which it could not yet inscribe once for all on its banner."

This had been the only correct course for proletarian revolutionists in Germany. "If we did not want to take up the movement, adhere to its already existing, most advanced, actually proletarian side and to push it further," he wrote, "then there was nothing left for us to do but to preach communism in a little provincial sheet and to found a tiny sect instead of a great party of action. But we had already been spoilt for the role of preachers in the wilderness; we had studied the Utopians too well for that, nor was it for that we had drafted our programme."[30]

In short, the question was how to carry out the most effective political action to advance the working class along the road toward power. First and foremost was the task of fighting alongside and pushing the radical democrats and the peasantry in order to destroy the common enemy—feudal prerogatives and monarchy.

THE PLATFORM of extreme democracy was the seventeen-point "Demands of the Communist Party in Germany," drafted by Marx and Engels in Paris as they were on their way back to Germany in March 1848. "It is in the interest of the German proletariat, the petty bourgeoisie and the small peasants to support these demands with all possible energy," the platform explained at its conclusion.[31]

The seventeen-point program began with the demand that, "The whole of Germany shall be declared a single indivisible republic."[32] It called for universal arming of the people and limitation of the right of inheritance. It demanded that all means of transport be taken over by the state; that the state guarantee jobs for all workers and provide for those unable to work; that a steeply progressive income tax be introduced; and that free, universal elementary education be established.

In relationship to the peasants and agricultural workers, it called for all feudal estates to be transformed into state property where "the estates shall be cultivated on a large scale and with the most up-to-date scientific devices in the interests of the whole of society." This was combined with a demand that all "mortgages on peasant lands shall be declared the property of the state," and that "interest on such mortgages shall be paid by the peasants to the state."[33]

These demands were championed by Marx and Engels in the *Neue Rheinische Zeitung*, as well. They sought to advance the bourgeois-democratic revolution as far as possible, and to win the most conscious workers to forging the alliances necessary and leading the mass fight for that political course.

Not all members of the Communist League, however, agreed with this course. League members such as Stephan Born in Berlin and Andreas Gottschalk in Cologne broke with Marx and Engels over this perspective. They charged Marx and Engels with turning their backs on the working class, and argued that communists should instead fight to orient workers' associations such as the Berlin-based Workers Brotherhood and the Cologne Workers Society toward immediate economic questions. Alliances with radical democrats and peasants' associations to fight for common political goals were of no interest to the working class, they held.

MARX, ENGELS, and their supporters fought for and won the leadership of the Cologne Workers Society soon after their return to Germany in April 1848. They vigorously opposed the narrow, economist perspective advocated by Gottschalk who—adapting to the political backwardness of the German petty-bourgeois artisans and skilled workers—had even muted his opposition to the Prussian monarchy. Under Gottschalk's leadership the Cologne Workers Society had been an obstacle to working-class political action. Under the leadership of Marx and Engels it was transformed into a vehicle for involving workers in the revolution and helping them to think politically. The Cologne workers began to forge an alliance with the peasants, educating about their conditions and demands and organizing in the countryside.

Marx and Engels had little direct political influence or support in Berlin, however, where Born's Workers Brotherhood was based. Engels's 1885 description of Born's activities provides an illuminating picture of the contrast between the strategy proposed by Marx and Engels, who sought to imbue the German working-class vanguard with the need to lead the fight for democracy and political fights against the autocracy, and that of the Menshevik-Economists of 1848 (to borrow the more familiar terms of the Russian revolution), who argued that the working class should abstain from political struggle.

> In the official publications of [Born's] association the views represented in the *Communist Manifesto* were mingled hodge-podge with guild recollections and guild aspirations, fragments of Louis Blanc and Proudhon, protectionism, etc. . . .
> In particular, strikes, trade unions and producers' co-operatives were set going and it was forgotten that above all it was a question of first conquering, by means of political victories, the field in which alone such things could be realised on a lasting basis. When, afterwards, the victories of the reaction made the leaders of the Brotherhood realise the necessity of taking a direct part in the revolutionary struggle, they were naturally left in the lurch by the confused mass

which they had grouped around themselves. . . .
In contrast to the great political movement of the
proletariat, the Workers Brotherhood proved to be
a pure *Sonderbund*.[34]

As Lenin aptly commented in 1905, "That is how Engels judged the two tactics of Social-Democracy in the democratic revolution!"[35]

By the beginning of 1849, as the counterrevolution gained momentum, Marx and Engels saw that the revolution was certain to suffer major defeats. They believed, however, that the downturn would be only a brief interlude. They anticipated a new revolutionary wave in which the working class, profiting from the experience and political consciousness gained through a year of intense struggle, would be capable of playing a more central leadership role.

To prepare for this anticipated next stage, Marx and Engels turned more attention toward organizing "the party of the people," which "exists as yet only in an elementary form."[36] Reaping the fruits of their work with the *Neue Rheinische Zeitung*, which had prepared a growing proletarian left wing of the democratic revolution, Marx and Engels now concentrated their energies on organizing and politically educating the workers' societies and peasant unions. They sought to draw together the vanguard of the coalition of class forces that would be capable of acting decisively and consistently against all feudal interests and the monarchy when the next revolutionary wave began.

It was at this point that the *Neue Rheinische Zeitung* serialized Marx's 1847 talks on "Wage Labour and Capital" in order "to deal more closely with the economic relations themselves on which the existence of the bourgeoisie and its class rule, as well as the slavery of the workers, are founded."[37]

The strongest resistance to the counterrevolution occurred in the southern German states of Baden and Palatinate, where provisional governments put armies into the field. But these governments also did not take the decisive steps proposed by Marx and Engels, including that of forging an alliance with the peasants in order to mobilize the broadest social movement. This, however, did not prevent Engels from accepting a commission in the Baden army in order to participate in the fight against reaction.

WITH THE REVOLUTION'S DEFEAT, thousands of revolutionary democrats, including Marx and Engels, were forced into exile. Yet, throughout the first half of 1850 Marx and Engels continued to think it was only an interlude, that a new revolutionary wave in Europe was imminent. They still expected this upturn would rapidly lead to proletarian victories in Britain or France. In Germany, the working class would be able to move into the leadership of the democratic revolution, assuring its victory. And, as the *Manifesto of the Communist Party* had said, that would be "but the prelude to an immediately following proletarian revolution."

As it turned out, this revolutionary revival anticipated by Marx and Engels was not on the agenda anywhere in Europe. By September 1850 they had recognized their misestimation and all expectation of imminent proletarian revolution had been jettisoned by Marx and Engels.

Correcting his previous assessment, Marx explained at a meeting of exiled Communist League members held in London in September 1850 that the working class, at least in Germany, would have to go through "15, 20, 50 years" of further developments and class battles "in order to alter the situation and to train [itself] for the exercise of power."[38]

In 1852, Marx wrote that while the June 1848 proletarian uprising in Paris had "indicated the general content of the modern revolution," it was "a content which was in most singular contradiction to everything that . . . could be immediately realised in practice."[39]

Throughout the second half of the nineteenth century, capitalist industrial development accelerated, and the proletariat throughout much of Europe, as well as in North America, grew in size, organization, combat experience, and class consciousness. Through their active participation in the workers movement, Marx and Engels developed an increasingly accurate assessment of the necessary preconditions and prospects for a victorious proletarian-led conquest of power.

For the communists, Engels wrote in 1884,

> February and March [of 1848] could have had the significance of a real revolution only if they had not been the conclusion but, on the contrary, the starting-point of a long revolutionary movement in which . . . the people would have developed further through its own struggles and the parties become more and more sharply differentiated until they had coincided entirely with the great classes, bourgeoisie, petty-bourgeoisie and proletariat, and in which the separate positions would have been won one after another by the proletariat in a series of battles.[40]

Conditions for a successful proletarian-led revolution did not ripen anywhere in the world while Marx and

Engels were alive. Engels came back to this question in 1895, the last year of his life, in an introduction to a new German edition of Marx's *The Class Struggles in France, 1848 to 1850.*

From the fact that the 1848 French revolution "had grouped all the other [nonfeudal and nonbourgeois] social classes, peasantry as well as petty bourgeoisie, round the proletariat," Engels explained, he and Marx had incorrectly concluded: "Was there not every prospect then of turning the revolution of the [proletarian] minority into a revolution of the majority?"

THAT WAS NOT TO BE. "History has proved us, and all who thought like us, wrong. It has made it clear that the state of economic development on the Continent at that time was not, by a long way, ripe for the elimination of capitalist production. . . . [It] still had great capacity for expansion."[41] Moreover, Engels added, this had not changed fundamentally by the time of the Paris Commune more than two decades later.

Neither the objective economic conditions in Europe nor the accompanying development of class relations were ripe for socialist revolution. Bourgeois-democratic revolutions on the continent had, to a greater or lesser extent, not gone all the way in sweeping aside the residue of feudal relations and royal absolutism, or they had gone through subsequent periods of reaction during which initial conquests were partially eroded. Throughout much of the nineteenth century, even the industrial bourgeoisie in England—by far the most developed capitalist country at the time—had not yet established its full political dominance over the landed classes of the old order.

In most countries the working class was increasing in

number and was going through its very first efforts to establish trade unions and political organizations. It was still learning who among the various social layers in the city and the countryside were its class enemies and who were its allies.

Why was it important for working-class revolutionists to recognize these political realities? Because, Engels emphasized in the 1895 introduction, the greater understanding afforded by further experience in the class struggle should serve to focus the attention and efforts of workers parties on winning necessary class allies in the fight for power. In Germany and France, for example, "the Socialists are realising more and more that no lasting victory is possible for them, unless they first win the great mass of the people, that is, in this case, the peasants."[42]

THIS QUESTION of the proletariat's attitude toward the peasantry—the centrality of the worker-peasant alliance and the kind of revolutionary struggles that could advance the proletariat to power at the head of a popular revolution—was one that Marx and Engels returned to repeatedly throughout their lifetimes, developing the initial lessons they had drawn from the 1848–49 revolutions.

During the mid-nineteenth century upheavals, Marx and Engels had already seen that an alliance with the exploited peasants was important to the working class in the fight to propel the democratic revolution to its completion. They had witnessed the disastrous consequences, especially in France, of the bourgeoisie's success in convincing large numbers of the rural toilers that their interests lay in preserving order and stability, which was being upset by the revolt of the workers and plebian masses in the cities. Marx dealt extensively with the question of the peasants in both his major works assessing the French revolution of 1848: *The Class Struggles in France, 1848 to 1850* and *The Eighteenth Brumaire of Louis Bonaparte*. He pointed out that, "It can be seen that [the French peasants'] exploitation differs only in *form* from the exploitation of the industrial proletariat. The exploiter is the same: *capital*. The individual capitalists exploit the individual peasants through *mortgages* and *usury;* the capitalist class exploits the peasant class through the *state taxes*. The peasant's title to property is the talisman by which capital held him hitherto under its spell, the pretext under which it set him against the industrial proletariat. Only the fall of capital can raise the peasant; only an anti-capitalist, a proletarian government can break his economic misery, his social degradation. The *constitutional republic* is the dictatorship of his united exploiters, the *social-democratic*, the Red republic, is the dictatorship of his allies."[43]

The German and French bourgeoisies, Marx and Engels concluded, had already proved to the peasants that they were, at best, an unreliable ally. In fact—as some peasants had begun to realize—the bourgeoisie were themselves ruthless exploiters waiting in the wings to replace feudal obligations and taxes with burdensome rents, new taxes, mortgage payments, and dispossession from the land.

Looking forward to the next revolutionary upsurge in Germany, Marx summed up the prospects in an 1856 letter to Engels: "The whole thing in Germany will depend on the possibility of backing the proletarian revolution by some second edition of the Peasant War. Then the affair will be splendid."[44]

The most thorough treatment of the strategic questions involved in forging a working-class alliance with the peasantry is contained in a major article by Engels written in 1894. Summarizing a half-century of experience, the article analyzes the social differentiations in the countryside—wage laborers, semi-proletarians, and the poor, middle, and rich peasants—and the significance of these differences for working-class strategy.

"In order to conquer political power," Engels wrote, the workers party "must first go from the towns to the country, must become a power in the countryside."[45] In order to accomplish this, "it is the duty of our Party to make clear to the peasants again and again that their position is absolutely hopeless as long as capitalism holds sway."[46]

Having conquered state power, he continued, the workers "shall not even think of forcibly expropriating the small peasants (regardless of whether with or without compensation), as we shall have to do in the case of the big landowners."

The working-class vanguard must continue to patiently explain the historically progressive character of large-scale agricultural production organized along socialist lines, Engels said. Nevertheless, he emphasized, "Our task relative to the small peasant consists, in the first place, in effecting a transition of his private enterprises and private possessions to co-operative ones, not forcibly but by dint of example and the proffer of social assistance for this purpose. . . ."[47]

"We of course are decidedly on the side of the small peasant," Engels said. A revolutionary workers party should pursue a course "to make his lot more bearable, to facilitate his transition to the co-operative should he decide to do so, and even to make it possible for him to remain on his small holding for a protracted length of time to think the matter over, should he still be unable to bring himself to this decision. . . .

"The greater the number of peasants whom we can save from being actually hurled down into the proletariat" by dispossession at the hands of the landlords, bankers, and middlemen, Engels wrote, "the more quickly and easily the social transformation will be accomplished." This, he said, "will effect a perhaps tenfold saving in the cost of the social reorganisation in general."[48]

The entire history of the socialist revolution in the twentieth century, with both positive and negative examples, confirms this line presented by Engels in 1894. Not until the next century would the "splendid affair" foreseen by Marx in 1856 be victorious, however. Not until 1917 in tsarist Russia did the working class, backed by a peasant war, succeed in leading the toilers to establish their own workers and peasants government, the first popular revolutionary dictatorship of the exploited, defend it against the combined forces of reaction at home and abroad, and march forward to consolidate the first dictatorship of the proletariat—the first workers state. It was, among other things, the capacity of the Bolshevik leadership of that revolution to absorb and apply the lessons about the worker-peasant alliance, accumulated through decades of struggle, that made these conquests possible.

III. THE PARIS COMMUNE: THE POLITICAL RULE OF THE PRODUCERS

THE FRENCH revolutionary upsurge of 1848 culminated in what Marx called "the first battle . . . between the two classes that split modern society." The heroic combat of the small working class of Paris in June

1848—"a fight for the preservation or annihilation of the *bourgeois order*"[49]—ended in the workers' defeat and a massacre carried out by an alliance of the big capitalists and monarchists. On the blood and bones of the Parisian workers, the Second French Empire of Louis Bonaparte was built.

By 1871, however, a new generation of working people in Paris was strong enough to renew the battle and they wrote a heroic chapter in the history of the modern working-class movement. The revolutionary upsurge of 1871 that led to the Paris Commune was precipitated by the defeat of the French armies in the Franco-Prussian War. "Storming heaven," as Marx put it,[50] the working people of Paris seized power, drove the government of the French bourgeoisie out of the city, and held the advancing Prussian army at bay.

"The political rule of the producers" was established, said Marx.[51] "The proletariat for the first time held political power."[52] The Paris Commune, "the glorious harbinger of a new society,"[53] showed the way forward for all humanity.[54]

As LEADERS of the International Workingmen's Association (later known as the First International), which had been founded seven years earlier, Marx and Engels tirelessly spread the truth about the Commune to the workers of the world. From England, where they were living and working, they participated in that great class battle by writing articles, raising funds, and helping their comrades organize meetings throughout Europe and North America to defend the Commune from the slander and vilification of the entire bourgeois world.

Marx and Engels also studied this first experience of

the political rule of the producers, in order to extract from it everything of value to the programmatic continuity of the international working-class movement. Many of these lessons were contained in a document on the Commune drafted by Marx for the General Council of the First International—*The Civil War in France.*

In the *Manifesto of the Communist Party* Marx and Engels had called attention to the need for the proletariat to replace the bourgeoisie as ruling class, "to win the battle of democracy." Later, drawing on the experiences of the 1848–49 upsurge, they were able to be more concrete about how this would be accomplished. The parasitic bureaucracy and the repressive institutions of the old order—army, police, courts, prisons—would have to be shattered and destroyed. New instruments of rule would have to be forged.

In the *Eighteenth Brumaire of Louis Bonaparte,* written in 1852, Marx explained that revolutionary classes in previous historical periods had not broken up the "enormous bureaucratic and military" apparatus they had inherited from the old order. Instead, they had sought to perfect and use it on their own behalf. The object of the proletarian revolution, in contrast, is to "concentrate all its forces of destruction against" this state apparatus.[55]

Returning to this theme in 1871 while the Commune was in power, Marx stressed that smashing this bureaucratic-military machine, rather than attempting to transfer it from one class to another, "is the precondition for every real people's revolution."[56]

The revolutions of 1848 failed to establish that precondition. They did not destroy the old repressive machine and open the way to "real people's revolutions." But the Paris Commune did establish that precondition. It went on to create a government of the Paris toilers, and thus gave working people—even if briefly—a glimpse into their own future.

So central was this lesson to the political strategy of the working class that Marx and Engels singled it out again in their 1872 preface to a new edition of the Communist Manifesto. "One thing especially was proved by the Commune," they wrote. Quoting from *The Civil War in France*, they underlined that "the working class cannot simply lay hold of the ready-made state machinery, and wield it for its own purposes."[57]

WHILE 1848 HAD TAUGHT the workers vanguard that the old state apparatus had to be destroyed, Marx and Engels did not attempt to predict what the new revolutionary government that would replace it would look like. The working class had not yet advanced far enough, had not yet lived and struggled through the experiences that could provide some initial, even if tentative, answers to that question.

As Lenin noted in *State and Revolution,* Marx "expected the *experience* of the mass movement to provide the reply to the question as to the specific forms this organisation of the proletariat as the ruling class would assume and as to the exact manner in which this organisation would be combined with the most complete, most consistent 'winning of the battle of democracy'."[58]

Marx "did not set out to *discover* the political *forms* of this future stage," Lenin said. "When the mass revolutionary movement of the proletariat burst forth" in 1871, however, "in spite of its failure, in spite of its short life and patent weakness," Marx set to work "to study the forms it had *discovered.*"[59]

What was Marx's conclusion? The secret of the Commune, as he put it in *The Civil War in France,* was that "it was essentially a working-class government."[60] By this Marx did not mean that the Commune was a minority government of Paris, a city that still had only a small industrial work force. Marx said that the Commune was a "government of the people by the people,"[61] a government of the producers. It was a government that led the nation.

The economic and social trajectory of this revolutionary dictatorship was clear. The Commune, Marx said, was "the political form at last discovered under which to work out the economic emancipation of labour." It was a tool for organizing and leading the transition from the society it inherited to a new order. The Commune, he emphasized, was "a lever for uprooting the economical foundations upon which rests the existence of classes, and therefore of class-rule."[62] That was not a task to be accomplished overnight. The Commune, however, showed the political form that would enable the exploited producers to organize to wrest from the exploiters, by degrees, the productive property rightfully theirs.

Marx carefully studied the actions of this first government of the producers, including those that pointed to its chief weaknesses.

"The first decree of the Commune," Marx noted, "was the suppression of the standing army, and the substitution for it of the armed people."[63] With that act—the precondition for a real people's revolution—a new government began to function, a revolutionary dictatorship whose legitimacy was based on the armed might of the popular majority.

The Paris Commune showed for the first time how a qualitatively new kind of political power begins to emerge as soon as the minority—the old ruling classes—no longer exercise a dictatorship suppressing the majority—the exploited classes.

It *was* still necessary, however, to suppress the armed resistance of the minority—the French bourgeoisie and landed property owners. Most of these exploiters fled Paris for nearby Versailles when the Commune took power. They continued to collaborate with the Prussian army, which was at the gates of Paris. As always, the old ruling classes, though shocked and stunned by the revolutionary victory of the people, were determined to restore their rule at any price.

It was in part what Marx called the "too great *decency*" of the Paris working people,[64] their reluctance to use decisive military force against their class enemies, that led to the Commune's early defeat after seventy-two days of tumultuous existence. The counterrevolutionary forces showed no such decency. They carried out one of the bloodiest slaughters ever inflicted on a city. The victorious forces of reaction ruthlessly murdered some 20,000 men, women, and children.

The Communards gave Adolphe Thiers, leader of the bourgeois reaction, time to concentrate his hostile forces, wrote Marx, by making two mistakes. "Firstly because they rather foolishly did not want to start a *civil war*—as if Thiers had not already started it by his attempt at the forcible disarming of Paris. . . . Secondly, in order that the appearance of having usurped power should not attach to them they lost precious moments (it was imperative to advance on Versailles immediately after the defeat . . . of the reactionaries in Paris) by the election of the Commune, the organization of which, etc., cost yet more time."[65]

The armed people inside Paris, organized and led by the Central Committee of the National Guard, began to assume all public functions. Through the institutions of the newly elected municipal government, the Paris Commune, the masses of working people were drawn into the tasks of deciding all questions affecting their daily lives—food distribution, education, health, public order and defense—and then implementing these decisions.

The Paris Commune was "no longer a state in the proper sense of the word," Engels wrote in 1875.[66] It was no longer an instrument for suppressing the majority, which had been the function of the state throughout all prior history. In place of a special coercive force, the armed population itself was organized through the Commune government and became the guarantor of popular majority rule.

In his 1891 introduction to the twentieth anniversary edition of *The Civil War in France,* Engels singled out three measures taken by the Commune which were decisive in preventing the "servants of society" from transforming themselves into its masters.

First, was the Commune's decision to "do away with all the old repressive machinery previously used" by the minority ruling classes against the majority. Second, the Commune "filled all posts—administrative, judicial and educational—by election on the basis of universal suffrage of all concerned, subject to the right of recall at any time by the same electors." Third, "all officials, high or low, were paid only the wages received by other workers."[67]

L‍ENIN CALLED ATTENTION again to these measures in 1917, in *State and Revolution,* summarizing their political significance.

1. The measures taken by the Commune to organize new state institutions, he said, were "simple and 'self-

evident', *democratic.*"But their simplicity is deceptive. The Commune "appears to have replaced the smashed state machine 'only' by fuller democracy. . . . But as a matter of fact this 'only' signifies a gigantic replacement of certain institutions by other institutions of a fundamentally different type. This is exactly a case of 'quantity being transformed into quality': democracy, introduced as fully and consistently as is at all conceivable, is transformed from bourgeois into proletarian democracy; from the state (a special force for the suppression of a particular class) into something which is no longer the state proper."[68]

2. This qualitatively transformed democracy, by its class nature, is inseparable from the social program it implements. In response to the most pressing needs of the majority, it begins to prepare the transition to a new economic order. The political measures of the Commune, Lenin noted, "acquire their full meaning and significance only in connection with the 'expropriation of the expropriators' either being accomplished or in preparation."[69] There can be no question of an abrupt, immediate abolition of private property in all the means of production, no "introduction" of socialism, ready or not. But the political and economic measures are necessarily interrelated. The course toward the new economic order must be consciously prepared and implemented. It may go faster or slower, depending on the concrete material conditions and class relations. What is decisive is the direction of motion.

3. The political measures taken by the Commune to reorganize the state, Lenin pointed out, served to *unify* the exploited producers, the workers and the majority of the peasants, who "are oppressed by the [capitalist] government and long for its overthrow, long for 'cheap' government." Cheap government—the destruction of

the large bureaucratic-military machine and its replacement by popular institutions of defense and administration—this "can be achieved *only* by the proletariat," Lenin added, "and by achieving it, the proletariat at the same time takes a step towards the socialist reorganization of the state."[70]

4. In other words, these "simple and 'self-evident' democratic measures" taken by the Commune in organizing the new state institutions are far-reaching transitional measures. "While completely uniting the interests of the workers and the majority of peasants, at the same time," Lenin said, they "serve as a bridge leading from capitalism to socialism."[71]

This is true because—to use Marx's words—"the political rule of the producer cannot coexist with the perpetuation of his social slavery."[72]

M ARX'S OBSERVATIONS on the Commune point to the importance of the measures taken to win the allegiance of the great majority of the middle classes, those in between the working class and the capitalists.

During its brief seventy-two days, the Commune was never able to break the siege of Paris. It was not able to extend the revolution to other cities or to the countryside in France. Nonetheless, through the measures it took and the program it projected, Marx said, the working class of Paris acted as "a truly national government."

In *The Civil War in France,* Marx explained that this "was the first revolution in which the working class was openly acknowledged as the only class capable of social initiative, even by the great bulk of the Paris middle class—shopkeepers, tradesman, merchants—the wealthy capitalists alone excepted."[73]

One of the Commune's most important political measures to alleviate the effects of the exploitation of the middle classes by the banks was its declaration of a three-year moratorium on the repayment of debts to the big banks and money lenders, and the cancellation of all interest on these debts.

But this was not the main reason the petty bourgeoisie rallied to the side of the working class, Marx pointed out. "They felt that there was but one alternative—the Commune, or the Empire—under whatever name it might reappear. The Empire had ruined them economically . . . suppressed them politically . . . shocked them morally . . . hand[ed] over the education of their children to [the church] . . . revolted their national feeling as Frenchmen."[74]

Just as the majority of the Parisian petty bourgeoisie supported the new state powers, so too, with time, the peasantry could have been convinced that a government of the producers, led by the working class, was *their* government. The Commune alone could have enabled the majority of the peasants to escape the exploitation of the landowners and banks, thus freeing them from debt slavery.

The Commune decreed that the costs of the Franco-Prussian War would be borne by the originators of the war—not by the peasants and workers through increased taxation. By this act, Marx noted, "the Commune would have delivered the peasant of the blood tax."

Moreover, Marx continued, the Commune would have given the peasant cheap government. It would have

> transformed his present blood-suckers, the notary, advocate [lawyer], executor, and other judicial vampires, into salaried communal agents, elected

by, and responsible to, himself. It would have freed him of the tyranny of the *garde champêtre* [rural police], the gendarme, and the prefect; would have put enlightenment by the schoolmaster in the place of stultification by the priest. And the French peasant is, above all, a man of reckoning. He would find it extremely reasonable that the pay of the priest, instead of being extorted by the taxgatherer, should only depend upon the spontaneous action of the parishioners' religious instincts. Such were the great immediate boons which the rule of the Commune—and that rule alone—held out to the French peasantry.[75]

The French bourgeoisie, Marx noted, was aware of the dangers posed to its continued rule by any such alliance between the exploited peasants in the provinces, and the workers, artisans, and small shopkeepers of Paris. This was, in fact, their chief fear. They knew, Marx wrote, "that three months' free communication of Communal Paris with the provinces would bring about a general rising of the peasants, and hence their anxiety to establish a police blockade around Paris."[76]

MARX CALLED ATTENTION to the other social and economic measures taken by the Commune that indicated "the tendency of a government of the people by the people." These included abolishing compulsory night work for journeymen bakers, prohibiting employers from fining workers and deducting the fines from their pay, and authorizing workers to reopen closed workshops and factories. The Commune also initiated the organization of the small but growing industrial working class of Paris into a single industrial union.

While Marx and Engels considered the heroic uprising of the Parisian workers to have been the greatest revolutionary action by any section of the international proletariat up until that time, they were by no means uncritical of the Commune's leadership or its policies. The Commune reinforced every lesson previously drawn concerning the need for an organized vanguard party of the proletariat, based on a scientific—not a utopian, petty-bourgeois—program.

In 1871 the task of the day was the defense of the Communards against the bloody repression they faced. Marx and Engels wrote sparingly of the Commune leaders' shortcomings in those days—even in their letters. In later years, however, they presented a more thorough evaluation. Writing in 1891, Engels explained some of the errors he and Marx thought the Commune leaders had made. "The members of the Commune were divided into a majority, the Blanquists . . . and a minority . . . chiefly consisting of adherents of the Proudhon school of socialism," Engels pointed out. "The great majority of the Blanquists were at that time Socialists only by revolutionary, proletarian instinct. . . ."[77]

THE PROUDHONISTS, on the other hand, did not even have the proletarian strengths of the Blanquists. They confined themselves to various petty-bourgeois schemes for attempting to limit the growth and consolidation of capital. Even more, their anarchistic opposition to organization or "authority" led them to lightmindedly ignore the need for decisive action to consolidate and defend the new state power.

Given the political combination of Blanquists and

Proudhonists, Engels remarked, the errors made were what you would expect. The most costly political error he singled out, following what Marx had written in *The Civil War in France,* was "the holy awe with which [Commune leaders] remained standing respectfully outside the gates of the Bank of France. . . .

"The bank in the hands of the Commune—this would have been worth more than ten thousand hostages," Engels continued. "It would have meant the pressure of the whole of the French bourgeoisie on the Versailles government in favour of peace with the Commune."[78]

"With a modicum of common sense," Marx insisted in a letter written in 1881, the Commune "could have reached a compromise with Versailles useful to the whole mass of the people—the only thing that was possible to reach at the time.

"The appropriation of the Bank of France alone would have been quite enough" to give the bourgeoisie pause, Marx said.[79]

The Communards had failed to use one of the weapons at hand that could have altered the course of the civil war to their favor. The criticisms concerning the Bank of France did not mean that the founders of the communist movement were reprimanding the Commune leadership for failing to begin the expropriation of the capitalist class. Marx and Engels had no ultraleft notions about what the Commune could have accomplished in the short run along these lines. Rather, their point was that strengthening the defense of the Commune through adequate measures against the onslaught of reaction could have prolonged the life of the Commune. The time bought for the Commune, in turn, could have opened the door to arousing and organizing the toilers in the countryside and in the other cities of France. If nothing else, more resolute policies could have lessened the price paid by Parisian working people for the subsequent reimposition of bourgeois political rule.

Engels returned to this question a few years later, arguing against anarchist notions prevalent in the workers movement that still echoed old Proudhonist concepts. "It was want of centralisation and authority that cost the Paris Commune its life," he wrote. "The fight needs to have all our forces brought together in a fist and concentrated at the central point of attack.

"And when I hear people speak of authority and centralisation as of two things deserving condemnation whatever the circumstances, I feel that those who say this either have no idea of what revolution is or are revolutionaries only in word."[80]

The Paris Commune, Lenin wrote in April 1917, was—like the soviets of workers, peasants, soldiers, and sailors then emerging in Russia—"a revolutionary dictatorship." This is "an entirely different kind of power from the one that generally exists in the parliamentary bourgeois-democratic republics of the usual type still prevailing in the advanced countries of Europe and America," Lenin noted.

What defines such a power, a revolutionary dictatorship?

"The fundamental characteristics" of a revolutionary dictatorship are: "(1) the source of power is not a law previously discussed and enacted by parliament, but the direct initiative of the people from below . . . ; (2) the replacement of the police and the army, which are institutions divorced from the people and set against the people, by the direct arming of the whole people; order in the state under such a power is maintained by the armed workers and peasants *themselves*, by the armed people *themselves*;

(3) officialdom, the bureaucracy, are either similarly replaced by the direct rule of the people themselves or at least placed under special control. . . ."
This, "and this *alone*," Lenin insisted, "constitutes the essence of the Paris Commune as a special type of state."[81]
The Commune was not a socialist dictatorship, however, nor could it have been. It did not attempt to "introduce" socialism. The manufacturers were not expropriated. The economic and social measures carried out were those of radical democracy: arming the people; establishing representative democracy based on universal suffrage; separation of church and state and confiscation of church property; shifting the tax burden off the backs of working people; decreeing a moratorium on debt foreclosures; cancelling interest payments and rents for a specific period of time in light of the economic collapse brought on by the war and siege of Paris.

These were measures that, as the 1848 Manifesto had explained, were by themselves "economically insufficient and untenable."[82] The very dynamic of their implementation by a revolutionary dictatorship, therefore, led toward further inroads on bourgeois property.

IT IS WORTH NOTING that among the many descriptions used by Marx to capture various aspects of the Paris Commune's significance, he nowhere described it as the dictatorship of the proletariat. Engels did describe it in these terms on one occasion twenty years later—in the final sentences of his introduction to the 1891 edition of *The Civil War in France*. He derisively pointed to the hypocrisy and spinelessness of those on the right wing of the German Social Democratic Party who feigned reverence for the Commune, but were "filled with wholesome terror at the words: Dictatorship of the Proletariat.

"Well and good, gentlemen," Engels rebuked them, "do you want to know what this dictatorship looks like? Look at the Paris Commune."[83]

As history has demonstrated, however, the revolutionary dictatorship established by the Commune was, more accurately, a transitional, revolutionary government of the producers—the first anticipation of what we today call a workers and farmers government. As such, it illuminated, briefly but brilliantly, the future not just for France and Europe, but for the world.

The logic of continued rule by the Commune was clear. It was a *lever* in the hands of the producing classes to begin uprooting the conditions of their social slavery. Had it survived long enough to realize its historic trajectory, Marx said, "The Commune intended to abolish that class-property which makes the labour of the many the wealth of the few. It aimed at the expropriation of the expropriators. It wanted to make individual property a truth by transforming the means of production, land and capital, now chiefly the means of enslaving and exploiting labour, into mere instruments of free and associated labour."[84]

Marx did not speculate on how long the transition to a new economic and social order would have taken, or what measures would have been required to carry it through. Only further historical experience could answer such questions. Blueprints for the future could be left to "bourgeois doctrinaires pouring forth their ignorant platitudes and sectarian crotchets in the oracular tone of scientific infallibility," Marx wrote in *The Civil War in France*.

The working class, Marx said. "did not expect miracles from the Commune." The workers "have no ready-made utopias to introduce *par décret du peuple* [by decree of the people]. They know that in order to work out their own emancipation, and along with it that higher form to which present society is irresistibly tending by its own economical agencies, they will have to pass through long struggles, through a series of historic processes, transforming circumstances and men. They have no ideals to realise, but to set free the elements of the new society with which old collapsing bourgeois society itself is pregnant."[85]

The historical significance of the Commune was that it did just that: "The great social measure of the Commune was its own working existence," Marx wrote.[86]

MARX AND ENGELS were well aware that the objective conditions for the emancipation of labor did not yet exist in 1871. The Commune was a historical "accident," Marx said, "merely the rising of a city under exceptional conditions." It came about not because of the general conditions of French society, but because the Prussian troops were at the gates of Paris, and the "bourgeois *canaille* [dogs] of Versailles . . . presented the Parisians with the alternative of either taking up the fight or succumbing without a struggle."[87]

The challenge to the Commune was to break the siege of Paris and extend the revolutionary dictatorship to the country as a whole. Even that step, however, would have posed the need to extend the revolution throughout Europe. Only risings in Berlin, London, Barcelona, or Rome could have made possible the consolidation of the new revolutionary government in Paris and opened the road to realization of the Commune's goals. But nothing of that order was yet on the historical agenda.

The Commune arose during a period of transition

in the international class struggle—*after* the European bourgeoisie had ceased to act any longer as a revolutionary class, but *before* capitalism had exhausted its progressive force as a social system; *after* the working class had emerged in struggle as the leading revolutionary class, but *before* it was of sufficient size, organization, revolutionary experience, and thus political consciousness to organize its allies and consolidate its own rule.

As Engels put it in his 1895 introduction to *The Class Struggles in France, 1848 to 1850,* history showed "once more that in Paris none but a proletarian revolution is any longer possible. . . . And once again it was proved how impossible even then, twenty years [after the 1848 revolutions] this rule of the working class still was."[88]

L ENIN MADE A SIMILAR POINT in an article commemorating the fortieth anniversary of the Commune in 1911. In modern society, he said, "the proletariat, economically enslaved by capital, cannot dominate politically unless it breaks the chains which fetter it to capital. That is why the movement of the Commune was bound to take on a socialist tinge, i.e., to strive to overthrow the bourgeoisie, the rule of capital, and to destroy the very *foundations* of the contemporary social order."[89]

Nothing more than that "socialist tinge" was yet possible, though, Lenin said. "Two conditions, at least, are necessary for a victorious social revolution—highly developed productive forces and a proletariat adequately prepared for it. But in 1871 both of these conditions were lacking.

"French capitalism was still poorly developed, and France was at this time mainly a petty-bourgeois country (artisans, peasants, shopkeepers, etc.)," Lenin pointed out. "On the other hand, there was no workers' party;

the working class had not gone through a long school of struggle and was unprepared, and for the most part did not even clearly visualise its tasks and the methods of fulfilling them. There was no serious political organisation of the proletariat, nor were there strong trade unions and co-operative societies."[90]

On this leadership level, Engels pointed out in an 1884 letter, the failure of the Commune was not an argument against building a party that could organize the working class to lead the toilers to power. That was the conclusion still being drawn by some French socialists from the bloody defeat of 1871. To the contrary, Engels noted, the Commune proved the opposite: that a proletarian communist leadership was needed. "The Commune was the grave of the *old,* specifically French socialism," he wrote, "while being the cradle of the international communism, which is new for France."[91]

The socialist revolution, the consolidation of a new proletarian economic and social order, was not on the agenda in Europe in 1871. But the first revolutionary dictatorship led by the working class *was,* even if briefly. The working people of Paris, through their initiative and capacity for struggle, advanced the entire world proletariat along its historic line of march.

"History has no like example of greatness," Marx wrote. "With the struggle in Paris the struggle of the working class against the capitalist class and its state has entered upon a new phase."[92]

If the Commune of the Parisian working people was the first historical step of the working class toward state power, it was the Russian workers and peasants who were to take the second. Out of their struggles a communist leadership equal to the task was forged. In 1917 soviet power—the first workers and farmers government—was born.

IV. THE LESSONS OF 1905

BETWEEN THE PARIS COMMUNE and the Russian revolutions of 1917, however, came the titanic revolutionary upheaval of 1905, a dress rehearsal of what was to culminate in victory in October 1917. The tsarist empire, which had been the bastion of feudal reaction for all of Europe since the French revolution, was shaken to its foundations.

Prior to 1905, Lenin wrote, all Marxists in Russia agreed that "the Russian revolution is a bourgeois revolution." The task was first and foremost to bring down the tsarist autocracy, establish a republic, abolish feudal obligations and privileges, destroy landlordism, and secure political liberties.

Fundamental questions of revolutionary strategy were posed for the working class. Should the vanguard of the proletariat, under these conditions, have a "nose for power"? Should the workers in backward Russia dare to win—to overthrow the tsar, lead the peasants to establish a revolutionary dictatorship, and wield it to defend the newly won republic? Should the representatives of the workers vanguard participate in a provisional revolutionary government that could arise under these conditions? Could they do so if representatives of workers parties were in a minority? Could participation in such a transitional government advance the proletariat along its historic line of march, even if the socialist revolution, the dictatorship of the proletariat, proved not to be immediately on the agenda?

The two major factions of the Russian Social Democratic Labor Party (RSDLP), the Bolsheviks and the Mensheviks, gave opposite answers to these questions.

The Bolsheviks answered yes. The Mensheviks, no.

Writing in 1918, Lenin summarized the differences between the Mensheviks and Bolsheviks as follows:

Since the tasks of the impending revolution were bourgeois-democratic, the Mensheviks argued that "the proletariat must not go beyond what was acceptable to the bourgeoisie and must pursue a policy of compromise with it," Lenin explained.

The Bolsheviks, however, "said this was a bourgeois-liberal theory. The bourgeoisie," they said, "were trying to bring about the reform of the state on bourgeois, *reformist*, not revolutionary lines, while preserving the monarchy, the landlord system, etc., as far as possible. The proletariat must carry through the bourgeois-democratic revolution to the end, not allowing itself to be 'bound' by the reformism of the bourgeoisie."

In sharp contrast to the Mensheviks, the Bolsheviks looked to the peasantry, not to the liberal bourgeoisie, as a revolutionary ally. "The Bolsheviks formulated the alignment of *class* forces in the bourgeois revolution as follows," Lenin wrote in the 1918 pamphlet. "The proletariat, winning over the peasants, will neutralise the liberal bourgeoisie and utterly destroy the monarchy, medievalism and the landlord system.

"It is the alliance between the proletariat and the peasants *in general* that reveals the bourgeois character of the revolution, for the peasants in general are small producers who stand on the basis of commodity production.

"Further, the Bolsheviks then added," Lenin wrote, "the proletariat will win over *the entire semi-proletariat* (all the working and exploited people), will neutralise the middle peasants and *overthrow* the bourgeoisie; this will be a socialist revolution, as distinct from a bourgeois-democratic revolution."[93]

Exactly how that strategy would unfold in practice,

how long or how short the different stages of the revolutionary process would be, could not be determined in advance. That would depend on the relative strength of the various class forces at the time, as well as the capacities of the proletarian vanguard. These factors could be determined only in struggle. One thing was certain, however. History would prove more creative than would anticipations of it.

IN 1905, ALL SOCIAL DEMOCRATS in Russia agreed on the historic goal of the dictatorship of the proletariat. Where they differed was on the strategic line of march of the working class in the coming bourgeois-democratic revolution. Which class forces must be mobilized, to accomplish what tasks? What is the relationship between the different stages of the revolutionary process?

While these stages may be more or less telescoped in practice, unless their distinctions are recognized and their interconnections understood, no revolutionary strategy is possible. It was on these points that Lenin could not have been more firmly grounded in the programmatic continuity of Marxism.

Nonetheless, the Mensheviks claimed that they, not the Bolsheviks, were applying the Marxist strategy. Menshevik leaders pointed in particular to writings by Marx and Engels in early 1850, when they were still expecting a revival from the 1848–49 defeats and a relatively rapid victory of the proletarian revolution in Europe.

Lenin replied that the Mensheviks were wrong on two counts. First, they misinterpreted these writings. Moreover, Lenin added, Marx and Engels during that period had not differentiated "between democratic dictatorship and socialist dictatorship." "They did not mention the former at all," Lenin said, "since they considered capitalism to be in a state of senile decay and socialism near."[94] Over the next decades of their lives, Lenin pointed out, Marx and Engels corrected this misestimation. If, at the time of the 1848 revolution, they had "realised that the democratic system was bound to last for a fairly long time," he said, "they would have attached *all the more* importance to the *democratic* dictatorship of the proletariat and the peasantry with the object of consolidating the republic, of completely eradicating all survivals of absolutism, and of clearing the arena for the battle for socialism."[95]

Recognizing the need for a revolutionary democratic dictatorship against tsarist autocracy and landlordism, Lenin wrote in another 1905 pamphlet, did not mean forgetting "that the proletariat will inevitably have to wage a class struggle for socialism even against the most democratic and republican bourgeoisie and petty bourgeoisie." From that fact, he said, comes the absolute necessity for a separate, independent proletarian party, and the temporary nature of the tactic of "striking a joint blow" in the struggle against tsarism together with those in the bourgeoisie who are willing to do so.

"However," Lenin continued, "it would be ridiculous and reactionary to deduce from this that we must forget, ignore, or neglect tasks which, although transient and temporary, are vital at the present time. The struggle against the autocracy is a temporary and transient task for socialists, but to ignore or neglect this task in any way amounts to betrayal of socialism and service to reaction. The revolutionary-democratic dictatorship of the proletariat and the peasantry is unquestionably only a transient, temporary socialist aim, but to ignore this aim in the period of a democratic revolution would be downright reactionary."[96]

The Mensheviks agreed that it was in the interests of the proletariat to fight alongside those in the bourgeoisie and petty bourgeoisie who were ready in deeds to actively oppose tsarism. However, the Mensheviks held that if a revolutionary uprising were successful, and the tsarist autocracy overthrown, it would be impermissible for representatives of the proletariat to participate in a provisional revolutionary government that would take the reins of power in the midst of that struggle.

In 1905 Lenin summarized the Mensheviks' argumentation as follows: "As the party of the proletariat, Social-Democracy cannot hold the power without attempting to put our maximum programme into effect, i.e., without attempting to bring about the socialist revolution. In such an undertaking it would, at the present time, inevitably come to grief, discredit itself, and play into the hands of the reactionaries. Hence, participation by Social-Democrats in a provisional revolutionary government is inadmissible."[97]

The Bolsheviks rejected this Menshevik position.

What was on the agenda in Russia was the revolutionary struggle to overthrow every vestige of feudalism and open the door to the revolutionary mass organization of the proletariat and its victory. "Our task as Social-Democrats," Lenin argued, "is to *drive* the bourgeois revolution onward as far as it will go, without ever losing sight of our *main* task—the independent organisation of the proletariat."[98]

The Bolsheviks agreed that if the goal was to overthrow the monarchy, not just to win concessions from it, then the working class had to provide an answer to the toilers about the kind of revolutionary government that would emerge from the initial victory over tsarism.

If the revolutionary people, the proletariat and the peasantry, "want to fight together against the autocracy,"

Lenin said, "we must fight against it together to the last, finish it off together, and stand together in repelling the inevitable attempts to restore it!"[99] That is the task of the revolutionary dictatorship.

"Is it not clear," Lenin insisted, "that as far as the proletariat is concerned the struggle for the republic is inconceivable without an alliance with the petty-bourgeois masses? Is it not clear that without the revolutionary dictatorship of the proletariat and the peasantry there is not a shadow of hope for the success of this struggle?"[100]

By declaring in advance that they would not participate in a revolutionary government, Lenin said, the Mensheviks were proclaiming that they would not carry the struggle through to the end. In reality, he said, the Mensheviks "shrink from the task which the proletariat, together with the peasantry, is called upon to shoulder—the task of the most radical democratic revolution; they shrink from the Social-Democratic leadership of this revolution and thus surrender, albeit unwittingly, the interests of the proletariat into the hands of the bourgeois democrats."[101]

LENIN EXPLAINED that the revolutionary democratic dictatorship of the proletariat and peasantry advocated by the Bolsheviks was not primarily an agitational slogan. Above all, he said, it was a scientific description of the class character of a popular revolutionary dictatorship that could replace the tsarist regime and advance the revolution as far as possible in the interests of the workers and exploited peasants.

To speak of a provisional revolutionary government, such as that called for by the Bolsheviks, Lenin said, was to stress two things: first, the origins of the governmental power—that it "originates, not from the law, but from the revolution"; and second, the transitional character of the regime and its limited tasks: "It is a temporary government committed to the future Constituent Assembly."

But, Lenin stressed, "whatever the form, whatever the origin, whatever the conditions, one thing at any rate is clear—that the provisional revolutionary government must have the support of definite classes. One has only to remember this simple truth to realise that the provisional revolutionary government can be nothing else but the revolutionary dictatorship of the proletariat and the peasantry."[102] No other revolutionary power could conceivably be victorious.

A DRAFT RESOLUTION submitted by Lenin to the Third Congress of the Russian Social Democratic Labor Party in April 1905 summarized the Bolsheviks' position on the character of the revolutionary democratic dictatorship of the proletariat and peasantry. It explained the conditions under which the proletarian vanguard would be able, indeed obliged, to participate in a provisional revolutionary government emerging from a mass insurrection that overthrew the tsarist regime.

> 1. Whereas a really free and open mass struggle of the proletariat against the bourgeoisie requires the widest possible political liberty and, consequently, the fullest possible realisation of republican forms of government;
> 2. Whereas various bourgeois and petty-bourgeois sections of the population, the peasantry, etc., are now coming out in increasing numbers with revolutionary-democratic slogans. . . .
> 3. Whereas international revolutionary Social-

Democracy has always recognised that the proletariat must render most energetic support to the revolutionary bourgeoisie in its struggle against all reactionary classes and institutions, provided that the party of the proletariat maintain absolute independence and a strictly critical attitude towards its temporary allies;

4. Whereas the overthrow of the autocratic government in Russia is inconceivable without its replacement by a provisional revolutionary government, and whereas only such a change can ensure real freedom and a true expression of the will of the whole people during the inauguration of the new political system in Russia and guarantee the realisation of our programme of immediate and direct political and economic changes;

5. Whereas without the replacement of the autocratic government by a provisional revolutionary government supported by all revolutionary-democratic classes and class elements in Russia, it will be impossible to achieve a republican form of government and win over to the revolution the backward and undeveloped sections of the proletariat and particularly of the peasantry....

6. Whereas with the existence in Russia of a Social-Democratic party of the working class, which, though only in the initial stage of its development, is nevertheless already organised and capable, particularly under conditions of political freedom, of controlling and directing the actions of its delegates in a provisional revolutionary government, the danger that these delegates may deviate from the correct class line is not insurmountable—

Therefore, the Third Congress of the R.S.D.L.P. holds that representatives of the Party may participate in the provisional revolutionary government for the purpose of relentlessly combating, together with the revolutionary bourgeois democrats, all attempts at counterrevolution, and of defending the independent class interests of the proletariat, provided that the Party maintain strict control over its representatives and firmly safeguard the independence of the Social-Democratic Labour Party, which aims at the complete socialist revolution and is in this respect hostile to all bourgeois-democratic parties and classes.[103]

This resolution was adopted amid the mounting struggles of the 1905 revolution in Russia. This challenge to the tsarist empire, which reached its high point between October and December 1905, brought with it peasant uprisings, mass strikes, and urban insurrections, and gave birth to new institutions of revolutionary struggle—the "soviets," councils of elected representatives of the working classes.

For a time, the impact of the new revolutionary situation narrowed the differences between the two factions of Social Democracy in Russia. "Old controversies of the pre-revolutionary period gave way to unanimity on practical questions," Lenin wrote. "The upsurge of the revolutionary tide pushed aside disagreements."[104]

Nonetheless, the differences between the Bolsheviks and Mensheviks over the class character of a provisional revolutionary government remained decisive. Bolsheviks, Lenin wrote in 1906, had regarded the soviets "as embryonic organs of revolutionary state power that united the proletariat with the revolutionary democrats."[105] They advocated the conquest of power by the soviets and establishment of a revolutionary democratic dictatorship of the proletariat and peasantry.

The Mensheviks, on the other hand, regarded the soviets "as organs of revolutionary local self-government,"[106] but they rejected any immediate perspective of the fight for a revolutionary dictatorship of the toiling classes. To cloak this stance in the mantle of Marxist orthodoxy, the Mensheviks argued that only their perspective would lay the groundwork to make possible, sometime in the future, the establishment of the Social Democrats' goal of a dictatorship of the proletariat.

LOOKING BACK ON THIS DEBATE, Lenin wrote in 1920 that the Bolsheviks had "emphasised that the Soviets of Workers Deputies [in 1905] were *'actually an embryo of a new revolutionary power.'*" The Mensheviks, on the other hand, "acknowledged the importance of the Soviets; they were in favour of 'helping to organise' them, etc., but they did not regard them as embryos of revolutionary power, did not in general say anything about a 'new revolutionary power' of this or some similar type, and flatly rejected the slogan of dictatorship."[107]

The Bolsheviks argued strongly for the need to broaden out the soviets beyond the workers' representatives, and incorporate into them representatives of other revolutionary democratic forces. The Mensheviks, on the other hand, insisted that the soviets were and should remain, above all, proletarian organizations.

"As a revolutionary centre providing political leadership," Lenin said in November 1905, the Soviet of Workers' Deputies "is not too broad an organisation, but on the contrary, a much too narrow one. The Soviet must proclaim itself the provisional revolutionary government, or form such a government, and must by all means enlist to this end the participation of new deputies not only from the workers, but first of all, from the sailors and soldiers, who are everywhere seeking freedom; secondly, from the revolutionary peasantry, and thirdly, from the revolutionary bourgeois intelligentsia. The Soviet must select a strong nucleus for the provisional revolutionary government and reinforce it with representatives of all revolutionary parties and all revolutionary (but, of course, only revolutionary and not liberal) democrats.

"We are not afraid of so broad and mixed a composition," Lenin pointed out. "Indeed, we want it, for unless the proletariat and the peasantry unite and unless the Social-Democrats and revolutionary democrats form a fighting alliance, the great Russian revolution cannot be fully successful."[108]

The Mensheviks and centrists objected that such a broad front of class forces could not agree on a "programme complete enough to ensure victory" for the revolution. Lenin answered, "Such a programme has already been advanced in full by reality": complete realization of political freedom; convocation of a national constituent assembly "with full authority and strength to establish a new order in Russia"; arming of the people; immediate granting of real and full freedom to the nationalities oppressed by the tsarist monster; implementation of the eight-hour working day and other urgent measures to curb the oppressive conditions of labor; and the transfer of all land to the peasants and establishment everywhere of revolutionary peasants committees.

That program, said Lenin, is what revolutionary democratic forces are already fighting for. It would be the program of a provisional government formed by the soviets, of the revolutionary democratic dictatorship of the proletariat and peasantry. "Even bourgeois liberals are willing to accept it in theory," Lenin said. "As for us, we must put it into practice with the help of the forces of the revolutionary people."[109]

The Mensheviks charged that the Bolsheviks' orientation would lead to a repeat in Russia of the traitorous action by French Socialist Alexandre Millerand. In 1899 Millerand, with the support of one faction of the divided French Socialist movement, joined the bourgeois government of France. (One of Millerand's fellow cabinet ministers was Gen. Gaston Galliffet, executioner of the Commune.) Millerand's class-collaborationist action was condemned by the overwhelming majority of the Second International.

In reply to the Mensheviks, Lenin pointed out that they were in effect equating two opposite experiences: on the one hand, Millerand's participation in a bourgeois government attempting to halt the advance of the working class during a period of rising discontent and revolutionary action; on the other hand, the participation of Louis-Eugène Varlin, the French communist worker and member of the First International, in the leadership of the Paris Commune—a revolutionary dictatorship of the Parisian working people who were fighting to defend and safeguard their new social order against the restoration of the Bonapartist dictatorship and domination by the Prussian monarchy.

THE LESSONS DRAWN by Marx and Engels from the Paris Commune, Lenin noted, pointed to exactly the opposite conclusions from those advanced by Menshevism. Actually, Lenin wrote in July 1905, the Commune teaches us "that the participation of representatives of the socialist proletariat with the petty bourgeoisie in a revolutionary government is in principle entirely permissible, and in certain conditions a direct obligation."[110]

Lenin also pointed to Engels's scathing denunciation of the role played by followers of the Russian anarchist Michael Bakunin in the defeat of the democratic forces in the Spanish republican uprising of 1873. At the time of these events, Engels wrote, Spain was still so undeveloped industrially that there could "be no question there of *immediate* complete emancipation of the working class." Spain would "first have to pass through various preliminary stages of development and remove quite a number of obstacles from its path. The Republic offered a chance of going through these stages in the shortest possible time and quickly surmounting the obstacles.

"But this chance could be taken only if the Spanish working class played an active *political* role," Engels stressed. "The labour masses felt this: they strove everywhere to participate in events, to take advantage of the opportunity for action, instead of leaving the propertied classes, as hitherto, a clear field for action and intrigues."

Despite this, Engels said, the Bakuninists "had been preaching for years, that no part should be taken in a revolution that did not have as its aim the immediate and complete emancipation of the working class."[111] The anarchists also opposed in principle participation by representatives of the proletariat in any government. They propagated the idea, as Engels put it, that "all revolutionary action from above was an evil, and everything should be organised and carried through from below."[112]

Pointing to the parallels with the debate raging in the Russian Social Democratic movement, Lenin explained that the Bakuninists' position in Spain "naturally and inevitably leads to the practical conclusion that the establishment of revolutionary governments is a betrayal of the working class." These are, Lenin continued, the same "'principles' which the new *Iskra* [Mensheviks] has arrived at, namely: (1) that only revolutionary action from below is admissible.... (2) that participation in a provisional revolutionary government is a betrayal of the working class. Both these new-*Iskra* principles are anarchist principles. The actual course of the struggle for the republic in Spain revealed the utter preposterousness and the utterly reactionary essence of both these principles."[113]

As it turned out, Engels demonstrated in his 1873 article, the anarchists—"as soon as they were faced with a serious revolutionary situation"[114]—ended up junking their previous "principles" regarding nonparticipation in revolutionary governments, but they did so in such a way as to totally disorient the working masses, fragment the revolutionary forces, and turn themselves into impotent hostages of the bourgeois forces. In short, Engels concluded, "the Bakuninists in Spain have given us an unparalleled example of how a revolution should *not* be made."[115]

THE DISASTROUS BOTCHWORK of the Spanish anarchists, however, gave no brief to the Mensheviks' warnings that participation by a workers party in a provisional revolutionary government in Russia in 1905 inevitably entailed unacceptable concessions to the class enemy. To the contrary, Lenin said, "Marx and Engels would have called the new *Iskra's* doctrinal position a contemplation of the 'posterior' of the proletariat, a rehash of anarchist errors."[116]

No one but a fool would contend that participation in a

provisional revolutionary government entails no dangers for Social Democracy, Lenin wrote, answering the Mensheviks. "There is not, nor can there be, any form of struggle, any political situation that does not involve dangers." But, Lenin pointed out, "If there is no revolutionary class instinct, if there is no integral world outlook on a scientific level, if . . . there are no brains in the head, then it is dangerous even to take part in strikes—it may lead to Economism; to engage in parliamentary struggle—it may end in parliamentary cretinism. . . ."

Applying these general considerations to the specific situation in tsarist Russia, Lenin continued:

> It goes without saying that if the Social-Democrats were to forget, even for a moment, the class distinctiveness of the proletariat vis-à-vis the petty bourgeoisie, if they were to form an ill-timed and unprofitable alliance with one or another untrustworthy petty-bourgeois party of the intelligentsia, if the Social-Democrats were to lose sight, even for a moment, of their own independent aims and the need (in all political situations and exigencies, in all political crises and upheavals) for attaching paramount importance to developing the class-consciousness of the proletariat and its independent political organisation, then participation in the provisional revolutionary government would be extremely dangerous. But under such circumstances, any political step, we repeat, would be equally dangerous.[117]

History had the final say on this dispute. The Mensheviks, despite their "ultraproletarian" and "ultraorthodox" line in 1905, expressed most sharply in their refusal to contemplate participation in anything but a "pure" workers government, wound up implementing a class-collaborationist line in 1917—the fate they had predicted for the Bolsheviks twelve years earlier. Like the Spanish anarchists, they found themselves supporting the counterrevolutionary "posterior"—a bourgeois government—while the Bolsheviks continued to advance the proletarian and peasant "head" of the revolution toward power.

V. FROM FEBRUARY TO OCTOBER 1917: THE DUAL POWER

THE STRATEGIC PERSPECTIVES of the Bolsheviks were tested in the crucible of revolutionary class struggle in 1905. That test confirmed the fundamental correctness of their program and provided rich experiences that enabled them to deepen their understanding of the class forces in the Russian revolution. Thus armed, the Bolsheviks were able to chart their course throughout the difficulties and complexities of the next decade.

Summarizing the Bolsheviks' strategic orientation in a 1909 article, Lenin wrote:

"Our Party holds firmly to the view that the role of the proletariat is the *role of leader* in the bourgeois-democratic revolution; that *joint actions* of the proletariat and the peasantry are essential to carry it through to victory; that unless *political power is won* by the revolutionary classes, victory is impossible."[118]

As the tsarist empire experienced accelerated capitalist development between 1905 and 1914, important changes took place in economic conditions, class relations, and the resulting political situation in Russia. The proletariat grew in size, and by 1912 there was a resurgence of workers' strikes and demonstrations. Alongside of and intertwined with the old feudal obligations and land ownership, economic and social relations in the countryside continued to be transformed in the direction of capitalist agricultural production.

The outbreak of the first interimperialist world war in August 1914, which pitted the backward tsarist empire against industrially advanced imperial Germany, sharpened the explosive contradictions in Russian society. As the bloodletting, hunger, and war-weariness grew in Russia, and, at a slower pace, across much of Europe, the only question was when the next phase of the Russian revolution would erupt. The answer came in February 1917.

THE FEBRUARY REVOLUTION brought down the tsarist regime, opening the tumultuous revolutionary upheaval that culminated eight months later in the Bolshevik-led October insurrection. The February mass upsurge, however, was not powerful enough to sweep aside the landlords and big capitalists, who sought to limit the scope of the revolution, continue the imperialist policies of the old regime, and compromise with the forces of reaction. The liberal bourgeois parties formed a provisional government to replace the tsar and his cabinet.

As in 1905, soviets sprang up. They emerged first in the cities, composed of workers, soldiers, and sailors. These were soon followed by peasant soviets in the countryside. All-Russia assemblies of delegates from these workers' soldiers, and peasants councils met in the capital city of Petrograd, where they established their headquarters.

The soviets were the organs of an incipient popular revolutionary dictatorship, drawing their authority from the revolutionary masses who looked to them for political leadership. For example, the soviets successfully blocked troop movements ordered by the capitalist Provisional Government that they believed endangered the survival of the revolution. In doing so they demonstrated their potential to rule. But state power was in the hands of the Provisional Government, which was made up of liberal members of the landed aristocracy, representatives of the bourgeois parties, and, after May, by leaders of the Mensheviks and the peasant-based Socialist Revolutionary Party. Before the soviets could become the governing power, and before the workers and peasants could exercise their dictatorship, the Provisional Government had to be overthrown through an insurrection.

Lenin pointed out that the revolutionary democratic dictatorship of the proletariat and peasantry had been partially realized with the rise of the soviets during the February revolution, although in an unforeseen form. It had come into existence as one pole of a dual power.

"The main feature of our revolution . . . is the *dual power* which arose in the very first days after the triumph of the revolution," Lenin wrote in April 1917.

"The class origin and the class significance of this dual power is the following: The Russian revolution of [February] 1917 not only swept away the whole tsarist monarchy, not only transferred the entire power to the bourgeoisie, but also *moved close towards* a revolutionary-democratic dictatorship of the proletariat and the peasantry. The Petrograd and the other, the local, Soviets constitute precisely such a dictatorship. . . .

"This remarkable feature," Lenin said, "unparalleled in history in such a form, has led to the *interlocking of two* dictatorships: the dictatorship of the bourgeoisie . . . and the dictatorship of the proletariat and the peasantry (the

Soviet of Workers' and Soldiers' Deputies). "There is not the slightest doubt that such an 'interlocking' *cannot* last long," the Bolshevik leader stressed. "Two powers *cannot exist* in a state. . . . The dual power merely expresses a *transitional* phase in the revolution's development, when it has gone farther than the ordinary bourgeois-democratic revolution, *but has not yet reached* a 'pure' dictatorship of the proletariat and the peasantry."[119]

While the old "formulas" of Bolshevism "have been found to be correct on the whole," Lenin said, "their concrete realisation *has turned out to be* different. Nobody previously thought, or could have thought, of a dual power."[120]

THE POPULAR REVOLUTIONARY DICTATORSHIP that existed alongside the bourgeois government displayed features of a state of a new kind, like the Paris Commune of 1871. *"Inasmuch as* [the soviets] are a power, we have in Russia a state of the *type* of the Paris Commune," Lenin wrote in April 1917. "I have emphasised the words 'inasmuch as', for it is only an incipient power."[121]

The class relations underlying the two alternative powers, and their relationship to each other, was crucial. The reason the two dictatorships were temporarily interlocked was that the "Petrograd Soviet of Soldiers' and Workers' Deputies, which . . . enjoys the confidence of most of the local Soviets, is *voluntarily* transferring state power to the bourgeoisie and *its* Provisional Government, is voluntarily *ceding* supremacy to the latter, having entered into an agreement to support it, and is limiting its own role to that of an observer, a supervisor of the convocation of the Constituent Assembly."[122]

This, in turn, was the result of the *"insufficient class-*

consciousness and organisation of the proletarians and peasants"[123]—itself a product of the level of economic development and revolutionary political experience. The decisive political dividing line was the war. The petty bourgeoisie—the vast majority of Russian society, and the vast majority of those deeply involved in the revolutionary upheaval—still supported the imperialist war against Germany, mistakenly judging it to be a war to defend the revolution.

"From the point of view of science and practical politics," Lenin wrote,

> one of the chief symptoms of *every* real revolution is the unusually rapid, sudden, and abrupt increase in the number of "ordinary citizens" who begin to participate actively, independently and effectively in political life and in the *organisation of the state*.
> Such is the case in Russia. Russia at present is seething. Millions and tens of millions of people, who had been politically dormant for ten years [since the 1905–7 upsurge] and politically crushed by the terrible oppression of tsarism and by inhuman toil for the landowners and capitalists, *have awakened and taken eagerly* to politics. And who are these millions and tens of millions? For the most part small proprietors, petty bourgeois, people standing midway between the capitalists and the wage-workers. . . .
> A gigantic petty-bourgeois wave has swept over everything and overwhelmed the class-conscious proletariat, not only by force of numbers but also ideologically; that is, it has infected and imbued very wide circles of workers with the petty-bourgeois political outlook.

> The petty bourgeoisie are in real life dependent upon the bourgeoisie, for they live like masters and not like proletarians (from the point of view of their *place* in social *production*) and follow the bourgeoisie in their outlook.
>
> An attitude of unreasoning trust in the capitalists—the worst foes of peace and socialism—characterises the politics of the *popular masses* in Russia at the present moment; this is the fruit that has *grown* with revolutionary rapidity on the social and economic soil of the most petty-bourgeois of all European countries. This is the *class* basis for the *'agreement'*, between the Provisional Government and the Soviet of Workers' and Soldiers' Deputies.[124]

This situation allowed the class-collaborationist Menshevik and Socialist Revolutionary parties to assume and maintain the majority leadership of the soviets. They backed the bourgeois government and rallied support for its continuation of the chauvinist war policies and expansionist aims of the fallen tsarist regime. Arguing that defense of the revolution against the armies of imperial Germany precluded fulfilling demands raised by the workers and peasants, the Provisional Government refused to grant demands for an agrarian reform, continued to oppress the peoples in the tsarist prisonhouse of nations, and pursued antilabor policies benefiting the employers. The Mensheviks and Socialist Revolutionaries backed these reactionary policies, seeking to convince working people that it was in their interests to postpone action on their demands until the military situation improved and a Constituent Assembly had been elected and convened.

Lenin was merciless in his condemnation of these "socialist" betrayers of the Russian workers and peasants. In April 1917 he waged a successful fight inside the Bolshevik Party against those who were adapting to "the gigantic petty-bourgeois wave," lending shamefaced support to the war being waged by the Provisional Government.

TOWARD THE WORKERS AND PEASANTS themselves, however, Lenin urged that the Bolsheviks' tactical course be "to patiently explain."[125] The war was not in the class interests of the exploited producers, and that would rapidly become apparent. Defensism, that is, support of the government war effort, would turn into defeatism. The experience of the class struggle itself, combined with comradely discussion, would bring the revolutionary masses to understand the need to overthrow the Provisional Government and transfer power to the workers and peasants. Experience would cure "the proletariat of the 'general' petty-bourgeois intoxication."[126]

Fine words in the mouths of Menshevik and Socialist Revolutionary leaders about "revolutionary democracy" and the "revolutionary people," Lenin argued, only served to conceal the conflicting interests of the bourgeoisie and the masses of workers and peasants.

The immediate task, he argued, was to build and extend the soviets as institutions of a revolutionary power. The real task of each local soviet, Lenin insisted, was not to busy itself passing resolutions calling for a constituent assembly. "The real work is to bring about the abolition of the standing army, the bureaucracy, and the police, and to arm the whole people."[127]

Should the bourgeois provisional government be overthrown immediately? This question could not be answered with a simple yes or no, Lenin said. The situation obliged communists to think more dialectically. He explained in early April:

> My answer is (1) it should be overthrown, for it is an oligarchic, bourgeois, and not a people's government, and *is unable* to provide peace, bread, or full freedom; (2) it cannot be overthrown just now, for it is being kept in power by a direct and indirect, a formal and actual *agreement* with the Soviets of Workers' Deputies, and primarily with the chief Soviet, the Petrograd Soviet; (3) generally, it cannot be "overthrown" in the ordinary way, for it rests on the *"support"* given to the bourgeoisie by the *second* government—the Soviet of Workers' Deputies, and that government is the only possible revolutionary government, which directly expresses the mind and will of the majority of the workers and peasants.[128]

The Bolshevik determination "to patiently explain" was based on the knowledge that no revolutionary dictatorship can survive unless it has broad popular support. "Only if power is based, obviously and unconditionally, *on a majority* of the population can it be stable during a popular revolution, i.e., a revolution which rouses the people to action," Lenin wrote.[129]

Insisting on the lessons of all previous revolutionary struggle, the Bolsheviks stressed that the class-conscious workers in Russia needed to win the *majority* of the people to their side. "We are not Blanquists," Lenin wrote, "we do not stand for the seizure of power by a minority. We are Marxists, we stand for proletarian class struggle against petty-bourgeois intoxication, against chauvinismdefencism, phrase-mongering and dependence on the bourgeoisie."[130]

It was possible to advance toward the undivided power of the soviets only "by *clarifying* proletarian minds, by *emancipating* them from the influence of the bourgeoisie," Lenin insisted.[131] And that meant first and foremost to "create a proletarian Communist Party." The core of that party has "already been created by the best adherents of Bolshevism," Lenin said. "Let us rally our ranks for proletarian class work; and larger and larger numbers from among the proletarians, from among the *poorest* peasants will range themselves on our side."[132]

It was precisely along those lines that the Bolsheviks advanced from April to October—from a clear understanding of dual power to the Bolshevik-led insurrection, which seized power from the Provisional Government and transferred it to the workers and peasants soviet majority.

VI. OCTOBER 1917: THE WORKERS AND PEASANTS REPUBLIC

BY THE FALL OF 1917 the majority of the working class had been convinced of the need to transfer all power to the soviets. That having been accomplished, Lenin insisted, the proletariat could win the peasant majority to its side only by proving that the soviets were strong enough to take power and would guarantee the peasants the right to work the lands they were seizing.

A decisive factor in convincing the Bolsheviks that there could be no delay in organizing an insurrection in the fall of 1917 was the rapid spread of peasant land seizures, which had broken out in virtually every part of Russia after the failure of the counterrevolutionary military coup by General Kornilov in August. Up until then, the peasantry had supported the Socialist Revolutionary and Menshevik conciliators in their subordination of soviet power to the bourgeois regime.

Lenin underscored the significance of these peasant rebellions. "In a peasant country," he wrote in early October, "and under a revolutionary, republican government which enjoys the support of the Socialist-Revolutionary and Menshevik parties that only yesterday dominated petty-bourgeois democracy, a *peasant revolt* is developing. Incredible as it is, it is a fact."[133]

A genuinely popular revolution, led by the proletariat and backed by a peasant war, was being realized in life, much as Marx had anticipated six decades earlier.

Such moments of revolutionary opportunity, however, pass quickly, in part because of the instability and vacillation of the nonproletarian layers of the population. The experience of the Russian revolution, Lenin wrote the month before the October insurrection, "has most strikingly and palpably confirmed the old Marxist truth that the position of the petty bourgeoisie is unstable."[134]

"Only the revolutionary workers, if supported by the peasant poor," Lenin said, "are capable of smashing the resistance of the capitalists and leading the people in gaining land without compensation, complete liberty, victory over famine and the war, and a just and lasting peace."[135]

The Russian peasants "must be wrested from the influence of the bourgeoisie," Lenin insisted in a pamphlet written a few days later in September. "That is the sole guarantee of salvation for the revolution."[136]

It is "only our victory in the metropolitan cities," he wrote in a September 1917 letter to the Bolshevik leadership, "that will carry the peasants with us."[137]

The question of "the firm course to take, of courage and resolve, is not a personal matter, but a question of which *class* is capable of manifesting courage and resolve. The only class capable of this is the proletariat."[138]

That was the *class* basis on which the Bolsheviks charted their course, not only throughout 1917 and in the years following the October revolution, but from their emergence as a distinct political current in 1903. They built a party of the revolutionary vanguard of the proletariat, based among the industrial workers, that could *lead* the entire working class despite its stratification and divisions, as well as the exploited petty bourgeoisie, rural and urban, toward power.

IN OCTOBER 1917, at the decisive turning point in the revolution, the Bolsheviks led the insurrection against the capitalist regime and declared that they were ready to establish a government of the new Bolshevik majority in the soviets alone, if no other soviet party would join them. The new workers and peasants government immediately began to implement radical policies that could "wrest" the majority of the peasantry from the tutelage of the bourgeoisie and its petty-bourgeois political servants. From that point on, the challenge before the working-class vanguard was to sustain and broaden the proletariat's alliance with the exploited peasants, on which the survival of the new power depended.

"Comrades, the workers' and peasants' revolution, about the necessity of which the Bolsheviks have always spoken, has been accomplished," Lenin said in the opening sentence of his speech to the victorious soviet congress on the night of October 25–26.

"What is the significance of this workers' and peasants' revolution?" he continued. "Its significance is, first of all, that we shall have a Soviet government, our own organ of power, in which the bourgeoisie will have no share whatsoever. The oppressed masses will themselves create a power. The old state apparatus will be shattered to its foundations and a new administrative apparatus set up in the form of the Soviet organisations.

"From now on," he said, "a new phase in the history of Russia begins, and this, the third Russian revolution, should in the end lead to the victory of socialism."

HAVING CONQUERED POWER, Lenin said, the first task of the new revolutionary government was "to put an immediate end to the war." Its proposal for an immediate and just peace, he said, would be welcomed by growing numbers of workers throughout Europe who were being driven toward revolution by the horrors and sacrifices of the war.

"Within Russia," Lenin said, "a huge section of the peasantry have said that they have played long enough with the capitalists, and will now march with the workers. A single decree putting an end to landed proprietorship will win us the confidence of the peasants. The peasants will understand that the salvation of the peasantry lies only in an alliance with the workers."

With this firm worker-peasant alliance, and the prospect of aid from revolutions elsewhere in Europe, Lenin said, "We must now set about building a proletarian socialist state in Russia."[139]

The government established on that night of October 25–26 was called on Lenin's proposal, "the provisional workers' and peasants' government" of the All-Russian

Congress of Soviets. The word "provisional" was dropped several months later.

What was the class nature of this new government? What was its relationship to the revolutionary democratic dictatorship of the proletariat and peasantry that the Bolsheviks called for from 1905 on, and that Lenin insisted was partially realized as one pole of the dual power that arose out of the February revolution?

Lenin and other Bolshevik leaders considered the revolutionary dictatorship that was born in October 1917 a dictatorship of the proletariat, in that the proletariat alone *led* that new power. Dual power having been resolved by the October insurrection, however, the first task of these triumphant workers, peasants, and soldiers councils was to implement the programs that the Bolsheviks had advocated for a revolutionary democratic dictatorship of the proletariat and peasantry since the early years of the century. These included total destruction of the old tsarist state apparatus, a thoroughgoing land reform, guarantees of self-determination for the oppressed nations, workers control over production to keep the factories in operation and prevent capitalist sabotage. Immediate steps to withdraw from the imperialist war and emergency measures to organize the distribution of food and other necessities were implemented.

As we will see, Lenin used many different terms in the years following the October victory to describe the revolutionary process the Bolshevik Party was leading: dictatorship of the proletariat, workers and peasants government, socialist state, soviet republic, dictatorship of the proletariat and poor peasants, proletarian state, etc. Some terms were more precise, others less so; some were seemingly contradictory. He used different ones for different situations. To try to settle on *the* term, *the* formulation, that the Bolshevik leaders should have definitively arrived at, thinking that by doing so we are gaining a better understanding of the class forces in the revolution, would be a barren and scholastic enterprise.

A MORE PRODUCTIVE APPROACH is to try to understand the particular aspects of the economic, social, and political reality that were being emphasized by the choice of one or another term at any specific juncture of this vast revolutionary process.

As the Bolsheviks had explained prior to 1917, it was impossible to specify in advance what the correlation of class forces would be in a future popular revolutionary dictatorship. The relative strength of the proletariat would depend on many factors: the development of capitalist industry and agriculture in Russia; the evolution of social differentiations and class struggle in the countryside; and the proletariat's social weight, its revolutionary experience and political maturity, and its organization and leadership.

Moreover, throughout the tumultuous several years following the October 1917 victory—as the revolution advanced and deepened, suffered setbacks, and organized retreats in order to move forward on other fronts—the balance of forces within the revolutionary dictatorship was constantly shifting. Within this living process, the Bolsheviks were constantly assessing their course, correcting errors, and making adjustments, as they provided leadership for the first workers and peasants government the world had seen.

With this reality in mind, let's look more closely at three elements of the revolutionary transition opened up by the victory in October.

1. The October revolution established a popular revolutionary dictatorship of the workers and peasants. Given the correlation of forces between these two classes that emerged at the end of 1917, the proletariat's weight was decisive. It led the new state power.

The immediate interests of the Russian proletariat coincided with the immediate interests of the overwhelming majority of Russian society, the peasantry. Thus, the proletariat was able to lead the seizure of power and the smashing of the old state apparatus. The road to a new historical epoch, an extended period of transition from capitalism to socialism, was opened. In this process, the proletariat was guided by a combat party, a political vanguard steeled over years of revolutionary battles, educated in the history of the class struggle, and grounded in scientific socialism.

"We know from our own experience—and revolutions all over the world confirm it if we take the modern epoch," Lenin stated in March 1921, that "the petty bourgeoisie in general, and the peasants in particular, have failed in all their attempts to realise their strength, and to direct economics and politics in their own way. They have had to follow the leadership either of the proletariat, or the capitalists—there is no middle way open to them.... Whenever the proletariat was unable to lead the revolution, this force always followed the leadership of the bourgeoisie."[140]

The proletariat is the only class that can lead the working and exploited people, Lenin stressed, because it "unswervingly follows its path without losing courage and without giving way to despair even at the most difficult, arduous and dangerous stages. Hysterical impulses are of no use to us. What we need is the steady advance of the iron battalions of the proletariat."[141]

2. If the proletariat *led* the new state, however, it was not for the purpose of making an immediate transition to proletarian property relations in Russia. The Bolsheviks were fully aware that property forms and the social relations based on them could not be transformed overnight. The new Soviet republic was an instrument whose purpose was to defend the new power against the onslaught of the old exploiting classes and their international allies, and to begin to carry out a social program in the interest of the great majority.

"Operating as it does in one of the most backward countries of Europe amidst a vast population of small peasants, the proletariat of Russia cannot aim at immediately putting into effect socialist changes," said the resolution adopted by the Bolsheviks in April 1917.[142]

"The Soviets must take power not for the purpose of building an ordinary bourgeois republic, nor for the purpose of making a direct transition to socialism," Lenin said that same month. "This cannot be. What, then, is the purpose? The Soviets must take power in order to make the first concrete steps towards this transition. . . ."[143]

The first decrees of the new Soviet government in October were measures of this type: withdrawal from the interimperialist war, nationalization of the land, institution of workers control in industry, and nationalization of the banking system to obtain needed control over financial and credit resources. They were steps to carry through the stalled bourgeois-democratic revolution and to protect working people against war-caused hunger and economic breakdown. Yet, these were measures that only the proletariat, with the support of the poor peasantry, could carry through to the end, because only those classes had no fear of mobilizing the masses of toilers to make these first despotic inroads on the sacred right of property.

3. The government established by the October insurrection was not a "workers' government," as that term had been used prior to 1917 by centrists in the Russian Social Democratic movement, who counterposed it to the Bolshevik governmental perspective of a democratic dictatorship of the proletariat and peasantry. The Bolsheviks had always strongly rejected this "workers' government" perspective, since it pointed away from the strategic tasks and class alliances that were key to the victory of the revolution in Russia.

LENIN REITERATED HIS OPPOSITION to this perspective during the battle for political clarification leading up to the October 1917 victory. In early April he answered those in the Bolshevik leadership such as Leon Kamenev who initially opposed the course advocated by Lenin of pursuing the fight for soviet power. By following this course, Lenin asked, would the Bolsheviks be "in danger of falling into subjectivism, of wanting to arrive at the socialist revolution by 'skipping' the bourgeois-democratic revolution—which is not yet completed and has not yet exhausted the peasant movement?

"I might be incurring this danger," Lenin continued, "if I said: 'No Tsar, but a *workers'* government.' But I did *not* say that, I said something else. I said that there *can be no* government (barring a bourgeois government) in Russia *other than* that of the Soviets of Workers', Agricultural Labourers', Soldiers', and Peasants' Deputies. I said that power in Russia now can pass from [the Provisional Government] to these Soviets. And in these Soviets, as it happens, it is the peasants, the soldiers, i.e., the petty bourgeoisie, who preponderate, to use a scientific, Marxist term, a class characterisation."[144]

Later that month, the Petrograd City Conference of the Bolshevik Party debated and adopted Lenin's proposed course. In the discussion, Lenin—again charged with having changed the strategic perspectives of Bolshevism with his April Theses—explained once more that his position had nothing in common with the slogan, "No tsar, but a workers' government."

"This is wrong," Lenin said. "A petty bourgeoisie exists, and it cannot be dismissed. But it is in two parts. The poorer of the two is with the working class."[145]

That reality continued to guide the new revolutionary dictatorship after it came to power. It was in *fact*, not just in name, a workers and peasants government, a two-class government.

The immediate interests of the workers and peasants coincided in the battle against landlordism and the monarchy. The historical trajectory of Russia's revolutionary classes, however, also involved conflicting interests, since a minority of the peasantry was made up of more or less well-off exploiters of agricultural laborers and tenant farmers. As the class struggle intensified between these rural exploiters and the producers exploited by them, survival of the Soviet republic demanded a proletarian vanguard strong enough numerically and mature enough politically to lead and consolidate its governmental alliance with the nonexploitative *majority* in the countryside.

From 1905 on the Bolsheviks worked to educate the working class in this spirit—not only to understand its tasks at each stage of the revolution, but to comprehend its responsibility to lead the other class forces necessary to maintain a popular revolutionary dictatorship. This education of the proletariat was indispensable not only to the victory of October but to the subsequent defense of the revolution.

Writing in 1919, Lenin pointed to a number of factors to explain to the workers of the world why the first successful socialist revolution had occurred in Russia. Among them was the fact that "Russia's backwardness merged in a peculiar way the proletarian revolution against the bourgeoisie with the peasant revolution against the landowners." But he also emphasized the long-term political training of the proletariat in an attitude of collaborative respect for the peasantry.

"From the beginning of 1905 the Bolsheviks advocated the idea of a revolutionary-democratic dictatorship of the proletariat and peasantry," Lenin noted. "The specific attitude of the proletariat towards the peasantry facilitated the transition from the bourgeois revolution to the socialist revolution, made it easier for the urban proletarians to influence the semi-proletarian, poorer sections of the rural working people."[146]

This political attitude of the proletariat towards its partnership in a revolutionary government with the other classes of exploited producers, especially the small peasants, continued to be the foundation of Soviet policy at each crucial stage of the initial years of the revolution.

4. Even though the Soviet government had barely begun the transition toward socialism, Lenin insisted in his January 1918 report to the Third All-Russian Congress of Soviets that the new state power was, and therefore should be called, a socialist republic.

"I have no illusions about our having only just entered the period of *transition* to socialism, about not yet having reached socialism," Lenin explained. "But if you say that our state is a socialist Republic of Soviets, you will be right. You will be as right as those who call many Western bourgeois republics democratic republics although everybody knows that not one of even the most democratic of these republics is completely democratic. . . .

"We know how difficult is the road that leads from capitalism to socialism," he continued. "But it is our duty to say that our Soviet Republic is a socialist republic because we have taken this road, and our words will not be empty words."[147]

By leading the toilers to establish a workers and peasants government, the working class of Russia had made it possible to begin "wresting by degrees" all productive property from the capitalist class and concentrating it in the hands of the state, in order to increase the total productive forces as rapidly as possible.

IN THE 1875 *Critique of the Gotha Programme,* Marx had explained that, "Between capitalist and communist society lies the period of the revolutionary transformation of the one into the other. Corresponding to this is also a political transition period," Marx wrote, "in which the state can be nothing but the *revolutionary dictatorship of the proletariat.*"[148]

Basing himself on this foundation of Marxist program and strategy, Lenin explained in his January 1918 speech to the Third All-Russian Congress of Soviets that, "The great founders of socialism, Marx and Engels, having watched the development of the labour movement and the growth of the world socialist revolution for a number of decades saw clearly that the transition from capitalism to socialism would require prolonged birth-pangs, a long period of the dictatorship of the proletariat, the break-up of all that belonged to the past, the ruthless destruction of all forms of capitalism, the co-operation of the workers of all countries, who would have to combine their efforts to ensure complete victory."¹⁴⁹

Lenin went on to explain that the transition would be particularly difficult given the material conditions existing in Russia. "It goes without saying," he pointed out, "that the transition to socialism in Estonia, that small country in which the whole population is literate, and which consists of large-scale farms, cannot be the same as the transition to socialism in Russia, which is mainly a petty-bourgeois country," with agriculture just emerging from semifeudal forms of organization, and a low level of literacy.¹⁵⁰

Confiscation of capitalist property was initially limited to cases where capitalists abandoned their factories, engaged in sabotage and decapitalization, or refused to abide by legislation ensuring workers control and better job conditions. The desire of the most militant workers to move faster with the expropriations required patient political leadership. Often the Bolsheviks' job was to slow them down, while educating them to organize and prepare for future measures.

In the early months of the Russian revolution it was common for workers to get together and demand that their factories be expropriated. "I told every workers' delegation with which I had to deal," Lenin said, "when they came to me and complained that their factory was at a standstill: you would like your factory to be confiscated. Very well, we have the blank forms for a decree ready, they can be signed in a minute. But tell us: have you learnt how to take over production and have you calculated what you will produce? Do you know the connection between what you are producing and the Russian and international market? Whereupon it turns out they have not learnt this yet; there has not been anything about it in Bolshevik pamphlets, and nothing is said about it in Menshevik pamphlets either."[151]

In pursuing this course, the Bolsheviks demonstrated their recognition not only that the transition from capitalism to socialism would take an entire historical epoch and was only possible on a world scale—the epoch of the dictatorship of the proletariat—but that even the transition in one country from capitalist to socialist property forms—that is, from private ownership to state property—would be accomplished over a more or less extended period, depending on the given country's degree of economic development.

It would take time for the Russian working class to acquire the consciousness, experience, and skills to begin managing state-owned factories and participating in the process of national economic planning. Meanwhile, it was to the benefit of the workers and peasants to take advantage of those few capitalists who would continue investing their capital in production, and, even more importantly, the much larger layer of managers and middle-class technicians whose skills were still needed by the revolution.

The decisive question was not the pace of the transition, but whose interests the new state power defended.

THE CLASS STRUGGLE does not end when the state power of the exploiters is overthrown, Lenin explained. "The dictatorship of the proletariat, is the *continuation* of the class struggle of the proletariat in *new* forms," he emphasized in the outline for a pamphlet on the dictatorship of the proletariat drawn up towards the end of 1919. "That is the crux of the matter."[152]

There is one decisive new fact, however. The proletariat now fights with a powerful weapon in its hands—a state, an instrument of coercion now to be used *against* the exploiters instead of on their behalf.

"The state is only a *weapon* of the proletariat in its class struggle. A special kind of *cudgel, rien de plus!*"[153] *A cudgel. Nothing more!*

The "suppression of the resistance of the exploiters," Lenin emphasized, is also the task of an entire epoch on a world scale. While the resistance of the exploiters begins before their overthrow, it intensifies even further afterward. Civil war today, he pointed out, takes on an intensity corresponding to the nature of capitalism at its highest stage. What the victorious proletariat must win is "civil war in the epoch of the international ties of capitalism." In other words, civil war intertwined with foreign imperialist aggression and the "inevitability of a combination of civil war with revolutionary wars."[154]

Crushing the resistance of the exploiters and their international allies, including militarily, cannot be accomplished, however, without simultaneously achieving other goals. In his 1919 outline on the dictatorship of the proletariat, Lenin stressed three new political tasks facing the working class in power.

1. To understand the contradictions among the petty-bourgeois producers, in particular, the class divisions within the peasantry—to separate "the peasant as a toiler" from the "peasant as an exploiter,"[155] and to win the active support of the poor peasants for the proletarian-led government, as well as the neutrality of most in the middle layers of the peasantry.

Lenin put this challenge succinctly in another article written at the end of 1919. Repeating a point he had explained time and again leading up to the October victory, Lenin stressed that the proletariat cannot win the majority of nonproletarian working people to support its leadership prior to taking state power. Only after a revolutionary dictatorship has been established can the working class begin to destroy "the influence of the bourgeoisie and petty-bourgeois compromisers over the *majority* of the non-proletarian masses by satisfying *their* economic needs *in a revolutionary way at the expense of the exploiters.*"[156]

"It is no use thinking," Lenin continued, "that the petty-bourgeois or semi-petty-bourgeois masses can decide in advance the extremely complicated political question: 'to be with the working class or with the bourgeoisie.' The *vacillation* of the non-proletarian sections of the working people is inevitable; and inevitable also is their own *practical experience,* which will enable them to *compare* leadership by the bourgeoisie with leadership by the proletariat."

This is lost sight of, he added, by those "who imagine that extremely important political problems can be solved by voting. Such problems are actually solved by *civil war* if they are acute and aggravated by struggle, and the *experience* of the non-proletarian masses (primarily of the peasants), their experience of comparing the rule of the proletariat with the rule of the bourgeoisie, is of tremendous importance in that war."[157]

2. To find ways to utilize the bourgeoisie and its more highly trained specialists and technicians, "setting them to work, compelling them to serve the proletariat."[158]

"When we rap the exploiters' knuckles," as Lenin put it somewhat later, "render them innocuous, overpower them, it is only half the job." In fact, "it is less than one fourth" the job. "We must make these hands work for us. . . ."

"The idea of building communist society exclusively with the hands of the Communists is childish, absolutely childish," Lenin told the Eleventh Congress of the Russian Communist Party in 1922. "We Communists are but a drop in the ocean . . . of the people." We may understand politics and history, but will we be able to supply the peasants with goods in exchange for their grain? If we cannot, "the peasants will say: 'You are splendid fellows; you defended our country. That is why we obeyed you. But if you cannot run the show, get out!' Yes, that is what the peasants will say.

"We Communists shall be able to direct our economy if we succeed in utilising the hands of the bourgeoisie in building up this economy of ours and in the meantime learn from these bourgeois and guide them along the road we want them to travel."[159]

3. To advance the political education and consciousness of the proletariat itself. The "inculcation of a new discipline" in the vanguard of the ruling class, a new confidence and understanding of its responsibilities to lead the toilers.[160]

VII. FROM WAR COMMUNISM TO THE NEW ECONOMIC POLICY

IN THE FIRST MONTHS following the October revolution, Lenin explained in 1921, the Bolsheviks had "expected a period in which peaceful construction would be possible."[161] But the class struggle did not give the communists in the new workers and peasants republic this opportunity to accomplish their immediate tasks and begin carrying through the economic and social transition in the least costly way.

The outbreak of civil war in mid-1918, and the desperate fight for survival against the invading forces of fourteen countries, which were organized and financed by the imperialist powers, forced the Soviet regime to change its original course and hastily erect the structures that became known as War Communism. Having begun in October 1917 with what were in effect the pressing tasks of a revolutionary *democratic* dictatorship of the proletariat and peasantry, the revolution was forced by mid-1918 to begin trying to accomplish more and more the tasks of the *socialist* revolution.

Most remaining privately owned industry was expropriated during the summer and fall of 1918. This was done for a combination of reasons. First, it was necessary to prevent sabotage of production by capitalists who were going over to the armed counterrevolution in growing numbers. The expropriations were also necessary to marshal the country's limited industrial capacity for war-related production. For the same reasons, all trade was centralized through the state. Individual marketing of foodstuffs or other products was declared illegal.

To defend the revolution, the Bolshevik-led government instituted compulsory military service. Soon afterward, conscription for industrial labor was instituted as an emergency measure, and factory work was reorganized along military lines. The trade unions strove to educate workers to understand why such drastic measures were being taken and helped to enforce military discipline in the workplaces.

THE ONSET OF THE CIVIL WAR and imperialist intervention in mid-1918 coincided with an intensification of the class struggle in the countryside. The agricultural workers and poor peasants were coming into increasing conflict with rich peasants, the kulaks, who exploited farm labor, rented land to their less well-off neighbors, and often engaged in usury. The exploited rural toilers began to break off from the peasants soviets if these were dominated by kulaks and to form Poor Peasants' committees to fight for their own demands. Given the hatred toward the landlords among the entire Russian peasantry, only a minority of the richer peasants actually joined the counterrevolutionary armies. Many more, however, resisted the economic sacrifices required by the war effort. In order to ensure sufficient food for the Red Army and for workers in vital war industries, the Bolshevik-led government had to institute compulsory requisitioning of all grain above that needed for subsistence. This military measure was often enforced by armed detachments of city workers and supporters of the Poor Peasants' committees.

Lenin believed that the intensification of class struggle in the countryside during 1918 marked an important turning point in the course of the new revolutionary government. In December 1918 he explained why to a congress of representatives of poor peasants.

"The first stage in the development of our revolution since October [1917] was mainly devoted to defeating the common enemy of all the peasants, the landowners," Lenin said.

The default of the capitalist Provisional Government following February proved that, "Only the October Revolution, only the victory of the urban working class, only the Soviet government could relieve the whole of Russia, from end to end, of the ulcer of the old feudal heritage, the old feudal exploitation, landed estates and the landowners' oppression of the peasants as a whole, of all peasants without distinction."

As long as the new workers and peasants soviet republic "had to exert every effort for the independent movement of the peasants, aided by the urban workers' movement, to sweep away and completely destroy the power of the landowners," Lenin said, "the revolution remained a general peasant revolution and could therefore not go beyond bourgeois limits." Up until that time, the revolution "had still not touched the more powerful and more modern enemy of all working people—capital."

The revolution "began to tackle this much more important and more difficult task this summer and autumn," of 1918, Lenin said. From that point on, "The village was no longer united. The peasants, who had fought as one man against the landowners, now split into two camps—the camp of the more prosperous peasants and the camp of the poor peasants who, side by side with the workers, continued their steadfast advance towards socialism and changed from fighting the landowners to fighting capital, the power of money, and the use of the great land reform for the benefit of the kulaks."

This "definitely put our revolution on the socialist road which the urban working class had tried so hard and vigorously to put it on in October," Lenin emphasized, "but along which it will not be able to direct the revolution successfully unless it finds firm, deliberate and solid support in the countryside."

SINCE THE POOR PEASANTS and middle peasants "do not exploit the labor of others and are not interested in exploitation," Lenin said, they can be won to support the proletarian-led workers and peasants government and its measures against the exploiting classes. "We have destroyed the monarchy and the medieval power of the landowners, and we are now getting down to the real work of building socialism," Lenin said. "This is the most difficult but at the same time the most important and very rewarding work in the countryside."¹⁶²

Lenin came back to this question in his report to the Eighth Congress of the Russian Communist Party several months later, in March 1919. He described the opening stage of the October revolution as one in which "the proletariat had to serve as the agent of a petty-bourgeois revolution." Our revolution, he went on, "was largely a *bourgeois* revolution until the Poor Peasants' committees were set up, i.e., until the summer and even the autumn of 1918. We are not afraid to admit that. We accomplished the October Revolution so easily because the peasants as a whole supported us and fought the landowners.

"Only when the October Revolution began to spread to the rural districts and was consummated, in the summer of 1918," Lenin concluded, "did we acquire a real proletarian base; only then did our revolution *become a proletarian revolution in fact*, and not merely in our proclamations, promises and declarations." ¹⁶³

During the 1918–20 civil war, the big majority of the peasants joined with the revolutionary workers in the life-and-death struggle against restoration of the landlords and the tsar. Their experiences with the White Guards, as the counterrevolutionary armies were known, served to solidify their support for the Soviet regime, as the only alternative to the return of landlordism.

As Lenin explained to the Fourth Congress of the Communist International in 1922, the Bolshevik-led government had been able to win the civil war "because the peasantry were on our side. Probably no one could have supported us more than they did. They were aware that the whiteguards had the landowners behind them, and they hate the landowners more than anything in the world. That is why the peasantry supported us with all their enthusiasm and loyalty."[164]

Despite this support for the Red Army, the compulsory requisitioning of grain surpluses was not popular with the peasants. "The basis of our economic alliance with the peasantry was, of course, very simple, and even crude," during the civil war, Lenin pointed out. "The peasant obtained from us all the land and support against the big landowners. In return for this, we were to obtain food. . . . We confess that the initial form of this alliance was very primitive and that we made very many mistakes. But we were obliged to act as quickly as possible, we had to organise supplies for the army at all costs."[165]

By the final months of 1920, however, as the acute military danger subsided, the toll taken by the war effort became more and more manifest. The continued use of the military methods of War Communism to attempt to run everything from the economy to the trade unions was bringing the workers and peasants regime face to face with a deep political crisis.

The mounting social pressures fostered anarcho-syndicalist tendencies in the working class and inside the leadership of the party. In late 1920 the party leadership was further divided by the so-called trade union debate.

"We must have the courage to face the bitter truth," Lenin said at the end of the year. "The Party is sick. The Party is down with the fever."[166] Spiralling factionalism in the leadership so endangered party unity, he warned, that it threatened to "cause a split and bring down the dictatorship of the proletariat."[167]

During the civil war, hundreds of thousands of the most conscious vanguard workers had fallen in battle or succumbed to disease or starvation at the front. The enormous economic and social costs of the struggle were exacerbated in 1920–21 by drought and famine.

"There was serious unrest among the peasantry," Lenin explained in his report on the Russian CP's tactics to the third Comintern congress in mid-1921, "and discontent was also rife among the workers. They were weary and exhausted. After all, there is a limit to human endurance. They had starved for three years, but you cannot go on starving for four or five years."[168]

Strikes occurred in some factories. Peasant revolts against the government gained momentum in parts of the countryside. At the Kronstadt naval garrison near Petrograd, a mutiny by troops, largely peasant and petty-bourgeois in composition, had to be militarily crushed.

LOOKING BACK on this period at the November–December 1922 Fourth Congress of the Comintern, Lenin explained that, "after we had passed through the most important stage of the Civil War— and passed through it victoriously—we felt the impact of a grave—I think it was the gravest—internal political crisis in Soviet Russia."

Lenin insisted that this crisis was not simply the inevitable result of war conditions, necessary emergency measures, and drought. As he explained to the 1922 Comintern congress, the degree of the economic and social dislocation was exacerbated by the fact that "in our economic offensive we had run too far ahead, . . . that the direct transition to purely socialist forms, to purely socialist distribution, was beyond our available strength, and that if we were unable to effect a retreat so as to confine ourselves to easier tasks we would face disaster."[169]

On Lenin's initiative, the Bolsheviks had begun to abandon the policies of War Communism by early 1921. The requisitioning of grain was replaced by a tax in kind on the peasants' surplus. Only a certain portion of the surplus, established by law, was taken by the state for distribution in the cities. The peasants kept the remainder for their own consumption or to sell on the open market, which was reestablished and encouraged.

"We shall make as many concessions as possible within the limits, of course, of what the proletariat *can* concede and yet remain the ruling class," Lenin explained in a 1921 article. "We shall collect the moderate tax in kind as quickly as possible and allow the greatest possible scope for the development, strengthening and revival of peasant farming."[170]

This was necessary to preserve the revolution's conquests. "The working class can heal its wounds, its proletarian 'class forces' can recuperate, and the confidence of the peasantry in proletarian leadership can be achieved *only* as real success is achieved in restoring industry," Lenin stressed in the same 1921 article, "and in bringing about a regular exchange of products through the medium of the state that benefits both the peasant and the worker."[171]

Along with the new policy toward the peasantry, the Soviet government adopted measures to help revive industrial production. One such measure was to make offers to lease some nationalized factories, mines, forests, and oil fields to foreign capitalists and to remaining entrepreneurs in Russia itself. Combined with this policy was an ambitious proposal to bring electrification to the entire country. This whole course became known as the New Economic Policy, or NEP.

The previous economic policies identified with War Communism were abandoned before the situation had spiralled beyond control. But the necessary retreat, nevertheless, took place "in extreme disorder," Lenin said.[172]

"We had to show the broad masses of the peasants immediately that we were prepared to change our policy, without in any way deviating from our revolutionary path," Lenin told the third Comintern congress in 1921, "so that they could say, 'The Bolsheviks want to improve our intolerable conditions immediately, and at all costs.'"[173]

LENIN SUMMED UP the significance of the New Economic Policy in a report given in October 1921. In the initial period after October 1917, "when we had only just completed the first stage in the work of building up the Soviet government and had only just emerged from the imperialist war, what we said about our tasks in the field of economic development was much more cautious and circumspect than our actions in the latter half of 1918 and throughout 1919 and 1920."[174]

"Partly owing to the war problems that overwhelmed us," against the White Guards and imperialist invaders in mid-1918, Lenin continued, "and partly owing to the desperate position in which the Republic found itself when the imperialist war ended—owing to these circumstances, and a number of others, we made the mistake of deciding to go over directly to communist production and distribution. We thought that under the surplus-food appropriation system the peasants would provide us with the required quantity of grain, which we could distribute among the factories and thus achieve communist production and distribution.

"I cannot say that we pictured this plan as definitely and as clearly as that," he continued, "but we acted approximately on those lines. That, unfortunately, is a fact. I say unfortunately, because brief experience convinced us that that line was wrong, that it ran counter to what we had previously written about the transition from capitalism to socialism. . . ."[175]

In part, the crisis that had welled up under War Communism had been exacerbated by the fact that the Bolsheviks, including Lenin, had drifted into the error of turning a necessity into a virtue. They had begun to expect that the emergency policies imposed to meet the needs of defense could somehow lay the foundation for a more rapid advance toward socialism.

The error could not be left at that, however, Lenin insisted. Some of the policies implemented between late 1918 and early 1920 were wrong even given the wartime conditions.

"In appraising our New Economic Policy," Lenin asked delegates to a Moscow party conference in 1921, "in what sense can we regard our former economic policy as a mistake? Would it be correct to say that it was a mistake? And lastly, if it was a mistake, is it useful and necessary to admit it?"

Lenin's answer was, yes. "Unless the mistake of the previous economic policy is clearly understood we cannot successfully accomplish our task of laying the foundations and of finally determining the direction of our New Economic Policy."[176]

THE CORRECTION OF the war-imposed attempt to somersault into "socialist forms of distribution" put the Soviet government back on the general course it had projected at the outset and had abandoned only in mid-1918. The NEP was the "economic path which [the government] would doubtless have pursued in 1918–1919 had not the implacable demand of the Civil War" forced a drastic change in direction, Russian Communist leader Leon Trotsky explained in a resolution on the NEP adopted by the Fourth Congress of the Communist International in 1922.[177]

Having defeated the White Armies and corrected their own errors in time, the Soviet Communist Party proved capable of leading the reorganization of the economy and reestablishing the proletariat's alliance with the peasantry on a more harmonious basis. "The most important political and economic result of the NEP," Trotsky told the Fourth Congress of the Comintern, "is our obtaining a serious and stable understanding with the peasantry who are stimulated to expand and intensify their work by gaining access to the free market."[178]

The economic recovery began, and this period of grave danger for the survival of the young Soviet republic passed into history.

Several additional points should be noted in regard to the New Economic Policy.

First, there were not a few ultraleft communists, both in Russia and especially in Communist parties in other countries, who vehemently opposed the adoption of the NEP. They considered it tantamount to abandoning the dictatorship of the proletariat, a betrayal of the revolution. Capitalism was being restored, they admonished.

Lenin, Trotsky, and other Bolshevik leaders considered such ultraleftism to be a supreme danger to the revolution. Opponents of the NEP revealed a total lack of comprehension of the real relationship of class forces that existed in Russia. They didn't understand the meaning of state power, of a revolutionary dictatorship of the workers and peasants. They couldn't recognize the fact that the cudgel had passed from the hands of the landlords and bourgeoisie to those of the workers and exploited peasants.

Trotsky explained these ABCs of state power in a

speech to a conference of young Russian Communists in 1922. When the bourgeoisie holds state power, he said, it

> makes concessions to the working class: universal suffrage, social and factory legislation, national insurance, the shortening of the working day. The bourgeoisie makes a retreat step by step; where necessary it grants a reform; when possible it puts on the pressure again and then makes a retreat.
> Why? It is manoeuvring; the ruling class is fighting for its rule, for the exploitation of the other class. Of course the reformists suppose that bit by bit they will remake the bourgeois system into a socialist one. And we reply to this: rubbish!— while power is in the hands of the bourgeoisie they will measure out each reform but they know up to what point they can grant a reform. And just for this purpose they have the power in their hands.
> The same interrelation between state power and reform exists with us too but with just that tiny difference that here the working class is in power and it likewise makes concessions to the bourgeoisie: trading concessions [licenses], free trade, the right to profit and the right to carry its bourgeois soul and its bourgeois body through the streets of Moscow with impunity. This considerable concession has been granted but it has been granted by the ruling working class which holds the debit and credit book of its state and which says: "To this line here I will make a concession but not any further."[179]

In a parallel way Lenin explained that the relationship between the proletariat and peasantry, the two partners in the revolutionary dictatorship, is also based on one overriding fact: the question of power. As the ruling class, the proletariat must have a historical perspective, discipline, and the capacity to lead. It is often obliged to undertake measures that are not in its immediate material interests, narrowly conceived, in order to preserve something that is more important: its alliance with the small producers, without which no popular revolutionary majority exists.

"The whole question is—whom will the peasantry follow?" Lenin emphasized in a 1921 speech on the NEP. "The proletariat, which wants to build socialist society? Or the capitalist, who says, 'Let us turn back; it is safer that way; we don't know anything about this socialism they have invented'?"[180]

In discussing the tax-in-kind policy, for example, Lenin explained to the Third Congress of the Comintern in 1921 that the framework for deciding on the new economic measures could not be to improve the lot of the working class, or to distribute the burdens of a ruined economy equally among the revolutionary classes.

THE NEW ECONOMIC MEASURES had to be adopted even if they meant added hardship and privation for the working class. "We must distribute the burdens in such a way as to preserve the power of the proletariat," Lenin said. "That is our only principle.

"We are helping the peasants because without an alliance with them the political power of the proletariat is impossible, its preservation is inconceivable," Lenin said. "It was this consideration of expediency and not that of fair distribution that was decisive for us. We are assisting the peasants because it is absolutely necessary to do so in order that we may retain political power. The supreme principle of the dictatorship is the maintenance of the alliance between the proletariat and the peasantry in order that the proletariat may retain its leading role and its political power."[181]

The political heart of the NEP, Lenin told the congress, is simple: "We tell the peasants quite openly that they must choose between the rule of the bourgeoisie and the rule of the Bolsheviks—in which case we shall make every possible concession within the limits of retaining power, and later we shall lead them to socialism."[182]

The alliance of revolutionary classes cannot be *imposed* by one of them on the other. Unless the revolutionary dictatorship is based on a genuine *agreement* between the proletariat and other producers—carrying out policies that are in the interests of the exploited, both proletarian and nonproletarian—it will be weakened and eventually overthrown.

As Cuban President Fidel Castro put it succinctly: "the building of socialism [is] the task of free men and women."[183]

From the price paid for the errors of War Communism and the experience of correcting them with the New Economic Policy, the Bolsheviks and the Comintern drew an important generalization for the world revolution. Every successful workers and peasants revolution, the Comintern leaders concluded, will have a transitional period in which policies comparable to the New Economic Policy will be necessary.

Speaking to the Fourth Congress of the Comintern, Lenin stated that the purpose of his report, which centered on the NEP, was "to draw very important practical conclusions for the Communist International," conclusions relevant "not only from the viewpoint of a country whose economic system was, and is to this day, very backward, but also from the viewpoint of the Communist International and the advanced West-European countries."[184]

THE BOLSHEVIKS RECOGNIZED, of course, that the exact character of the transition and of the measures carried out by a revolutionary government would vary widely from country to country, depending on the level of economic and social development inherited by the workers and farmers. Lenin, however, had something more fundamental in mind in drawing out the international implications of Russia's New Economic Policy. In the "Theses for a Report on the Tactics of the Russian Communist Party," prepared by Lenin and adopted by the third Comintern congress, he drew out the significance of these policies for the proletariat's attitude toward the middle classes in general.

"The internal political situation in Soviet Russia," the theses stated, "is determined by the fact that here, for the first time in history, there have been for a number of years, only two classes—the proletariat . . . and the small peasantry, who constitute the overwhelming majority of the population."

This being the internal situation in Russia, Lenin's theses continued, "the main task now confronting her proletariat, as the ruling class, is properly to determine and carry out the measures that are necessary to lead the peasantry, establish a firm alliance with them and achieve the transition, in a series of gradual stages, to large-scale, socialised, mechanised agriculture."

This is a particularly difficult task in Russia, Lenin commented, because of her backwardness and extreme state of ruin. But it is "one of the most difficult tasks of socialist construction that will confront all capitalist countries, with perhaps, the sole exception of Britain. However, even in regard to Britain it must not be forgotten that, while the small tenant farmers there constitute only a very small class, the percentage of workers and office employees who enjoy a petty-bourgeois standard of living is exceptionally high, due to the actual enslavement of hundreds of millions of people in Britain's colonial possessions.

"Hence, from the standpoint of development of the world proletarian revolution as a single process, the epoch Russia is passing through is significant as a practical test and a verification of the policy of a proletariat in power towards the mass of the petty bourgeoisie."[185]

The attitude of the proletariat toward the middle classes, especially the exploited rural producers, and the centrality of this question in charting the strategic line of march of the working class toward political power, were questions that the leadership of the Communist International dealt with at some length between 1919 and 1923.

VIII. THE COMINTERN AND THE WORKERS AND FARMERS GOVERNMENT

THE TASK OF ORGANIZING and politically leading the first four congresses of the Communist International, which met in Moscow during the difficult early years of the revolution, represented a colossal endeavor on the part of the Bolsheviks. As a growing vanguard of the international working class was won to the revolutionary perspective opened by the October victory, the Communist International expanded in breadth and influence. Through its congresses, special conferences, and leadership gatherings, the Bolsheviks sought to educate these diverse forces in Marxism and pass on to them the rich lessons of Soviet Russia's revolutionary experiences. Virtually every question of working-class strategy was debated. The Comintern resolutions, reports, and discussions between 1919 and 1923 remain, for revolutionists today, one of the most valuable repositories of the communist program—a legacy of the lessons learned by the proletariat in the course of its struggle for emancipation.

The Comintern dealt with the strategy of the road to power, including what kind of government Communist parties should advocate and fight to bring into being. Several reports and resolutions dealt directly with the slogan of a workers and peasants government. Others emphasized that the political example of the Soviet republic, as well as its existence as a powerful bastion of the world revolution, opened the perspective of soviet governments coming to power not only in developed capitalist countries, but also in economically undeveloped countries, including colonial countries where the working class had only begun to be formed.[186] The Comintern gave a genuinely worldwide perspective to the fight for revolutionary dictatorships of the workers and peasants.

The Fourth Congress of the Communist International, held in November–December 1922, discussed and adopted a set of "Theses on Tactics" that included a section proposing the call for a workers government, or a workers and peasants government, as a transitional slogan. This document, as well as a resolution adopted by the subsequent meeting of the Executive Committee of the Communist International (ECCI), in June 1923, incorporated lessons drawn by the Bolsheviks not only from their own revolution, but also from other experiences of the international working class since the beginning of World War I.

On the one hand, there had been numerous betrayals by parties of the Second International. During and after the imperialist war, Social Democratic parties had participated in bourgeois governments in Germany and elsewhere in Europe, helping to contain and crush workers' struggles. The Australian Labour Party had gained office through elections and administered the capitalist state on behalf of the exploiters, and "there may also be [such a government] before very long in England," the fourth Comintern congress resolution noted.[187]

On the other hand, workers and peasants governments based on soviets and involving coalitions between Communists and centrist Social Democrats, had come to power briefly in Hungary and Bavaria in 1919. In both cases, the class-collaborationism of the centrists, combined with ultraleft errors by the young Communist parties, were in part responsible for bloody defeats of the workers and peasants at the hands of capitalist reaction.[188]

THE COMINTERN'S 1922 "Theses on Tactics" presented a revolutionary alternative to the class-collaborationist course being pursued by the Social Democratic misleaders throughout Europe, within the framework of a united front policy aimed at influencing the mass of workers still in the ranks of these parties.

"To the coalition between the bourgeoisie and the Social Democrats, whether it be open or concealed," the theses explained, "the Communists counterpose the united front of all workers and the political and economic coalition of all workers parties against bourgeois power, in order to overthrow the latter once and for all."[189]

What program would be carried out by a workers government of the kind advocated by the Comintern?

"The most elementary program of a workers government must consist in arming the proletariat, disarming the counterrevolutionary bourgeois organizations, installing supervision over production, insuring that the main burden of taxation falls on the rich, and smashing the resistance of the bourgeois counterrevolution.

"A government of this sort is only possible if it emerges from the struggle of the masses themselves," the theses stated, "if it is based on working-class organizations that are suited for combat and formed by the broadest layers of the oppressed working masses." The continued existence of such a government, "carrying out a revolutionary policy must lead to a fierce struggle and eventually to civil war with the bourgeoisie."[190]

The Fourth Congress resolution also discussed the approach that communists should take toward participation in such a government.

"In certain circumstances," the theses said, "Communists should declare that they are prepared to form a government with workers parties and organizations that are non-Communist. But they can take such an action only when guarantees are given that these workers governments will really carry out a struggle against the bourgeoisie in the sense indicated above."[191]

If that is done, the resolution said, then the workers government or the workers and peasants government can "serve as a point of departure for attaining" the dictatorship of the proletariat.

Pointing to the examples of the Australian Labour Party government and the Social Democratic-led coalition in Germany, however, the theses warned that not "every workers government is actually proletarian, that is, a revolutionary instrument of proletarian power." Some, instead, are "governments that camouflage a coalition between the bourgeoisie and the counterrevolutionary leaders of the working class."

Communists, the theses explained, "must not participate in such governments. To the contrary, they must relentlessly expose to the masses the real character of these phony 'workers governments.'"[192]

Summing up the debate on the theses at the Fourth Congress, Comintern leader Gregory Zinoviev concluded, "We must educate the working class by explaining, 'Yes, dear friends, to establish a workers' government, the bourgeoisie must first be overthrown and defeated.' . . .

"The International must follow a correct strategy, but there is no strategy with which we can avoid civil war and slip directly over to a workers' government. No such possibility exists. What is decisive is the struggle, the overthrow of the bourgeoisie. After it is defeated, various forms of the workers' government may be established. . . ." Whatever the exact form, its role is to serve as a transition to the dictatorship of the proletariat, "a concrete road to the realization of the proletarian revolution."[193]

Trotsky was another Russian Communist leader who played a leading role at the fourth Comintern congress. Subsequently, he spoke at a December 1922 Bolshevik gathering to report back the results of the congress. In that speech, Trotsky put the discussion and decisions of the Fourth Congress in the framework of the Bolsheviks' own experience following the October revolution. "Under certain conditions the slogan of a workers' government can become a reality in Europe," Trotsky said. "That is to say, a moment may arrive when the Communists together with the left elements of the Social Democracy will set up a workers' government in a way similar to ours in Russia when we created a workers' and peasants' government together with the Left Social-Revolutionaries.

"Such a phase," Trotsky said, "would constitute a transition to the proletarian dictatorship, the full and completed one."[194]

At the Fourth Congress, the Comintern took up the governmental question primarily from the standpoint of an extension of the united front tactic. In that context, the terms "workers government" and "workers and peasants government" were used somewhat interchangeably, the latter slogan pertaining to countries with large peasant populations, or revolutionary peasant-based parties.

At the subsequent meeting of its Executive Committee in June 1923, the Comintern's leadership returned to the discussion. This time they approached the question from a different point of view: that of the central importance of the worker-peasant alliance, and the policy the proletariat must carry out to establish and maintain that alliance. This had been discussed at the second and fourth congresses of the Comintern. By thus shifting the axis of the discussion of the workers and peasants government question, the Comintern leadership reached a deeper understanding of the importance of the governmental slogan, its application in every country, and its connection to the strategic line of march of the proletariat toward state power.

They looked at the workers and peasants government in the context of generalizing the understanding by the parties of the Communist International that the New Economic Policy in Russia represented a necessary stage and policy that would have its counterpart in every anticapitalist revolution. They sought to use the discussion on the governmental question to sharpen the orientation toward power by communist workers around the world, to teach them to think not as sectarian "preachers in the wilderness," to use Engels's phrase, but as leaders of forces determined to become "a great party of action."[195]

"The Communist Parties must not regard themselves as the parties of the extreme proletarian opposition *within* bourgeois society, as was the case during the period of the development of the Second International," the 1923 resolution stated, "The Communist Parties must develop in themselves the psychology of parties which sooner or later will lead the toiling masses into the fight against bourgeois society, to overthrow the bourgeoisie and to replace it as the rulers of the State."

The narrow social vision and conservatism of the more privileged craft workers, which dominated the old parties of the Second International, the resolution said, "must be replaced by the psychology of parties which possess the will to power...

"A Communist Party," the resolution continued, "must prepare itself to defeat the bourgeoisie tomorrow and *therefore* today adopt aims common to all the people. It must therefore attempt to attract to the support of the proletariat all those sections which because of their social position, will be able at the critical moment to support the proletarian revolution in one way or another."

Reiterating the transitional character of the workers and peasants government, the resolution stated:

"The slogan of the 'Workers and peasants Government', like that of the Workers government in its time, does not in any way replace or put in the background the agitation for the dictatorship of the proletariat: the foundation of foundations of Communist tactics. On the contrary, the slogan of the Workers and peasants Government, by extending the basis of the tactic of the united front—the only correct tactic for the present epoch—is the path to the dictatorship of the proletariat.

"The correct interpretation of the slogan of the Workers and peasants Government will permit the Communists not only to mobilise the proletarian masses of the towns," the resolution added, "but also to create valuable points of support in the countryside and thus prepare the ground for the seizure of power."[196]

The resolution pointed to the failure of most of the newly formed Communist parties to pay sufficient attention to forging a worker-peasant alliance. With regard to work in rural districts, it said, "the great majority of the sections of the International have hitherto displayed an attitude which is extraordinarily inert and extremely harmful to our cause." This it attributed to "the unhappy traditions" of the Second International; "an incorrect theoretical attitude towards the peasantry which professes that from an 'orthodox Marxian' standpoint the party of the workers has no connection with the peasantry"; and a "narrow craft conception of the class struggle of the proletariat."[197]

THE 1923 RESOLUTION quoted a resolution adopted by the Second Congress of the Comintern: "The industrial workers, however, cannot carry out their world-historical task of freeing humanity from the yoke of capitalism and war if these workers remain locked within the framework of the narrow interests of their craft and trade union, complacently limiting themselves to efforts to improve their often somewhat tolerable petty-bourgeois living conditions.

"The proletariat can only be a genuinely revolutionary class, acting in a truly socialist fashion," the Second Congress resolution had said, "if it acts as the vanguard of all the toilers and all the exploited, and as leader of the struggle to overthrow the exploiters."[198]

The workers and peasants government slogan, the ECCI resolution explained, was not limited in its application to countries with majority peasant populations. While it "will be of the greatest significance" in such countries, "the victory of the proletarian revolution and its consolidation will nowhere be possible without some assistance from the peasantry. In this sense the slogan of a 'Workers and Peasants Government' must be the general slogan of the Communist Parties!"[199]

Propaganda and agitation around this transitional slogan, the ECCI resolution added, "must be adapted to the conditions prevailing in each country, for instance, in the United States it will apply to working farmers."[200]

IN HIS REPORT on this resolution to the June 1923 ECCI meeting, Zinoviev insisted that one of the main reasons the Comintern should "broaden the watchword 'workers' government' to 'workers' and peasants' government'" was the need to educate the parties of the International that without winning the leadership of the peasantry they would never be capable of defeating the bourgeoisie.

"We need parties which understand not only how to fight for the eight-hour day, but that also understand how to organize the workers in order to fight for the conquest of the majority of the working masses," he emphasized.

"We must not remain exclusively an urban party, if we want to defeat the bourgeoisie; we must become the party of the urban proletariat which, at the same time, remains in close touch with the village," Zinoviev added. "The Russian Communist party was a purely urban party for at least two decades. It was capable of defeating the bourgeoisie only after it had established close ties with the peasantry through millions of soldiers and peasants."

The fight for a workers and peasants government did not imply that any class other than the proletariat was capable of leading the forces necessary to establish a popular revolutionary dictatorship, Zinoviev said. "The only truly and consistently revolutionary class is the working class."[201]

It is self-evident, the resolution stated, "that penetration into the heart of the masses of the peasantry and the slogan of 'Workers' and peasants' Government' by no means imply the conversion of our party from a workers' party into a 'party of labour' or a 'workers' and peasants' party.' Our party, as far as its composition and aims are concerned, must remain a party of the working class."

But we are the party "of a working class which draws in its wake all sections of the working population and leads them into the fight against capitalism," it explained.[202]

Building on the theses adopted at the fourth Comintern congress, the ECCI resolution stressed that this transitional slogan should be used to advance the revolutionary struggle for power, not "to replace mass revolutionary work amongst the lower sections of the working peasantry by parliamentary combinations, based on no principles, with the so-called 'representatives' of the peasantry which often are the most reactionary elements of the bourgeoisie."[203]

Both the resolution and Zinoviev's report related the workers and peasants government to the lessons of the New Economic Policy, and the experiences leading to it that the Russian revolutionaries went through. The slogan was intended to help *educate* the working class about the character of its alliance with the peasantry after the overthrow of the bourgeoisie, as well. Its purpose was to counter ultraleft ideas still rampant in the International, and to explain the need for economic policies based not on coercion, but on the interests of the small producers, implemented with their agreement and support.

"The slogan of a 'Workers and peasants Government'," the ECCI resolution explained, "will render good service to the communist parties even after the seizure of power by the proletariat; for it will remind the proletariat of the necessity to harmonise its movements with the sentiments of the peasantry in their respective countries, to establish a correct coordination between the victorious proletariat and the peasantry, and to observe a rational policy in the gradual introduction of the economic measures of the proletariat, such as was arrived at by the victorious proletariat of Russia in that period of the Russian revolution which is called the New Economic Policy."[204]

"At the World Fourth Congress," Zinoviev said in his report, "we explained to you, why in our opinion the New Economic Policy of the Soviet government is an international phenomenon and not merely an episode in the Russian Revolution. We have proved to you that almost every country after the revolution will have to go through a more or less long phase of this type of policy . . . and that the victorious proletariat of any country will have to face the problem of the appropriate unification of the working class and the peasantry when the time comes.

"If this is so," Zinoviev said, "and we do not doubt it, the logical conclusion to be drawn is the necessity of a workers' and peasants' government.

"If we consider conditions in a number of countries, we

do not see a single country for which this solution would not be the most fitting. We now say to the backward workers and peasants: we want to destroy the state of the rich, and we want to create a state of workers. Let us decide to add: for this reason we suggest the formation of a workers' and peasants' government."[205]

IX. THE WORKERS AND FARMERS GOVERNMENT TODAY

THE BOLSHEVIKS COULD NOT have foreseen—and would not have tried to predict—the actual paths to power and the forms taken by the workers and peasants governments that have emerged in the course of revolutionary struggles in more than a dozen countries in the post–World War II period. The Bolsheviks knew that the road laid down by the class struggle always contains more twists and turns, more detours, than can be seen in advance. The extent of the continuing lag in revolutionary developments in the imperialist countries, the victories that have been achieved in bringing workers and peasants governments to power despite leadership obstacles, the way in which some of these governments have come to power—none of these could have been predicted.

But the strategic line of march of the world working class explained by the Comintern—the line of march toward the seizure of power and the institution of a revolutionary dictatorship of the majority, the toilers—remains the foundation of revolutionary proletarian strategy today. It has been enriched by the lessons of the past forty years of international class struggle that have become part of our theoretical heritage and programmatic continuity.

The strategic orientation toward soviet power—the revolutionary political rule of the workers and peasants—was presented by the Comintern as a possibility on a world scale. It was meant not only for the economically advanced imperialist countries, but for the colonial and semicolonial world as well. With aid from the Soviet workers and peasants republic, Lenin stressed, the toilers in even the most economically backward countries, where precapitalist economic forms predominated, could organize themselves into soviets and follow the course to power charted by the Russian people.

This world perspective became realistic because the proletarian victory in Russia fundamentally changed the relationship of class forces everywhere. For the first time in history, the recognition of the *Manifesto of the Communist Party* that, as yet, "the working men have no country,"[206] fortunately ceased to be true. A workers state had come into being—one that could aid the toilers' struggle everywhere.

N OWHERE IS THIS LEGACY of the Comintern more valuable today than in understanding the process unfolding on the front lines of the world revolution in Nicaragua, where a popular revolutionary dictatorship—a workers and peasants government—emerged from the victory over the Somozaist tyranny in July 1979.

The Nicaraguan Government of National Reconstruction emerged "from the struggle of the masses themselves," to use the words of the 1922 Comintern resolution. It is "based on working class organizations that are suited for combat and formed by the broadest layers of the oppressed working masses." Under the leadership of the Sandinista National Liberation Front

(FSLN), it is carrying out a program of "arming the proletariat, disarming the counterrevolutionary bourgeois organizations, installing supervision over production, insuring that the main burden of taxation falls on the rich, and smashing the resistance of the bourgeois counterrevolution."

This has led to a "fierce struggle" with a large layer of the bourgeoisie. This involves large-scale armed attacks along both Nicaragua's borders, as well as a deepening class polarization inside the country. And we are now seeing Washington press to deepen this conflict into a civil war of the kind Lenin described in 1919: "a civil war in the epoch of the international ties of capitalism," a civil war inevitably intertwined with imperialist aggression and revolutionary war.

The Nicaraguan workers and peasants government is attempting "to observe a rational policy in the gradual introduction of the economic measures of the proletariat," in harmony with the sentiments of the peasants as well as the working class. As Nicaraguan leader Tomás Borge told a visiting delegation of Canadian trade unionists in 1983, there is a mixed economy in Nicaragua, but one that is qualitatively different from the mixed economy of other countries in Latin America. "This is a mixed economy within the revolution," he pointed out, "a mixed economy at the service of the workers." Elsewhere "it is a mixed economy at the service of the bourgeoisie."[207]

The Nicaraguan government is a popular power that is determined to end centuries of brutal national oppression of the native Indian peoples and the Black, English-speaking minority on the Atlantic Coast. It is pursuing policies aimed at ending the second-class status of women, doing what is possible within the economic resources available to draw women into the work force, provide education and training, and ease the burden of child care and other household labor.

The revolutionary vanguard of Nicaragua more and more is composed of the most conscious workers. They are striving to organize, unify, and raise the consciousness and discipline of the entire working class. It is above all through the Sandinista Workers Federation, the CST, that the understanding is being forged of the leading role of the working class in the march toward a socialist Nicaragua.

The weight of the proletariat is growing within the worker-peasant alliance that is in power in Nicaragua. The role of the industrial workers in the government and in defending the revolution is expanding. This is occurring simultaneously with the deepening of the ties between the working class and other toilers throughout the country, including the poorest peasants and the Indian and Black populations concentrated on the Atlantic Coast.

Under the conditions of intensifying revolutionary struggle a mass proletarian party, the Sandinista National Liberation Front, is being constructed. The most conscious workers are being incorporated into the ranks of the FSLN, as are the leaders coming forward in the mass organizations of peasants, women, youth, and the oppressed nationalities.

This deepening proletarianization, which is being consciously advanced by the Sandinista leadership, is strengthening the workers and peasants rule.

The defeat in Grenada stands as a fresh reminder that initial victories can be reversed. The politically displaced exploiters, with their powerful international ties, will turn every weakness to their advantage.

A workers and farmers government stands at the head of a turbulent, transitional process, during which the old ruling classes still retain significant advantages. Their economic power, reinforced by imperialism, is constantly being regenerated by the operation of the laws of commodity production and exchange. A revolutionary government at such a stage is inevitably more vulnerable to counterrevolutionary overthrow than a popular power that has successfully led the struggle across a second qualitative threshold: the expropriation of industry and establishment of a planned economy based on state property in the basic means of production—that is, to the establishment of a workers state. This transformation, growing out of the deepening proletarianization of the revolution, marks a further strengthening of the rule of the toilers. Two workers and farmers governments, Algeria and Grenada, have been overthrown in the last twenty years. But no revolution that succeeded in establishing a workers state has yet been overthrown.

THE EXAMPLE OF CUBA serves as a beacon for Nicaragua today. The survival and continuing advance of the revolutionary Cuban workers state offers living proof that imperialism is not all-powerful, that the workers and peasants of a small and economically impoverished nation can take their own destiny in hand and move forward.

In this way, too, the world perspectives laid out by the Comintern are being confirmed, and advanced, in Central America and the Caribbean. The victory, consolidation, and defense of the conquests of the October revolution have made possible the military and economic aid from the Soviet workers state that has enabled the Cuban revolution to survive and accomplish as much as it has.

Nicaragua, in its turn, would face qualitatively worse odds in its life-and-death struggle with Yankee imperialism were it not for the internationalist aid of socialist Cuba and other workers states, as well as the changed relationship of forces that the existence of these workers states imposes on the world class struggle.

For proletarian revolutionists in North America, the fight for a workers and farmers government is not a distant perspective—either in time or geography. It is a political orientation that guides everything we do right here today to build our party.

A VICTORIOUS REVOLUTION of the workers and farmers of the United States will be achieved only by smashing the capitalist state that wields the military might of U.S. imperialism and by destroying the economic power of America's sixty families. That revolution will create the preconditions for the working class and the producers on the land to unleash the vast productive potential of the U.S. economy, placing it at the service of the workers and peasants of the world.

The internationalist perspective embodied in the fight for a world federation of workers and farmers republics is the negation of the selfish concern of an aristocracy of labor, seeking to improve its often quite tolerable conditions of life, as the Comintern resolution said. With a government of their own in power, the workers and farmers of the United States will seek to advance to a society of socialist abundance not *ahead of* the toilers of the world—but *together with them.*

Our fight for a workers and farmers government serves to educate the vanguard of the U.S. working class in a spirit of hatred for all national chauvinism, narrow-minded arrogance, and craft smugness. It advances and deepens a truly proletarian attitude of respect toward all working people, here and the world over. Without such training, the bourgeoisie will never be defeated. No new social order will ever be built.

The working class, because it owns no capital and exploits no one, is the only class that is able, by abolishing the conditions of its own exploitation, to emancipate all humanity from inequality and all its attendant barbarities. For that reason, it is the only thoroughly and consistently revolutionary class. It has no need to impose a new social order on its allies. The working class needs only *to lead*, with the self-confidence born of the certainty that it can truly speak for and does represent the interests of humanity.

That is why the fight to establish a workers and farmers government is necessarily interlinked with the perspective of fighting to build a party that is proletarian in its composition, program, and attitudes—a party deeply rooted in the organizations of the industrial working class, with strong ties to the other exploited producers. Nowhere is that more true than right here in the citadel of U.S. imperialism.

The advance toward a world federation of workers and farmers republics is inseparable from the fight to build an international movement of the toilers of the whole world, one that in every country, in its composition, leadership, and daily work—as the 1920 statutes of the Communist International put it—"breaks once and for all with the traditions of the Second International, which, in reality, only recognized the white race."[208]

With such a perspective we can advance against the most powerful imperialist rulers on earth, and open the door to the socialist future.

NOTES

(As a rule, we have taken quotations by Marx and Engels and by Lenin from their Collected Works, although many of their writings are also available in other collections. The works cited here by Marx, Engels, Lenin, Trotsky, Zinoviev, and Castro can be obtained through Pathfinder Press, at www.pathfinderpress.com.)

1. Elizabeth Stone (ed.), *Women and the Cuban Revolution* (New York: Pathfinder Press, 1981), p. 129.

2. Frederick Engels, "The Communists and Karl Heinzen" in Marx and Engels *Collected Works* (hereinafter *MECW*) (New York: International Publishers, 1976), vol. 6, pp. 303–4.

3. Some of the ways in which this cumulative experience has contributed to an evolution of our thinking were outlined in a report entitled "For a Workers and Farmers Government in the United States," which was adopted by the Socialist Workers Party National Committee in March 1982 (available in an Education for Socialists bulletin published by the SWP). This report is now under discussion in the SWP, leading up to the party's August 1984 national convention. Aspects of these questions were also discussed in the article entitled "Their Trotsky and Ours: Communist Continuity Today," by Jack Barnes, in the first issue of *New International*.

4. V.I. Lenin, "A Contribution to the History of the Question of the Dictatorship" in Lenin, *Collected Works* (hereinafter *LCW*) (Moscow: Progress Publishers, 1974), vol. 31, p. 354.

5. Ibid., pp. 360–61.

6. Lenin, "The Third Congress of the R.S.D.L.P.: Report on the Question of the Participation of the Social-Democrats in a Provisional Revolutionary Government," in *LCW*, vol. 8, p. 385.

7. Lenin, "A Contribution to the History of the Question of the Dictatorship" in *LCW*, vol. 31, p. 340.

8. Here, as elsewhere, I use the term dictatorship of the proletariat to indicate a state that is based on and defends

state property in the means of production, a state monopoly of foreign trade, and a planned economy. Such a social dictatorship has been referred to as a workers state by our movement since the mid-1930s, when we were challenged—following the consolidation of the privileged bureaucratic caste led by Stalin—to explain the class nature of the Soviet Union. What conquests of the proletarian revolution remained? What had to be defended by the workers there and around the world?

Our answer has been that, although the Soviet working class had been demobilized and demoralized, its political power usurped by a petty-bourgeois social layer, the dictatorship of the proletariat, a workers state, remains because of the socialist property relations on which it continues to be based and continues to defend. "The class nature of the state," Trotsky explained in 1937, is "determined not by its political forms but by its social content; i.e., by the character of the forms of property and productive relations which the given state guards and defends.... The regime which guards the expropriated and nationalized property from the imperialists is, independent of political forms, the dictatorship of the proletariat." (*Writings of Leon Trotsky [1937–38]*, New York: Pathfinder Press, 1976, pp. 61–62.) This is the fundamental criterion for what constitutes a proletarian state in the historical transition from capitalism to socialism.

For further discussion of this question and its decisive political implications, see *In Defense of Marxism* by Leon Trotsky (New York: Pathfinder Press, 1973) and *Dynamics of the Cuban Revolution* by Joseph Hansen (New York: Pathfinder Press, 1978).

I make this clarification because quotations from Marx, Engels, Lenin, and others elsewhere in this article generally use the term dictatorship of the proletariat in a sense that also encompasses a state in which political power has been wrested from the exploiting classes and taken into the hands of the proletariat and its allies, but in which socialist property forms do not yet predominate.

Part I. Foundations of the modern communist movement

9. Marx, "Herr Vogt" in *MECW*, vol. 17, p. 19. Marx and Engels were recruited to the Communist League by revolutionary-minded workers, who succeeded in convincing them that only by being part of a workers party could they implement the communist program they were working to develop.

Engels later recalled the decisive influence these workers' leaders had on him, and on Marx. Writing of the time he first came to know Karl Schapper, Joseph Moll, and Heinrich Bauer in 1843, Engels explained, "They were the first revolutionary proletarians whom I met, and however far apart our views were at that time in details—for I still owned, as against their narrow-minded equalitarian communism, a goodly dose of just as narrow-minded philosophical arrogance—I shall never forget the deep impression that these three real men made upon me, who was then still only wanting to become a man." (Engels, "On the History of the Communist League," in Marx and Engels, *Selected Works* [Moscow: Progress Publishers, 1977], vol. 3, p. 175.)

10. "Rules of the Communist League," (June 1847) in *MECW*, vol. 6, p. 585.

11. "Rules of the Communist League," (December 1847) in *MECW*, vol. 6, p. 632.

12. Marx and Engels, "Manifesto of the Communist Party" in *MECW*, vol. 6, p. 498.

13. Ibid., p. 504.

14. Ibid., pp. 505–6.

15. Ibid., pp. 494–95.

16. Marx, letter to Joseph Weydemeyer of March 5, 1852, in *MECW*, vol. 39, pp. 62–65. Emphasis in original; the translation has been slightly revised.

17. Lenin, "State and Revolution" in *LCW*, vol. 25, p. 430.

18. Ibid., p. 422.

Part II. The lessons of 1848

19. Marx and Engels, "Manifesto of the Communist Party" in *MECW*, vol. 6, p. 519.
20. Engels, "Marx and the *Neue Rheinische Zeitung* (1848–1849)" in *Selected Works*, vol. 3, p. 165.
21. Marx, "The Crisis and the Counter-Revolution" in *MECW*, vol. 7, p. 431.
22. Marx and Engels, "The Programmes of the Radical-Democratic Party and of the Left at Frankfurt" in *MECW*, vol. 7, pp. 49–50.
23. Marx, "The Assembly at Frankfurt" in *MECW*, vol. 7, p. 16.
24. Marx, "The Bourgeoisie and the Counter-Revolution" in *MECW*, vol. 8, p. 178.
25. Ibid., p. 161.
26. Ibid., pp. 161–62.
27. Ibid.
28. Engels, "Marx and the *Neue Rheinische Zeitung* (1848–1849)" in *Selected Works*, vol. 3, pp. 165–66.
29. Marx, "The Bourgeoisie and the Counter-Revolution" in *MECW*, vol. 8, pp. 175–76.
30. Engels, "Marx and the *Neue Rheinische Zeitung* (1848–1849)" in *Selected Works*, vol. 3, pp. 165–66.
31. Marx and Engels, "Demands of the Communist Party in Germany" in *MECW*, vol. 7, p. 4.
32. Ibid., p. 3.
33. Ibid.
34. Engels, "On the History of the Communist League" in *Selected Works*, vol. 3, pp. 185–86. The Sonderbund (separatist league) was the reactionary association of Catholic-controlled Swiss cantons formed in 1843 to oppose progressive bourgeois-democratic reforms and defend the powers of the church of Rome and the Jesuit order in Switzerland. Marx and Engels often used it as a term to refer to petty-bourgeois sectarian currents splitting from the communist movement.
35. Lenin, "Two Tactics of Social-Democracy in the Demo-

cratic Revolution" in *LCW*, vol. 9, p. 140.

36. Marx and Engels, "Stein" in *MECW*, vol. 8, p. 390.

37. Marx, "Wage Labour and Capital" in *MECW*, vol. 9, p. 198.

38. "Meeting of the Central Authority, September 15, 1850" in *MECW*, vol. 10, p. 626.

39. Marx, "The Eighteenth Brumaire of Louis Bonaparte" in *MECW*, vol. 11, p. 109.

40. Engels, "Marx and the *Neue Rheinische Zeitung* (1848–1849)" in *Selected Works*, vol. 3, p. 169.

41. Engels, Introduction to "The Class Struggles in France, 1848 to 1850" in *Selected Works*, vol. 1, pp. 191–92.

42. Ibid, p. 200.

43. Marx, "The Class Struggles in France, 1848 to 1850" in *MECW*, vol. 10, p. 122.

44. Marx, letter to Engels of April 16, 1856, in Marx and Engels, *Selected Correspondence* (Moscow: Progress Publishers, 1975), p. 86. The text of the letter is also contained in *MECW*, vol. 40, pp. 37–41.

45. Engels, "The Peasant Question in France and Germany" in *Selected Works*, vol. 3, p. 458.

46. Ibid., p. 472.

47. Ibid., p. 470.

48. Ibid., pp. 471–72.

Part III. The Paris Commune:
The political rule of the producers

49. Marx, "The Class Struggles in France, 1848 to 1850" in *MECW*, vol. 10, p. 67.

50. Marx, letter to Ludwig Kugelmann of April 12, 1871, in *Selected Correspondence*, p. 247.

51. Marx, "The Civil War in France," in *Selected Works*, vol. 2, p. 223.

52. Marx and Engels, "Preface to 1872 Edition of the Communist Manifesto" in *Selected Works*, vol. 1, pp. 98–99.

53. Marx, "The Civil War in France" in *Selected Works*, vol. 2, p. 241.

54. In September 1870 the French empire of Louis Bonaparte, facing imminent defeat in a war with the Prussian monarchy, collapsed. A bourgeois republic headed by Adolphe Thiers replaced it. In Paris working people formed a National Guard to defend the city from the impending German assault. At the beginning of 1871, the new French government signed a peace accord with its Prussian counterparts, but German troops remained near Paris for several more months. On March 18 the new bourgeois regime tried to disarm the National Guard, which it saw as a threat to the consolidation of capitalist political power.

The National Guard ranks and elected leadership, its Central Committee, refused to give up their arms, however. At that point, the bourgeois politicians took refuge in nearby Versailles. The Central Committee of the National Guard became the provisional revolutionary government of Paris.

Eight days later the Central Committee held elections for a municipal council (the city had previously been governed directly by the national government). This new municipal council was called the Paris Commune, "commune" being the term used in many European cities to describe the local government. The Central Committee ceded its powers over the National Guard to this newly elected body.

In this article, and in the writings of Marx, Engels, and Lenin, the term Paris Commune is used to refer not just to the Paris municipal council elected on March 26, but to the new state power that came into existence on March 18 based on the working people organized and armed through the National Guard.

55. Marx, "The Eighteenth Brumaire of Louis Bonaparte" in *MECW*, vol. 11, p. 185.

56. Marx, letter to Kugelmann of April 12, 1871, in *Selected Correspondence*, p. 247.

57. Marx and Engels, "Preface to 1872 Edition of the Com-

munist Manifesto" in *Selected Works*, vol. 1, p. 99.
58. Lenin, "State and Revolution" in *LCW*, vol. 25, p. 422.
59. Ibid., p. 437.
60. Marx, "The Civil War in France" in *Selected Works*, vol. 2, p. 223.
61. Ibid., p. 227.
62. Ibid., p. 223.
63. Ibid., p. 220.
64. Marx, letter to Wilhelm Liebknecht of April 6, 1871, in *Selected Correspondence*, p. 246.
65. Ibid.
66. Engels, letter to August Bebel of March 18–28, 1875, in *Selected Correspondence*, p. 275.
67. Engels, Introduction to "The Civil War in France" in *Selected Works*, vol. 2, pp. 187–88.
68. Lenin, "State and Revolution" in *LCW*, vol. 25, p. 424.
69. Ibid., p. 426.
70. Ibid.
71. Ibid.
72. Marx, "The Civil War in France" in *Selected Works*, vol. 2, p. 223.
73. Ibid., p. 224.
74. Ibid., p. 225.
75. Ibid., pp. 225–26.
76. Ibid., p. 226.
77. Engels, Introduction to "The Civil War in France," in *Selected Works*, vol. 2, pp. 185–86.
78. Ibid., p. 186.
79. Marx, letter to Domela Nieuwenhuis of February 22, 1881, in *Selected Correspondence*, p. 318.
80. Engels, letter to Carlo Terzaghi of January 14–15, 1872, in *Marx and Engels on the Paris Commune* (Moscow: Progress Publishers, 1971), p. 292.
81. Lenin, "The Dual Power" in *LCW*, vol. 24, pp. 38–39.
82. Marx and Engels, "Manifesto of the Communist Party" in *MECW*, vol. 6, p. 504.

83. Engels, Introduction to "The Civil War in France" in *Selected Works*, vol. 2, p. 189.
84. Marx, "The Civil War in France," in *Selected Works*, vol. 2, p. 223.
85. Ibid., p. 224.
86. Ibid., p. 227.
87. Marx, letter to Kugelmann of April 17, 1871, in *Selected Correspondence*, p. 248.
88. Engels, Introduction to "The Class Struggles in France, 1848 to 1850" in *Selected Works*, vol. 1, p. 193.
89. Lenin, "In Memory of the Commune" in *LCW*, vol. 17, p. 140.
90. Ibid., p. 141.
91. Engels, letter to Bebel of October 29, 1884, in *Marx and Engels on the Paris Commune*, p. 294.
92. Marx, letter to Kugelmann of April 17, 1871, in *Selected Correspondence*, p. 248.

Part IV. The lessons of 1905

93. Lenin, "The Proletarian Revolution and the Renegade Kautsky" in *LCW*, vol. 28, pp. 294–95.
94. Lenin, "On the Provisional Revolutionary Government" in *LCW*, vol. 8, p. 471.
95. Ibid., p. 472.
96. Lenin, "Two Tactics of Social-Democracy in the Democratic Revolution" in *LCW*, vol. 9, pp. 85–86.
97. Lenin, "The Revolutionary-Democratic Dictatorship of the Proletariat and the Peasantry" in *LCW*, vol. 8, p. 294.
98. Lenin, "A Revolution of the 1789 or the 1848 Type?" in *LCW*, vol. 8, p. 258.
99. Lenin, "The Revolutionary-Democratic Dictatorship of the Proletariat and the Peasantry" in *LCW*, vol. 8, p. 299.
100. Ibid., p. 298.
101. Lenin, "Social-Democracy and the Provisional Revolutionary Government" in *LCW*, vol. 8, pp. 281–82.

102. Lenin, "The Revolutionary-Democratic Dictatorship of the Proletariat and the Peasantry" in *LCW*, vol. 8, p. 302.

103. Lenin, "Draft Resolution on the Participation of the Social-Democrats in a Provisional Revolutionary Government" in *LCW*, vol. 8, pp. 379–80.

104. Lenin, "The Victory of the Cadets and the Tasks of the Workers party" in *LCW*, vol. 10, p. 252.

105. Ibid.

106. Ibid.

107. Lenin, "A Contribution to the History of the Question of the Dictatorship" in *LCW*, vol. 31, p. 343.

108. Lenin, "Our Tasks and the Soviet of Workers' Deputies" in *LCW*, vol. 10, pp. 23–24.

109. Ibid., pp. 24–25.

110. Lenin, "The Paris Commune and the Tasks of the Democratic Dictatorship" in *Lenin on the Paris Commune* (Moscow: Progress Publishers, 1970), p. 120.

111. Engels, "The Bakuninists at Work" in Marx and Engels, *Anarchism and Anarcho-Syndicalism* (New York: International Publishers, 1972), p. 138.

112. Ibid.

113. Lenin, "On the Provisional Revolutionary Government" in *LCW*, vol. 8, p. 477.

114. Engels, "The Bakuninists at Work" in *Anarchism and Anarcho-Syndicalism*, p. 144.

115. Ibid., p. 146.

116. Lenin, "On the Provisional Revolutionary Government" in *LCW*, vol. 8, p. 481.

117. Lenin, "The Revolutionary-Democratic Dictatorship of the Proletariat and the Peasantry" in *LCW*, vol. 8, pp. 300–301.

Part V. From February to October 1917: The dual power

118. Lenin, "The Aim of the Proletarian Struggle in Our Revolution" in *LCW*, vol. 15, p. 379.

119. Lenin, "The Tasks of the Proletariat in Our Revolution" in *LCW*, vol. 24, pp. 60–61.
120. Lenin, "The Dual Power" in *LCW*, vol. 24, p. 38.
121. Ibid., p. 39.
122. Lenin, "The Tasks of the Proletariat in Our Revolution" in *LCW*, vol. 24, p. 60.
123. Lenin, "The Dual Power" in *LCW*, vol. 24, p. 40.
124. Lenin, "The Tasks of the Proletariat in Our Revolution" in *LCW*, vol. 24, pp. 61–62.
125. Lenin, "The Seventh (April) All-Russia Conference of the R.S.D.L.P.(B.): Report on the Current Situation" in *LCW*, vol. 24, p. 236.
126. Lenin, "The Tasks of the Proletariat in Our Revolution" in *LCW*, vol. 24, p. 63.
127. Lenin, "The Petrograd City Conference of the R.S.D.L.P. (Bolsheviks): Concluding Remarks on the Report of the Present Situation" in *LCW*, vol. 24, p. 149.
128. Lenin, "The Dual Power" in *LCW*, vol. 24, p. 40.
129. Lenin, "One of the Fundamental Questions of the Revolution" in *LCW*, vol. 25, p. 371.
130. Lenin, "The Dual Power" in *LCW*, vol. 24, p. 40.
131. Ibid., p. 41.
132. Ibid., p. 40.

Part VI. October 1917:
The workers and peasants republic

133. Lenin, "The Crisis Has Matured" in *LCW*, vol. 26, p. 77.
134. Lenin, "The Lessons of the Revolution" in *LCW*, vol. 25, p. 242.
135. Ibid., p. 243.
136. Lenin, "The Impending Catastrophe and How to Combat It" in *LCW*, vol. 25, p. 368.
137. Lenin, "The Bolsheviks Must Assume Power" in *LCW*, vol. 26, p. 20.

138. Lenin, "One of the Fundamental Questions of the Revolution" in *LCW*, vol. 25, p. 376.

139. Lenin, "Meeting of the Petrograd Soviet of Workers' and Soldiers' Deputies October 25 (November 7), 1917: Report on the Tasks of the Soviet Power" in *LCW*, vol. 26, pp. 239–40.

140. Lenin, "Speech Delivered at the All-Russia Congress of Transport Workers" in *LCW*, vol. 32, pp. 277–78.

141. Lenin, "The Immediate Tasks of the Soviet Government" in *LCW*, vol. 27, p. 277.

142. Lenin, "The Seventh (April) All-Russia Conference of the R.S.D.L.P.(B.): Resolution on the Current Situation" in *LCW*, vol. 24, p. 311.

143. Lenin, "The Seventh (April) All-Russia Conference of the R.S.D.L.P.(B.): Report on the Current Situation" in *LCW*, vol. 24, p. 241.

144. Lenin, "Letters on Tactics" in *LCW*, vol. 24, p. 48.

145. Lenin, "The Petrograd City Conference of the R.S.D.L.P. (Bolsheviks): Concluding Remarks in the Debate Concerning the Report on the Present Situation" in *LCW*, vol. 24, p. 150.

146. Lenin, "The Third International and Its Place in History" in *LCW*, vol. 29, pp. 310–11.

147. Lenin, "Third All-Russia Congress of Soviets of Workers', Soldiers' and Peasants' Deputies: Report on the Activities of the Council of People's Commissars" in *LCW*, vol. 26, pp. 464–65.

148. Marx, "Critique of the Gotha Programme" in *Selected Works*, vol. 3, p. 26.

149. Lenin, "Third All-Russia Congress of Soviets of Workers', Soldiers' and Peasants' Deputies: Report on the Activities of the Council of People's Commissars" in *LCW*, vol. 26, p. 471.

150. Ibid., p. 457.

151. Lenin, "Session of the All-Russia C.E.C.: Report on the Immediate Tasks of the Soviet Government" in *LCW*, vol. 27, p. 297.

152. Lenin, "The Dictatorship of the Proletariat" in *LCW*, vol. 30, pp. 95–96.
153. Ibid., p. 96.
154. Ibid., pp. 96–97.
155. Ibid., p. 98.
156. Lenin, "The Constituent Assembly Elections and the Dictatorship of the Proletariat" in *LCW*, vol. 30, p. 266.
157. Ibid., p. 267.
158. Lenin, "The Dictatorship of the Proletariat" in *LCW*, vol. 30, p. 98.
159. Lenin, "Eleventh Congress of the R.C.P.(B.): Political Report of the Central Committee of the R.C.P.(B.)" in *LCW*, vol. 33, pp. 290–91.
160. Lenin, "The Dictatorship of the Proletariat" in *LCW*, vol. 30, p. 98.

Part VII. From War Communism to the New Economic Policy

161. Lenin, "The New Economic Policy and the Tasks of the Political Education Departments" in *LCW*, vol. 33, p. 62.
162. Lenin, "Speech to the First All-Russia Congress of Land Departments, Poor Peasants' committees and Communes" in *LCW*, vol. 28, pp. 338–41.
163. Lenin, "Eighth Congress of the R.C.P.(B.): Report of the Central Committee" in *LCW*, vol. 29, p. 157.
164. Lenin, "Fourth Congress of the Communist International: Five Years of the Russian Revolution and the Prospects of the World Revolution" in *LCW*, vol. 33, p. 427.
165. Lenin, "Third Congress of the Communist International: Report on the Tactics of the R.C.P." in *LCW*, vol. 32, p. 487.
166. Lenin, "The Party Crisis" in *LCW*, vol. 32, p. 43.
167. Lenin, "The Second All-Russia Congress of Miners: Report on the Role and Tasks of the Trade Unions" in *LCW*, vol. 32, p. 54.

168. Lenin, "Third Congress of the Communist International: Report on the Tactics of the R.C.P." in *LCW*, vol. 32, p. 494.

169. Lenin, "Fourth Congress of the Communist International: Five Years of the Russian Revolution and the Prospects of the World Revolution" in *LCW*, vol. 33, p. 421.

170. Lenin, "New Times and Old Mistakes in a New Guise" in *LCW*, vol. 33, p. 28.

171. Ibid., p. 29.

172. Lenin, "The New Economic Policy and the Tasks of the Political Education Departments" in *LCW*, vol. 33, p. 64.

173. Lenin, "Third Congress of the Communist International: Report on the Tactics of the R.C.P." in *LCW*, vol. 32, p. 487.

174. Lenin, "The New Economic Policy and the Tasks of the Political Education Departments" in *LCW*, vol. 33, p. 61.

175. Ibid., p. 62.

176. Lenin, "Seventh Moscow Gubernia Conference of the Russian Communist Party: Report on the New Economic Policy" in *LCW*, vol. 33, p. 84.

177. "Theses on the Economic Situation of Soviet Russia from the Standpoint of the Socialist Revolution" in *Theses, Resolutions and Manifestos of the First Four Congresses of the Third International* (London: Ink Links, 1980), p. 341.

178. Leon Trotsky, "Report on the New Soviet Economic Policy and the Perspectives of the World Revolution" in *The First Five Years of the Communist International* (New York: Monad Press, 1972), vol. 2, p. 269.

179. Quoted in Mary-Alice Waters, *Proletarian Leadership in Power* (New York: Education for Socialists, 1980), p. 9.

180. Lenin, "The New Economic Policy and the Tasks of the Political Education Departments" in *LCW*, vol. 33, p. 65.

181. Lenin, "Third Congress of the Communist International: Report on the Tactics of the R.C.P." in *LCW*, vol. 32, pp. 489–90.

182. Ibid., pp. 495–96.

183. *Fidel Castro Speeches: Cuba's Internationalist Foreign Policy 1975–80* (New York: Pathfinder Press, 1981), p. 278.

184. Lenin, "Fourth Congress of the Communist International: Five Years of the Russian Revolution and the Prospects of the World Revolution" in *LCW*, vol. 33, p. 420.

185. Lenin, "Third Congress of the Communist International: Theses for a Report on the Tactics of the R.C.P." in *LCW*, vol. 32, pp. 455–56.

Part VIII. The Comintern and the workers and farmers government

186. See "Preliminary Draft Theses on the National and the Colonial Questions" drafted by Lenin and adopted by the Second Congress of the Communist International, and Lenin's report on these theses (*LCW*, vol. 31, pp. 144–51 and 240–45); and the "Theses on the Eastern Question" adopted by the fourth Comintern congress (*Theses, Resolutions and Manifestos of the First Four Congresses of the Third International*, pp. 409–19).

187. Excerpts from "Theses on Tactics" in Joseph Hansen, *The Workers and Farmers Government* (New York: Education for Socialists, 1974), p. 40.

188. For a more extensive discussion of the lessons of the Hungarian and Bavarian revolutions, see Farrell Dobbs, *Revolutionary Continuity: Birth of the Communist Movement, 1918–1922* (New York: Monad Press, 1983), pp. 117–22, 137–39.

189. *The Workers and Farmers Government*, p. 39.

190. Ibid.

191. Ibid.

192. Ibid., p. 40.

193. *Protokoll des IV. Weltkongresses der Kommunistischen Internationale* (Hamburg: Carl Hoym, 1923), pp. 194–95.

194. Trotsky, "Report on the Fourth World Congress" in *The First Five Years of the Communist International*, vol. 2, p. 324.

195. Engels, "Marx and the *Neue Rheinische Zeitung* (1848–

1849)" in *Selected Works*, vol. 3, p. 166.

196. *International Press Correspondence,* July 23, 1923, p. 539. It is also contained in Jack Barnes, *For a Workers and Farmers Government in the United States* (New York: Education for Socialists, 1982), pp. 48–50.

197. Ibid.

198. *Protokoll des II. Weltkongresses der Kommunistischen Internationale* (Hamburg: Carl Hoym, 1921), p. 767.

199. *International Press Correspondence,* July 23, 1923, p. 539.

200. Ibid.

201. Reprinted in Barnes, *For a Workers and Farmers Government in the United States*, p. 51.

202. *International Press Correspondence,* July 23, 1923, p. 540.

203. Ibid.

204. Ibid., p. 539.

205. Reprinted in Barnes, *For a Workers and Farmers Government in the United States*, pp. 51–52.

Part IX. The workers and farmers government today

206. Marx and Engels, "Manifesto of the Communist Party" in *MECW*, vol. 6, p. 502.

207. *Intercontinental Press*, September 19, 1983, p. 516.

208. *The Second Congress of the Communist International* (London: New Park Publications, 1977), vol. 2, p. 145.

BASIC WORKS OF MARXISM

The Communist Manifesto
KARL MARX AND
FREDERICK ENGELS

Communism, say the founding leaders of the revolutionary workers movement, is not a set of ideas or preconceived "principles" but workers' line of march to power, springing from a "movement going on under our very eyes." $5. Also in Spanish, French, Farsi, and Arabic.

The Origin of the Family, Private Property, and the State
FREDERICK ENGELS

The emergence of class-divided society gave rise to repressive state bodies and the oppression of women to enable the ruling classes to pass along wealth and privilege. Engels discusses the consequences for working people of these class institutions—from their ancient forms to their modern versions. $15. Also in Spanish and Farsi.

Socialism: Utopian and Scientific
FREDERICK ENGELS

"To make men the masters of their own form of social organization—to make them free—is the mission of the modern proletariat," writes Engels. A classic guide to the operations of capitalism and struggles of the working class. $10. Also in Farsi.

WWW.PATHFINDERPRESS.COM

Join the PATHFINDER READERS CLUB

BUILD A MARXIST LIBRARY!

25% OFF ALL PATHFINDER BOOKS AND PAMPHLETS

30% DISCOUNT ON MONTHLY SPECIALS

Get your annual card for only *US$10*.
Available at
www.pathfinderpress.com
or at Pathfinder book centers around the world.

THE RUSSIAN REVOLUTION'S WORLD EXAMPLE

Lenin's Final Fight
Speeches and Writings, 1922–23

V.I. LENIN

In 1922 and 1923, V.I. Lenin, central leader of the world's first socialist revolution, waged what was to be his last political battle—one that was lost following his death. At stake was whether that revolution, and the international communist movement it led, would remain on the revolutionary proletarian course that brought workers and peasants to power in October 1917. $17. Also in Spanish, Farsi, and Greek.

The History of the Russian Revolution
LEON TROTSKY

How, under Lenin's leadership, the Bolshevik Party led millions of workers and farmers to overthrow the state power of the landlords and capitalists in 1917 and bring to power a government that advanced their class interests at home and worldwide. Unabridged, 3 vols. in one. Written by one of the central leaders of that socialist revolution. $30. Also in French and Russian.

The Revolution Betrayed
What Is the Soviet Union and Where Is It Going?

LEON TROTSKY

In 1917 workers and peasants of Russia were the motor force for one of the deepest revolutions in history. Yet within ten years a political counterrevolution by a privileged social layer, whose chief spokesperson was Joseph Stalin, was being consolidated. The classic study of the Soviet workers state and its degeneration. $17. Also in Spanish, Farsi, and Greek.

WWW.PATHFINDERPRESS.COM

NATIONAL LIBERATION AND SOCIALISM IN THE AMERICAS

by Manuel Piñeiro

Revolutions of national and social liberation

Each epoch leaves its imprint on the social revolutions that occur within it. The same is true for the struggles for national liberation. Lenin stressed this idea when he said: "The era 1789–1871 was of special significance for Europe. That is irrefutable. We cannot understand a single national liberation war, and such wars were especially typical of that period, unless we understand the general conditions of the period."[1]

In the premonopoly phase of capitalism, national liberation revolutions were part of the great antifeudal transformations which had a bourgeois-democratic content. Their social character was predominantly capitalist. Consequently the tasks they were to carry out were part

---

This article is the text of a presentation to an April 1982 conference in Havana sponsored by the Communist Party of Cuba and the magazine World Marxist Review. *It was published in the September–October 1982 issue of* Cuba Socialista *and the July–August 1983 issue of* Casa de las Américas. *The translation from the Spanish is by Michael Baumann.*

ENDNOTES BEGIN ON PAGE 212

and parcel of the worldwide development of the capitalist system. We should not overlook that these anticapitalist national liberation struggles occurred within the context of the expansion and development of the capitalist socioeconomic formation. At the same time, however, we should note that each process embodied its own particularities. These particularities were conditioned by the character of foreign domination, the historical circumstances, and the specific economic and sociological configuration of the countries involved. The national factor thus represented the particular, distinctive ingredient of these revolutions, while the insertion of these countries in the capitalist system represented the more general underpinnings.

IN EXAMINING the many experiences of the struggles for freedom in our own countries in the nineteenth century we should keep both these factors in mind. It will help us avoid the error of seeking to view these struggles as equal with the European revolutions of the same historical period.

It would not be valid—either now or then—to mechanically apply to each specific situation, without distinctions, a general conception of a single type of revolution. Borne out here, perhaps more clearly than in any other field, is the well-known Leninist assertion: Concrete analysis of the concrete situation is the soul of Marxism.

In our era, national liberation revolutions have also presented particular characteristics. These are determined by the general crisis of capitalism, the existence of a powerful and developing socialist system, and the historic confrontation between those two systems. These factors are the origin of the great differences between the present national liberation struggles and those of capitalism's premonopoly stage. Imperialism creates and sustains the oppression of nations through new relations of domination—centered on state monopoly capital. But it is also true that the revolutions taking place in underdeveloped countries are fundamentally aimed at destroying these premises. Accordingly, their distinctive feature is their anti-imperialist character.

At the same time, and because of this anti-imperialist nature, contemporary national liberation revolutions are also links in the process of transition from capitalism to socialism. And precisely here the most important particularities of these revolutions originate, both in terms of their objectives, social composition, and tasks, as well as their strategic historical direction. They are more advanced than their predecessors; yet they also maintain a continuity with these earlier revolutions that culminates in a dialectical leap. Sooner or later, and in many different forms, the dominant material realities impel these countries to liquidate the foundations of their entire oppression. This is the inevitable solution for dependent countries facing the crossroads, that imperialist exploitation has brought them to.

That is why the national liberation revolutions of our time have a profound social content that converts them into events of worldwide importance. They are an indivisible part of a single international revolutionary process in which the fundamental contradiction—socialism *versus* capitalism—is in turn sharpened by the very advance of these revolutions.

Their anti-imperialist course and their anticapitalist tendency place them among the principal forces to transform the bourgeois system, alongside the world socialist system and the international workers movement.

The revolutions for national and social liberation in

Latin America and the Caribbean are a clear expression as well as constituent elements of these general circumstances.

They also embody characteristics that are significant in relation to the present liberation process in Africa and Asia. Our revolutions, like those of Africa and Asia, are also advancing along the world historical path that began in October 1917. They form a part of the three underdeveloped continents that are confronting imperialism. But the material premises created by capitalist domination in our countries (a level of development that on average is superior to that of Asia and Africa) have created better conditions for a more intense and radical advance of our revolutions. These revolutions, in their dialectical course, take on tasks of a democratic, popular, and anti-imperialist content in their first stage. As they develop, they tend to carry out clearly socialist tasks—as an indissoluble part of their own process and in accordance with their general historical character.

On this point, the Programmatic Platform of the Communist Party of Cuba says: "There is no insurmountable barrier between the democratic-popular and anti-imperialist stage and the socialist stage. In the era of imperialism, both are part of a single process, in which national-liberation and democratic measures—which at times have already a socialist tinge—pave the way for genuinely socialist ones. The decisive and defining element of this process is who leads it, which class wields political power."[2]

That is why the national and social liberation movements on this continent have to directly and immediately confront imperialism. In particular this means U.S. imperialism, in its capacity as the system of domination conditioning the physiognomy of capitalism in Latin America and the Caribbean. Despite their distortions, bourgeois-national states (formed more than 150 years ago) have matured in the majority of our countries. There exists in these countries a formidable variety of experiences in national and class struggles. This was brought out most clearly with the triumph of the first socialist revolution in the hemisphere, which unmistakably reveals the degree of maturity reached by these societies.

In Our America the proletariat—the main historical agent of the new society—is the most important social force. This is true not only because of its qualitative merit but also because of its size in various countries of the region, a point that in no way diminishes the extraordinary significance of the poor peasantry and other popular forces. Finally, to cite another relevant factor: foreign domination on this continent is exercised by the strongest imperialist power, which, because of its overall interests, attributes a geopolitical strategic character to the struggle. This makes the liberation of our peoples more difficult—but also more radical and urgent.

THESE REALITIES have not ceased to be expressed in a contradictory fashion over the last twenty-five years, with advances and retreats. But at the end of the last decade and increasingly in the early years of this one, our region demonstrated the revolutionary movement's highest level of acceleration in the underdeveloped areas, including on a world scale.

From the factors we have pointed out, there flows an original combination of democratic and popular tasks on the one hand, and economic, political, and social demands on the other—all of which contribute to the historic socialist course of the revolution. It is a combination of anti-imperialist, national liberation tasks alongside the consolidation of power by workers, peasants, and other toiling layers against latifundist and capitalist exploitation. In a nutshell, what we have in some countries is a complex and dynamic overlapping or interweaving of the class struggle and the anti-neocolonial or anticolonial struggle. In his main report to the First Congress of the Communist Party, Commander-in-Chief Fidel Castro referred to the experience of Cuba: "Our national and social liberation were indissolubly linked, to advance was a historical necessity, to stop was cowardice and treachery that would have again turned us into a Yankee colony and slaves of the exploiters."[3]

It is worthwhile to investigate the material and historical realities that explain the intensity, scope, depth, and perspectives of the present class struggle in our societies. This will help identify the objective and subjective factors that lie behind the present structural crisis of capitalism on the continent, the rise of various revolutionary processes, and the growth in the combative movement of the popular masses.

The crisis of capitalism and the revolutionary processes in Latin America and the Caribbean

There exists in Latin America and the Caribbean, as a reflection of what is happening in reality, a crisis in the capitalist models of economic development. Schemes for independent development (efforts by the national bourgeoisies of various countries from the 1930s to the 1950s, along with a few later development-oriented variants) have been frustrated one after the other because of the asphyxiating limits imposed by foreign monopoly capital. With the cancellation of these options, variants for development were reduced to a single alternative:

Either the imperialist transnational enterprises and the international economic relations they represent; or the revolutionary program of the popular classes, in the first place the proletariat: the socialist path. The first choice operates within the network of capitalist structures imposed by region-wide imperialist domination. It involves the reproduction of well-known deforming and deformed socioeconomic conditions. It also accentuates and complicates the contradictions of underdevelopment in Latin America and the Caribbean. Fundamentally it leads to a polarization of the class struggle as an inevitable expression of the concentration and centralization of capital. The other choice permits attaining independent development—that is, genuine development—and flows from the very contradictions generated by the system of oppression and exploitation. Socialism thus emerges as the sole historical solution making it possible to overcome the tremendous obstacles of underdevelopment, obstacles that are insoluble under capitalism.

As part of the worldwide capitalist system, the economies of Latin America and the Caribbean have been subject since the 1970s to the process of the establishment of a new capitalist international division of labor, promoted by the leading countries of this system. This has brought about, first and foremost, the consolidation of the domination of big monopoly and finance capital, which has definitively become the determining axis of the majority of the region's economies. In this way, and as never before, the fate of the economic evolution of the area depends on the overall dynamic of capitalism on a world scale. Moreover, the prolonged crisis that has affected capitalism in recent years has repercussions in Latin America and the Caribbean that are even more direct and brutal.

Scarcely a single country has been spared from the process of transnationalization of the Latin American and Caribbean economies. To take an example, this is reflected in the final integration—or rather in the structural dependency—of the continent's bourgeoisies with relation to big monopoly and finance capital. In this way the pattern of capital accumulation inherent in the establishment of a new capitalist international division of labor has given rise to a greater integration of the national economies for the developed countries. This new capitalist international division of labor presupposes specialization in the production of more technologically complex goods and the perfection of science and technique, with the aim of maintaining control over the most advanced technology. At the same time, the service sector grows, and there is a general increase in the activities of a parasitic character by the monopoly economy, thus confirming the tendency of imperialism that Lenin pointed to.

The underdeveloped countries are "elevated" to a more modern rung of the ladder through the incorporation of new production techniques. Such techniques are channeled there by the industrialized countries because of the greater relative density of the work force these techniques require. This is why it is more profitable to exploit these techniques in dependent countries, where the working class has much lower wage levels. Accordingly, one of the formulas that in recent years has received the most support from transnational capital is the return to liberal economic relations. As the Chilean case clearly shows, this represents an extreme variant of dependency on foreign capital; of concentrating and centralizing national wealth in its hands, in association with "national" big capital; and of enforcing the highest rates of superexploitation of workers ever registered in the history of our region. Some variants of state capitalism, including state monopoly capitalism (which are also dependent because of the nature of the society from which they emerged) rest on the same principle of modernization through attracting foreign capital. On occasion, however, contradictions arise with foreign capital as a consequence of possible differences in interests that can become quite significant.

IT IS NOT OUR AIM to treat extensively the complexity of this process but rather to point out its importance for examining the theme before us. This importance stems from the contradictions and new consequences this process gives rise to. These include, in particular, the tendency toward reducing bourgeois democracy and the establishment of repressive military regimes. Such consequences, in our opinion, increase conditions that are favorable for the tasks of the revolutionary vanguards. At the same time, they demand of these vanguards the highest capacity of struggle on all fronts and a scientific understanding of capitalism's new adjustments in their various manifestations, both global and national.

In this context we would like to point out some of the contradictions that can be observed in this process. In one form or another, they are present in the majority of countries of the region.

There is an initial contradiction that arises between the necessity of the area's economies to increase investment so as to attain development, and the limits imposed on these economies by the narrowness of the internal market—precisely because of the domination of that market by the foreign monopolies.

Paradoxically, the effects of the modern technology

used in new investments by the transnational enterprises are minimal in terms of the internal market of the country on the receiving end. This technology does not tend to increase sources of employment. And at times, in displacing old technologies and artisanal activities, its impact on the internal market is totally negative.

On the other hand, as a consequence of their monopoly control of prices, their absolute domination of finances, and the possibility of expansion because of the bankruptcy of competitors, the transnational enterprises have no special interest in breaking up traditional agrarian relations based on latifundism.

So these archaic agrarian structures continue to survive, although with relative modernization as a result of other factors that we will analyze later. And there is a sustained increase in unemployment and underemployment, whose most visual manifestation are the inhuman marginal barrios. Both factors impose very strict limits on the expansion of investment. And this in turn results in greater stagnation of the economy.

ANOTHER SIGNIFICANT contradiction arises out of the transnational enterprises' primary interest in attaining high profits. They seek to recover rapidly the capital they have invested and to increase dividends. The profits they make are not reinvested in the country from which they originate. Therefore, the limits of that country's internal market determine that the transnational enterprises must channel their profits toward new markets in other countries. These circumstances are the origin of an antagonism between the underdeveloped countries' need to increase investments, and the interests of the transnational enterprises to increase their overall profits, including by deepening the decapitalization and financial dependency of the underdeveloped countries.

One result of the new capitalist international division of labor are endemic deficits in the Latin American countries' commercial balances and their balance of payments. These in turn are manipulated even more intensively by the International Monetary Fund and private international banks. This is done with the systematic aim of imposing a policy in accordance with the interests of big imperialist capital.

This type of modernizing neodevelopment of dependent capitalism has elevated to higher and decisive levels the transnationalization of our economies, affecting nearly all the countries of the continent. On the one hand, the dominance of monopoly and finance capital, as the leading center of the economies in the region, has been consolidated. On the other, there has been a strengthening of the alliance between foreign capital and sectors of big local capital, in a process where denationalization is reflected in greater degrees of submission to the pattern of imperialist accumulation. Such a dynamic, unfolding in the present stage of capitalist crisis and recession, has definitively exhausted the previous stages of relative national industrial development, which were based on import substitution and broadening of the internal market. In the political sphere, it has tended to provoke a crisis in multiclass groupings of a populist nature, as well as in the bourgeois-democratic state order.

On the level of classes there has been an accelerated tendency toward polarization in the social structure, resulting in clearer demarcations between the conflicting forces. Defined more clearly in the majority of our countries are two large class blocs: first, the classes and sectors linked organically to foreign capital; the second, broadly based, is made up of the working class first of all, the peasantry, the unemployed, the underemployed, and growing segments of what are called the middle sectors.

The crisis of capitalist development models in the region has thrown into sharper relief and prominence the question of socialist development as the only alternative to the underdevelopment capitalism generates.

In the last two decades, economic and political reformism has put into practice different policy variants aimed at diminishing the effects of the implantation of the new pattern of capitalist accumulation. All these variants, however, have met failure one after the other since they were too weak to confront the economic, political, and social structures that sustain the system of capitalist domination in the region. One aim of the reformist schemes has been to attenuate the class struggle. But this has been attained only in a few cases and for brief periods of time. For the masses tend to radicalize their tasks even more when they are unable to resolve underlying problems, and this in turn increases their consciousness concerning the way to resolve them.

One fact has been demonstrated in different countries and at different times: reformism's aspirations are limited to destroying the traditional export economy and sharing economic power with the foreign monopolies, opposing to them the forces of state capitalism. There is no question of attaining independence, which they know to be unobtainable. They accept dependency on foreign capital as a premise, and try to attain maximum profit for the national economic interest they claim to represent.

The social layers that sustain this position are normally the civil and military bureaucracies, backed in a partial and temporary way by strata of the middle sectors. Under the new conditions, they seek to inherit the functions of the national bourgeoisie, whose schemes failed in the decades from the 1930s to 1950s. Today, the dominant material situation renders more fatal the negative results of those schemes. Accordingly, their weakness is not just economic. In the political sphere they are also accustomed to accepting as inevitable the imposition of restrictions on bourgeois democracy and the use of state repressive mechanisms. Both are seen as necessary to assure the high levels of exploitation and poverty to which the popular masses are subjected.

COINCIDING in recent years with the deepening of the world capitalist economic crisis, the negative consequences of the new capitalist international division of labor have become visible in the area. These include the exhaustion of reformist efforts, the decline of bourgeois-democratic regimes, and the tendency of dictatorial military governments to replace such regimes. All of this marks the end of a historic stage on the continent. It also foreshadows a new scenario for the class struggle in which the peoples and their revolutionary organizations encounter greater possibilities for developing their struggles. These struggles are more radical because of the nature of the material bases that condition them. And, as a consequence, they become more complex and diverse in their national expressions. They have a common objective: definitive solution of the contradictions of the system of imperialist oppression and exploitation through the path of revolutionary transformations of their economic and political structures. This road is already being taken by Nicaragua and Grenada—at their own pace and with their own forms—while El Salvador and Guatemala can be seen advancing in a very promising way. Cuba, in the vanguard historically, has shown the viability of the alternative and continues following it victoriously.

Latin America and the Caribbean thus began, in the mid-1970s, a stage of deep polarization of their social structures, accentuation of political confrontations, and an increasingly well-defined antagonism between revolution and counterrevolution.

To sum up, the material bases of the present revolutionary processes in Latin America and the Caribbean have been created by the changes that occurred in economic and social relations in our countries, especially since the 1950s. These transformations have brought levels—and means—of capitalist development of a deformed and deforming variety that must be very carefully considered so as to define the character of the revolutions for national and social liberation in this part of the world.

The economic growth of capitalism in the region has provoked the growth of underdevelopment because of imperialist domination and the lack of an essential break in archaic agrarian relations based on latifundism. These circumstances accentuate without interruption the contradiction between the character and development of the productive forces and the relations of production, both of which are molded by foreign capital in association with the local bourgeoisie and landowners. What has occurred is a process of capitalist socioeconomic formation subordinated to the world imperialist system through neocolonial relations.

Here precisely lies the historic nature of the present crisis of Latin American and Caribbean societies—historic because in addition to being economic and social, there will be no substantial change in the continent's future without anti-imperialist and anticapitalist transformations.

That is why the present crisis in the region is at one and the same time a crisis of imperialist domination, of obsolete agrarian relations, and of the network of dependent capitalism's relations of production. It is simultaneously a crisis of all these structures linked to a political, juridical, and ethical crisis. It is an overall crisis of the society, deepened by the growing negative effects of the general crisis of capitalism.

THE CONVERGENCE of these factors and processes determines the historical character of the contemporary revolutions of our continent. This character does not exclude but rather presupposes the possibility of varied forms and rhythms of moving toward socialism, and of different national paths facilitating access to an initial anti-imperialist, democratic, and popular stage of the revolution.

It is important to stress, however, that in the majority of the countries on the continent the material bases created by the development of capitalism have established the conditions necessary to permit triumphant revolutions to advance in an uninterrupted manner—although by stages—in a single historical process, toward socialism.

The many experiences accumulated by our peoples in their intense and varied struggles, especially since 1959, are a factor favoring this possible outcome. Since then, we have witnessed the collapse of bourgeois-democratic reformist movements and various nationalist experiments, followed by the search for options for obtaining development, independence, and self-determination. The activity of the working class has been incessant, along with the advance of the rest of the people's movement. Formidable examples have been accumulated in the revolutionary use of arms by the vanguards and the peoples. We have lived through an interesting and useful experience toward attaining socialism—in Chile. Military dictatorships of the old and new type have proliferated. There have been uprisings by patriotic military men and the establishment of nationalist governments led by them. There has been a notable incorporation into the struggle of Christian, progressive, and revolutionary sectors. Nicaragua and Grenada, with their victorious revolutions, have reaffirmed the validity of the road to power opened by Cuba and have enriched the heritage of the continent's revolutionary culture.

These nearly twenty-five years of battle and sacrifice, impregnated with the blood of thousands of combatants, represent today's best school for the revolutionary movement of Our America. Today, in addition to the theoretical and scientific certainties, in addition to the rich experiences accumulated by our peoples since the wars of independence, they also have at their disposal a number of revolutionary situations which they and various revolutionary generations in struggle have lived through—experiences that have been sufficiently broad and clear in their fundamental lessons. We have a diversity of experiences and situations that include both undeniable advances and temporary setbacks. But one truth has been reaffirmed again and again, becoming irrefutable: The historical course toward socialism does not depend solely on the objective laws of the capitalist system; in crystallizing this course, the revolutionary vanguards have the first and decisive responsibility for impelling the process forward, and this must be demonstrated above all in their capacity to lead the peoples to the conquest of power. This is the cardinal problem of every revolution. It synthesizes the different aspects that must be considered and correctly resolved, in order to increase the possibilities of that crucial moment—the end of a complex process and the guarantee of its development.

Among the many factors linked to the struggle for power, we consider it essential to examine first the structure of the classes and social forces that objectively tend to participate in the revolution.

Structure of the classes and forces that are motors of the revolution

We are not going to spend a great deal of time on this theme because we have already discussed it at some length in the theoretical conference held in 1980. Our interest here, in connection with the main objective of the conference, is to identify the principal actors in the present class struggle on our continent.

When analyzing the structure of classes one cannot separate out the struggles of these classes. For these struggles, in the course of their development, modify all of the society's structures. Accordingly, the first element to be considered is imperialist domination, to which we attribute the function of being the main conditioning factor in the class structure and class struggle on our continent. Let us look first at the bloc of ruling classes.

The modernizing economic processes we described earlier have led in recent years to the formation of a new oligarchy representing the different factions of the big bourgeoisie—industrial, commercial, financial, and agrarian. This new oligarchy is subordinated to and shares the same strategy of development and domination as imperialist capital. On occasion, however, there may appear certain differences of interests that should not be overlooked in terms of the tactical struggle of the revolutionary movement.

Another element of the bloc of exploiting classes is the declining middle, or national, bourgeoisie, substantially weakened by the rigors of its alliance with the big bourgeoisie and the transnational enterprises. In general, this middle bourgeoisie has been reduced to the most traditional industrial sector—nondurable consumer goods—and is gradually losing its possibilities for economic reproduction. These circumstances mean that many sectors of the middle bourgeoisie may become important allies of the revolutionary process. This, however, does not always depend so much on correct tactics toward them as on the interweaving of their interests with different branches of the economy, ideological factors, and specific situations of struggle.

The third element in this grouping of forces is the landowners. In some countries they have retained their power, based fundamentally on control of landed property. In other countries, however, various capitalist reforms carried out in the countryside have affected this class, disintegrating or modifying it in one way or another. In almost all cases a capitalist agro-export business sector has arisen, that is, a sector of modern ranchers and agro-industrialists. However, a layer of landowners of the traditional type still subsists—latifundists—many of whom turn to renting out their land. This process of dissolution of the landowning class is still inconclusive in the majority of countries and will continue at many different paces and rhythms, depending on the circumstances in each country. But in its general direction, it is useful to stress that the modernizing faction (the big rural bourgeoisie we mentioned) tends to tighten its links with sectors of the local commercial and financial bourgeoisie. And they too, in the last analysis, subordinate themselves to the interests and accumulation patterns of the imperialist bourgeoisie, which becomes the beneficiary and principal decision-making center of the new relations of capitalist exploitation in Latin American agriculture.

It should be noted that this process of transformation in the countryside generates contradictions between the sectors of "modernizing" capital and the landowners who defend traditional latifundism. The latter react forcibly against certain aspects of agrarian reform, and above all against those modifications that alter their position. This accentuates their reactionary role in class struggles, and in many countries they make up a significant part of the counterrevolution.

TO SUM UP, there is an observable tendency toward homogenization of the ruling classes, as never before seen in the history of the continent. This is determined by the international processes of capitalism mentioned above. At the same time, however, it should be kept in mind that varying levels of economic development in subregions and countries preclude an absolute generalization—for example, in comparing the situation in some countries of Central America and the Caribbean with others on the continent. It is also useful to point out, because of its evident practical value, that the transformations operating in the capitalist system in our region are generating various contradictions inside the bloc of ruling classes. Among them, we can point to the following:

• The struggle between sectors of the local big bourgeoisie and foreign monopoly capital, as both seek the best economic possibilities in the international market.

• Differences of interests between the latifundists and the big agrarian bourgeoisie.

• The conflict of the middle bourgeoisie with the big

bourgeoisie or new oligarchy, as well as with transnational capital.

- Middle sectors that are part of the system and defenders of it, but who also aspire to reform and renegotiate their dependency on transnational capital.

It is useful at this point to take a general look at what are called the middle sectors. In Latin American societies, perhaps even more than in other capitalist countries, defining these forces is an extremely complex task. This stems from the diversity of the elements that make them up, the limited economic stability of many of them, and other factors in the dynamic of the class struggle. Because of these characteristics, it is very difficult to place all these sectors in either the bloc of ruling classes or in the bloc of exploited classes. It is valid, however, to identify them on the basis of their *class standpoint*. We share the assessment that they, in and of themselves, do not make up an organic social class. The fundamental component of this social force is the urban petty bourgeoisie, comprising small businessmen and entrepreneurs, professionals with private practices, and so forth. Added to this are such diverse layers of the population as government functionaries, students, public employees, skilled workers, professionals, etc.

The distinctive feature of the middle sectors is their socioeconomic heterogeneity, which determines their extremely contradictory content. Flowing from this, the middle sectors are incapable of formulating an independent historical program, and it is common knowledge that they have to make an alliance with one class or another.

On the one hand, they have an average standard of living that is higher than that of manual workers. They are usually susceptible to influence by bourgeois ideology and assume values and expectations that stem from this ideology. Some of these layers serve as administrators of the capitalist state and have fully committed themselves to this.

On the other hand, many members of these sectors are wage earners or small entrepreneurs who are not linked with either monopoly capital or the local oligarchy. In both cases they suffer the consequences of the system's crisis and of the imposition of the new pattern of accumulation. This either reduces them to poverty or diminishes considerably their standard of living. Furthermore, the absence of individual guarantees and institutionalized democracy is keenly felt by sectors in this position when they come up against the system. These factors, among others, give rise to the possibility that many members of the middle sectors will adopt a progressive stance, including identifying with the interests of the working class.

IT IS THE TASK of the political forces of the bourgeoisie on the one hand, and of the exploited classes on the other, to attract the members of the middle sectors who—for the reasons noted above—lean toward one direction or the other, or one or another class point of view. In these sectors (which are numerous in the majority of our countries and have a qualitative role that is still quite important) there is to be found a force that can be decisive for the victorious outcome of the Latin American revolutions. This explains the priority attention given them by the parties and organizations that represent the exploited classes. The aim is to isolate the reactionary layers, neutralize and draw in as much as possible the ambivalent elements, and win over to the revolution those who are objectively in a position to be incorporated into this historical undertaking. Often, large components of the middle sectors can become part of the leading force. They can serve as catalysts in the revolutionary struggles of their peoples, with a significant presence in the vanguards.

ALONG WITH the transformations that have taken place in recent years in the capitalist structures in Latin America and the Caribbean, there have also been some changes in the relationship of forces inside the bloc of exploited classes. There has been a notable increase in the level of relative and absolute pauperization among all the oppressed classes and sectors.

Because of the new process of industrialization we have already discussed, the working class tends to be more heterogeneous in the composition of its sectors. This contributes to making the class more representative of the overall interests of the people. At the same time, it is necessary to understand that the industrialization process under way tends to concentrate the sector of workers associated with it, and to stratify them in relation to the rest of the class. This is accentuated wherever the importance of other economic sectors (such as medium and small national industry, or the mines) either disappears or is reduced. It is useful to take such differences into consideration in order to avoid having them become obstacles to the unity of the industrial working class.

The rural sector of the proletariat has also been modified. The expansion of capitalist relations in the countryside gives rise to a relative increase in this vital segment of the working class. Even more importantly, it generates a greater concentration of such workers within the framework of the big haciendas. This increases their capacity for class organization, which on occasion is also enhanced by attainment of greater skills and by links with the urban industrial proletariat.

The broad peasant masses—poor peasants—constitute the other fundamental class within the popular bloc. The peasantry in our countries continues to be made up of diverse segments: tenant farmers, sharecroppers of various sorts, small proprietors, those who simply make use of property whose ownership is not defined, and so forth. But the common factor characterizing them is their extreme and growing poverty. The most inhuman forms of this poverty continue to be concentrated among the Indian masses, who are subjected to the highest levels of exploitation and social marginalization.

In various countries of the region the peasantry remains numerically the most important class among the rural population. In other countries this is already no longer the case because of capitalist transformations that have taken place in the field of agriculture. One impact of these transformations is that the segment of peasant proprietors suffers the pressure of competition from the big productive haciendas, often resulting in their ruin or displacement from their parcel of land. In general this process implies a tendency toward elimination of the peasantry, since capitalist modernization of agriculture tends to reduce the size of this class. This occurs through proletarianization and semiproletarianization of part of it, and expulsion toward the cities (mainly to their marginal outskirts) of another part. At the same time, in a number of regions the amount of land the peasants have access to has either been notably reduced—or remained the same. This combined with the population increase means that the smaller properties can no longer serve as the basis for family subsistence farming. This whole complex situation broadens the consciousness of the peasantry about the necessity of carrying out profound agrarian reforms. It increases the potential of their struggles for economic demands and those of a revolutionary character. And it objectively increases the possibilities for development of their alliance with the working class.

Alongside these exploited classes (often part of one or another of them, or separated by very subtle demarcations) is the urban and rural subproletariat. This sector represents a numerous part of the population in Latin America and the Caribbean. Unstable by nature, it is in the course of transition toward either the marginal population and lumpen-proletariat or toward joining the productive system. These social forces are pressing to resolve their problems (for urbanization of their settlements, among other things), pressure that is on occasion dramatized by violent explosions. Because of their composition and conditions, they are usually inconsistent and subject to manipulation by the parties of the system. But it has also been shown that it is possible to orient them toward revolutionary objectives when effective work is carried out with them, for example, in the marginal settlements.

To complete the broad range of forces that make up the social base of the present revolutionary processes on our continent, it is necessary to include the large and growing mass of unemployed—extreme victims of the capitalist system who do not have access to even minimal possibilities of subsistence.

This grouping of classes, layers, and sectors share a similar standard of living and a situation of exploitation, with no possible solution under the reigning system. In addition, they are often subjected to the terrible severity of reactionary dictatorial governments. These layers can only enter into radical contradiction with the existing socioeconomic formation.

These forces thus constitute the historical protagonist of the present revolutions on our continent. The working class is the fundamental center of this multifaceted collection of forces, but all are important in the struggle for power and in the later development of socialist construction. It is impossible to define uniformly the role of each one of these forces in all countries. It is up to the vanguards in these countries to make this analysis and to attain the correct relationship in its tactics in order to gain their effective participation in the different stages and settings of the struggle.

In the particularities and nuances of this relationship, conditioned by the general and decisive historical confrontation of our time—that between the bourgeoisie and proletariat—there is to be found indispensable support for the triumph of revolutions on the continent. In this regard, it is worthwhile to stress the outstanding role peasants have played in revolutions that have been victorious, and in those today developing in El Salvador and Guatemala. In the latter country, incorporating the Indians is decisive to the struggle for power.

Strategy and tactics of the revolution: General considerations

Let us begin with a fundamental truth: the class struggle can neither be planned nor programmed; the triumph of revolutions even less so. We should also base ourselves on another well-known truth: when revolutions are authentic, they always respond to universal laws; but their very authenticity also makes them unique in terms of their national outlines.

It is not our intention to examine exceptional factors or the contributions that have been made by Latin American revolutions that are victorious, postponed, or under way. This task is of great importance for the revolutionary movement of this continent's collective heritage of political culture, and we will surely have analysis here by other delegates on this theme.

We would simply like to take up our considerations on a few more general factors and problems that are present in the processes occurring today in the region. These common ingredients, while also exhibiting their national characteristics, have been confirmed with the triumph of Cuba, Nicaragua, and Grenada. They are also being clearly repeated in El Salvador and Guatemala; and they are demonstrating their existence in other developing processes.

For Marxist-Leninists, the central problem of the revolution is the seizure of power. This means encouraging the material and subjective conditions that will make it possible to advance the process, in an uninterrupted manner, toward the socialist stage. The first and most important of these conditions is the destruction of the bourgeois state apparatus and its replacement by a revolutionary state based on the hegemony of the proletariat in close alliance with the other popular classes and sectors. In any genuine revolution there is no substitute for this historic break.

Not all components of the bourgeois state can be destroyed at the same time, or with the same methods. However, the nucleus of the state apparatus—its repressive force—is the key to attaining domination over the rest of the state body. Hence destruction of it is the indispensable and definitive priority for the triumph of any revolution. The repressive apparatus is, in the last analysis, what guarantees the bourgeoisie its continuation in power, what it turns to in situations of crisis. It is possible, to be sure, to encounter substantial differences when comparing the forms of political and ideological domination of various bourgeois regimes. But differences are minimal when it comes to the forms of organization and use of the repressive apparatus by this type of state. So, the problem of power rests above all on the validity of the strategy for reaching this goal. Accordingly, revolutionary strategy must at minimum fulfill the following requisites: defining the character of the revolution; assessing the world, regional, and national relationship of forces; identifying the main enemy, its allies, and the contradictions among them; defining the leading class of the revolution, its allies, and the points of convergence and divergence among these forces; elaborating the main outlines of the fundamental path of the struggle that has been chosen, as well as of other complementary forms that are indispensable for advancing the revolution.

THE STRATEGY of the revolutionary movement is based on scientific considerations that are, for this very reason, effective only to the extent that they are adapted to the specific realities of each country. Development of the revolution presupposes the maturation, over a more or less lengthy period, of the forces that will lead the dual task of destroying the old order and building the new one. The multiple tasks faced by these forces range from economic struggles to political and military objectives. These in turn generate, at a determined moment, the opening of a prerevolutionary period, characterized by a high degree of class confrontation and by a crisis of bourgeois power. In this process the incessant activity of parties and organizations of the left is decisive.

It is then that wider possibilities for the revolutionary triumph emerge. The attempt to seize power becomes the definitive test of the effectiveness of the strategy that has been worked out, and of the tactical capacity of the vanguard to lead the masses to the decisive goal.

In the first instance, the basis of all strategy lies in the objective conditions that define it and provide its historical viability. Consequently, if the subjective conditions do not correspond to the strategy that has been outlined, this does not mean that the strategy has to be replaced by one of lesser scope. In such cases, and this in fact is what happens most often, what is required is the use of tactics that are adequate to bringing about a *practical* understanding of the *viability* and *necessity* of the chosen strategy. This understanding emerges out of a complex and dynamic direct participation by the masses who, consciously or unconsciously, assimilate and adopt as their own the strategy worked out and led by the vanguard.

The masses do not act solely out of conviction injected into them from outside—without belittling the importance of revolutionary propaganda. They do not enter into combat because of simple faith in the promises of a better world or a future ideal. It is the experience they accumulate in the confrontation between their own vital interests and the economic and political realities they live through that serves as their main school. That is how they learn the strategic road to their liberation and the practical means for advancing along it. In short, the problem of how to bring the strategy to fruition can only be resolved through the various tactics of struggle.

Consequently, the elaboration and victorious application of revolutionary tactics is the most complex and definitive test of a vanguard. In real life there is no task more difficult than deriving tactics that are adequate to the strategic line that has been adopted. For while the latter rests on a scientific analysis of reality, the former must also take into account a multiplicity of conjunctural factors that are both difficult to control and of little scientific predictability. Day-to-day activity, then, requires a vanguard that is both well grounded in theory and has a special capacity and sensibility for capturing concrete reality. Only in this way is it possible to master the dialectic of struggle with sufficient flexibility to be able to implement rapid and effective decisions as events develop. This is especially true in revolutionary periods, which frequently present situations of a brand new type.

In reality, vanguards and individual leaderships emerge precisely where, in addition to a correct strategy, correct tactics of struggle are defined and developed at each moment. This, therefore, is the fundamental attribute of a legitimate vanguard.

That is, the decisive challenge for every vanguard is the elaboration of tactics adjusted to both concrete circumstances and to the strategic objectives of the revolution. We do not seek to standardize the factors that must be taken into account in formulating tactics. But experience indicates that there are certain points of reference that are useful to consider because of their general value. These include, among others: the relationship of forces at every moment of the struggle; contradictions inside the ruling classes; tactical objectives of the enemy's political gambits; the organization, consciousness, tradition of struggle, and social psychology of the masses; and the overall cohesion and strength of the vanguard.

As is well known, none of these factors are static. For example, it would be a metaphysical approach to always attribute to the ruling class a strength superior to that of the oppressed classes. In actuality the relationship of forces is characterized by its dynamism. Timely and audacious action by revolutionary detachments can, with the support of the masses, bring about abrupt changes in their favor. The same thing occurs, but inversely, when revolutionary actions are inadequate or do not match the level and creativity demanded by a given conjuncture. History shows the high price paid by the peoples in such cases, because each error, deficiency, and failure of the revolutionary movement is exploited to the hilt by the adversary.

Finally, it is important to note that it is often not possible to define the limits between strategy and tactics. They are interrelated and complement each other reciprocally.

In elaborating their strategy and tactics of struggle, the revolutionary movements in Latin America and the Caribbean confront two conditioning factors that are fundamental and permanent: the character of imperialist domination on the continent and the policy of the North American government.

For the United States, our region is part of the internal nucleus, the core, of its world strategy. North American imperialism has an integral policy toward our continent, containing all elements necessary for the conservation of its control of the hemisphere. Being part of an overall strategy, the policy of the United States with respect to neighbors to the south is based on principles that are both international and continental. In addition, in a few cases, there are particular approaches to relations with given countries and subregions.

Alongside the economic, military, and political importance the United States attributes to our countries, a significant role is also played by its arrogance in refusing to accept the triumph of liberating revolutions inside what it considers to be the borders of its national security.

These circumstances determine the increasingly sharp confrontations between the democratic, popular, and revolutionary processes on the one hand, and North American imperialism on the other.

That is why, on the level of strategy, the popular vanguards pay special attention to anti-imperialist objectives. Such objectives become the principal line of revolutionary combat, both strategic and tactical.

Revolutionaries also know that the crisis of North American imperialism will engender internal political currents and forces with varying points of view as to the most adequate forms for resolving the crisis and maintaining world domination. Thus, it may be possible to note genuine differences of nuance between one and another North American government—as well as inside each of them—differences that will logically be expressed in their policy toward our region. Experience teaches that in their handling of tactics, revolutionaries must pay the most painstaking attention to the policy developed by North American administrations so as to identify its weakest aspects and draw from them the greatest fruit. Both Cuba and Nicaragua have given us valuable experiences in how to correctly understand and use appropriate tactics in taking advantage of openings provided by different U.S. governments.

FROM ALL THE ABOVE it follows that in the strategic conception and tactics, the revolutionary processes of Latin America and the Caribbean must adopt, as their principal line, unity in the effort to defeat the overall enemy. This point of view is shared by all revolutionary parties and organizations in the region.

The socioeconomic and political changes these societies require have as a prerequisite the liquidation of North American imperialist domination over each one of these countries. This in turn requires removing imperialism's representatives from power.

To accomplish this, solidarity between all anti-imperialist forces is a historical necessity, an unavoidable condition for attaining the national and social liberation of our peoples.

Unity, the masses, and arms in the struggle for power

The experiences of the victorious revolutions and of the many processes that are developing on this continent confirm the general criteria formulated by Comrade Fidel Castro regarding the three ingredients decisive to attaining revolutionary triumph: unity, the masses, and arms.

It is useful to examine the specific importance of each one of these factors separately.

Life shows that it is not enough to proclaim the need for unity in order to advance toward achieving it. It is precisely in this manner that the real maturity of a vanguard and its full commitment to the cause of its people is tested. Individual passions, sectarian deviations, and other limitations must bow before the collective interests of the masses.

The process of building unity encompasses all the motor forces of the revolution and the allied democratic sectors. But its vital nerve center is the solid unity of the vanguard. The truth is that when the different detachments of the left succeed in cementing unity in action, have a consistent strategy, and put forward common tactics of struggle, the popular masses—who are instinctively for solidarity among themselves—increase this unity, to the point of making it virtually irreversible. And the broader the scope of the forces—national and international—taking part in the struggle against the immediate enemy, the greater is the imperative of the unity of the vanguard.

At this point in Latin American and Caribbean revolutionary history, this means objectively recognizing that in the majority of our countries, other left parties and organizations have grown up alongside the experienced Communist parties. These organizations have won in struggle the respect of their peoples, and many times also represent exemplary detachments in leading the people along the road of their final liberation. Therefore, the unity of these parties and organizations amongst themselves, and their unity with the Communist parties, is the primary guarantee for advancing the democratic, popular, and anti-imperialist revolutions in our continent.

It is necessary to realistically understand the processes of unity, and to avoid taking superficial steps that later turn out to be counterproductive. It is indispensable, at the same time, to make sure that the nonsectarian spirit of effective collaboration spreads through all levels of the parties and organizations, bearing in mind that many times in real life, the various groups carry out their activities in geographical spaces and social sectors that turn out in the long run to be complementary in the development of the revolution.

In those countries where military dictatorships rule, the field of unity broadens. It embraces even sectors interested solely in the destruction of the repressive, fascist-like structures, and in the return to bourgeois-democratic constitutional norms. In those cases the ground is even more fertile for the creation of antidictatorial democratic fronts, but on the condition that the revolutionary parties and organizations succeed in previously consolidating the leadership nucleus in such fronts.

We must emphasize that the proletarian revolution

in Latin America and the Caribbean is at the same time eminently a people's revolution. To take power and keep it, the working class needs to weave close political, ideological, and military ties with the rest of the masses. The unity of the working class and its allies must be pushed strongly through a mass policy, because that unity will not arise spontaneously from common economic interests, nor from the propagandistic invocation of those interests.

Certainly, the potential for unity in action by the popular masses exists in the economic basis of the system. But the process that leads to this unity in the political and ideological fields depends on the action of the vanguards; it is these vanguards, and not some economic predestination, that are responsible in practice for the achievement of democratic and revolutionary unity.

Today in various countries of the region the problem of unity is the principal obstacle to the advance of the revolution. This being plainly true, there is evidence that it also represents a spur for overcoming the harmful tendency toward the division of the left in some of our countries. Every step forward in unity is a step forward on the road of the revolution.

Inertia, delay, or deviation from the united road is a gift from the revolutionary movement to the enemy.

It is common knowledge that the best form of advancing unity is through collaboration in concrete struggles. This direct relationship between the development of the revolutionary processes and the levels of unity of the vanguards is right now being demonstrated in El Salvador, Guatemala, and in the other countries of Central America, such as Honduras. The Sandinista triumph reaffirmed, among other important questions, the crucial value of the unity of the vanguard as the nucleus providing cohesion and orientation to the antidictatorial, democratic, anti-imperialist, and revolutionary forces as a whole. We also see in Chile advances toward unity that are promising for the future of the struggles of this people.

THE UNITY of the revolutionary movement inside the borders of a country is a contribution to the broader unity on a continental and world scale. In regard to our region, the historic and economic factors, the confrontation with a similar enemy, and the political interrelation of our societies fosters an identity in proposals and reciprocal solidarity of the left. But here too, these elements are potential, and by themselves they cannot move forward the effective collaboration of the revolutionary forces in action.

There has to be an individual and collective will that demonstrates in action the proclaimed Latin Americanism and internationalism. There are many examples of solidarity and they are well-known. We Latin American and Caribbean revolutionaries have offered convincing demonstrations of our understanding of internationalism. However, internationalism is of such importance for achieving the triumph of national revolutions in one or another historic moment, and the role of concrete solidarity toward one or another process is so complex and dynamic, that we must still ask ourselves how far we have to go to advance and perfect the collaboration between all the revolutionary parties and organizations of the area.

Sometimes, although in Latin America it does not occur to the same degree as in other regions, there are confusions or deviations regarding the necessary and healthy independence that parties of the left have the right and the duty to preserve. Real sovereignty of these parties and movements, however, far from excluding it, presupposes the need to join collectively to confront common international problems and to collaborate in support of the revolutionary processes that most need solidarity at a given moment.

Finally, together with united work, it is indispensable to give special emphasis to activity to take advantage of the contradictions within the ruling classes in each country and those that arise on an interimperialist scale or between the countries in the region.

IN THIS SENSE, the Latin American experience confirms the ideas of Lenin: "The more powerful enemy can be vanquished only by exerting the utmost effort, and by the most thorough, careful, attentive, skillful and *obligatory* use of any, even the smallest, rift between the enemies, any conflict of interests among the bourgeoisie of the various countries and among the various groups or types of bourgeoisie within the various countries, and also by taking advantage of any, even the smallest, opportunity of winning a mass ally, even though this ally is temporary, vacillating, unstable, unreliable and conditional. Those who do not understand this reveal a failure to understand even the smallest grain of Marxism, of modern scientific socialism *in general*. Those who have not proved *in practice*, over a fairly considerable period of time and in fairly varied political situations, their ability to apply this truth in practice have not yet learned to help the revolutionary class in its struggle to emancipate all toiling humanity from the exploiters."[4]

Although there are many differences in the various countries and subregions, it is possible to offer a general characterization of four fundamental forces with which revolutionary forces in Latin America and the Caribbean have to develop tactical or strategic alliances. We are referring to Social Democracy, Christian Democracy, the Christian movement, and progressive military sectors.

Our position in regard to the activity and ideological and political content of the Social Democracy was clearly expressed by Comrade Fidel Castro in the main report to the Second Congress of the Communist Party of Cuba.

We take into account that the Social Democracy is not a homogeneous political current but rather one that inevitably reflects the different social forces that make it up on a world and regional scale, as well as interimperialist contradictions. This explains why, despite common political and ideological views, these parties adopt stances that are not always identical, and on many occasions notoriously divergent, with regard to the various revolutionary struggles. For that reason, an alliance with Social Democratic forces has to be based on clear and honest principles of collaboration, without impairing the final objectives the revolutionaries are fighting for. Accordingly, we must stress this collaboration in the political aspects that unite us rather than stress the ideological differences that separate us. For while the latter cannot be avoided, they should not be allowed to become insurmountable obstacles to united action in favor of coinciding objectives.

In contrast, the most general tendency of Christian Democracy is to lean toward active collaboration with the policy and interests of North American imperialism. But it is not correct to deduce, from such an extreme, a position that excludes all Christian Democratic forces. Inside the Christian Democracy there also exist important sectors that are genuinely democratic and Christian, and on occasion these sectors are forced to break openly with the official, compromised leaderships of their parties. In such cases, keeping in mind specific national situations, it is our responsibility to approach them frankly and free of prejudice, with the aim of working in common agreement on all tasks that it is possible to share. And this includes the strategic line for the conquest of power and the construction of a new society.

It is well known that we take a broad approach to the Christian movements, which include priests and members of the Catholic hierarchy who identify with the human, political, and economic aspirations of their peoples. On various occasions Comrade Fidel Castro has stressed the decisive character of unity between Marxist-Leninist forces and Christians who are acting together with their peoples for essentially the same objectives. These Christians we consider brothers in struggle for great historical changes on the continent. There will be no victorious revolutions without the participation of the immense Christian masses that populate our countries. Consequently, it is natural for the vanguards to open their doors to rank-and-file Christians, to priests and members of the church hierarchy who are committed—often at the cost of their lives—to the struggle for the emancipation of Latin America and the Caribbean. We believe that in a number of countries the revolutionary movement has not yet made the advance that is both necessary and possible in terms of collaboration with and integration of these forces. In some cases, it is these Christian forces who show a greater readiness for unity, and a more correct understanding in practice of their revolutionary role.

Another question that is important to take up is that of relations with progressive military sectors. In our opinion, the conduct of the armed forces cannot be analyzed apart from the historical context of each country or from its class confrontations. Regardless of the general function that the military apparatus is supposed to carry out within the bourgeois state, it would be erroneous to view every man in uniform as an unconditional servant of the state. In this aspect as well, accumulated experiences indicate the usefulness of making a distinction with regard to the progressive elements of the armed forces, an important sector in some countries. The aim should be to get to know the practical possibilities of collaboration with them in the development of anti-imperialist, democratic, and revolutionary struggles.

A CORRECT POLICY toward the military sectors cannot be based on rigid, exclusionary schemas. It must emerge from each specific reality and take into account all the factors that make up such an institution. Nor would it be valid, on the other hand, to overlook the fundamental principles of Marxism-Leninism, which teach that it is an imperative necessity to destroy the repressive machinery of the state in order to attain complete control over the state and replace it with one of a new type.

Let us now focus on the role the masses must play. The incorporation of the masses into the revolution is the sole motor force capable of guaranteeing the achievement of power and its subsequent preservation. But as we know, it is not enough simply to call on the working class and the rest of the people to overthrow the bourgeoisie for the masses to respond to that call. Lenin taught us, and life confirms, that propaganda and agitation are not sufficient by themselves to make the people understand revolutionary activity and involve themselves in it. For this, the political experience of the masses themselves is needed, Lenin asserted. And he concluded: This is the fundamental law of the great revolutions.

The problem, then, is to contribute to these experiences of the masses, to help them develop their revolutionary energies through the most fitting channels at each stage of the development of the class struggle. This cannot be derived from the desires and final aspirations of the revolutionary movement.

Subjectivism can lead to substituting the vanguard for the role of the masses or to precipitating decisive actions of the masses, which should be held for opportune moments. Just as bad, subjectivism can also lead to a metaphysical view of postponing certain actions again and again, using the subterfuge that the masses are not adequately prepared to move toward the conquest of power.

THERE ARE NO RECIPES or general formulas to resolve the crucial question of incorporating the masses into the tasks of their revolution. Nevertheless, there are experiences that are useful to consider. For example the revolutions in Cuba, Nicaragua, and Grenada show that a program of struggle against the dictatorship and for democracy has the greatest possibilities to mobilize the broad masses of the people and other allied political forces.

We think that under present conditions in the majority of our countries, the decisive thing is not to stress the final or long-term objectives of the struggle, but rather unifying slogans linked directly to the circumstances that most strangle the life of the people, in the economic, social, and political realm.

Focusing the central activity of the masses on achieving their antidictatorial, democratic aspirations, and on solving their most pressing human problems (jobs, health, education, among others), increases the possibility of their acting. With this comes an increase in the revolutionary movement's potential in the struggle to achieve power and initiate the democratic and anti-imperialist phase of the revolution.

The third and final factor—along with unity and the masses—that guarantees the triumph of genuine revolutions is the correct and timely use of arms. This does not represent a dogma, but rather results from the system of domination that exists in the majority of Latin American and Caribbean countries. It would be a grave attitude of voluntarism to try to sketch out a single continental strategy for such a geographically extensive span of national societies, enriched by their own historic struggles and sociological peculiarities. But at the same time, there are certain principles of every revolution that cannot be forgotten.

Arms are indispensable to securing the victory of any liberating revolution in the continent, and, even more important, to preserve its continuity and achieve its full realization. This statement does not disregard the objective reality of different countries. In some countries where there are regimes of the far right—nearly always military dictatorships of a fascist cut—the use of forms of armed struggle or the correct preparation of the vanguard for their use is a virtually inescapable imperative.

In other countries, where democratic norms of life predominate and the vanguards have constitutional channels adequate for carrying out their activity, the role of arms will be shaped not by their inopportune use but rather by psychological preparation and the creation of the consciousness in all militants that—at some point, in some form—military confrontation will be indispensable, even though it would not be valid under existing circumstances. What is involved, therefore, is to create an attitude in all revolutionaries, and to move forward as much as possible in the revolutionary military preparation of the cadres and militants.

Furthermore, at the moment when political conditions demand the selection of the armed road, that decision must not be subordinated to the survival of some democratic forms, which would compromise the strategic actions of the revolutionary and people's movement.

AND, FINALLY, in the daily events of the class struggle, one must tenaciously forge the conditions that will help to advance along the road to the conquest of power. This conquest of power, in one or another variant, and with its national modalities, has always been due to the creation and development of its own military force.

On occasion, of course, false dichotomies have been put forward that counterpose armed and nonarmed forms of struggle. A struggle is not reformist simply because it is legal or because it seeks to open a democratic space, nor can a struggle be called revolutionary simply because it has an armed character. In our opinion, the revolutionary content of any form of struggle is measured by its results, that is, by the advance or retreat it implies for the final objectives of the popular masses.

The leadership capacity of the vanguards rests in their overall preparation to utilize all forms of struggle, permitting them to articulate energetic and opportune responses to the diverse twists and turns that the class confrontation imposes. In that respect, the experiences of various revolutionary processes in the area show that a division between the political and military functions (particularly when determined and popular use of arms is required) gives rise to a mutilation of both functions. Therefore only a political-military strategy, and the corresponding formation and preparation for it, provides the vanguards with the flexibility to undertake a new form of principal struggle in accordance with the stage and conjuncture of each national process.

At times the necessary use of arms is incorrectly identified with the mechanical application of one or another experience of armed struggle. The revolutions in Cuba, Nicaragua, and Grenada present well-known differences, but among other similar elements, have the common stamp of the use of arms. At the same time, along with specific common bases (especially in the cases of Cuba and Nicaragua), they show differences in military tactics employed, in insurrectional forms, etc. For example, in El Salvador creative revolutionary formulas are being applied in the use of arms, based on the closest links with the masses and in adverse geographic conditions—including among other factors the country's small territorial dimensions.

All the revolutions of our continent will have their own characteristics and will undoubtedly bring with them new contributions to the world revolutionary heritage. There won't be schemas capable of guiding the processes of national liberation and the construction of socialist societies in the Americas. Each people will make their revolution and will reach socialism by taking nourishment from the roots of its own national, Latin American, and Caribbean history. And this will not be a contradiction, because every real social revolution is, at the same time, also a daughter of the universal laws discovered by Marx, Engels, and Lenin.

In that sense, our Commander-in-Chief Fidel Castro asserted:

"Modern revolutionaries are indebted to the theoreticians of scientific socialism—Marx, Engels, and Lenin—for the immense treasure of their ideas. We are absolutely sure that, without them, our people would not have been able to achieve such a tremendous leap in the history of their social and political development. But, even with them, we would not have been capable of achieving it without the fertile seed and the unlimited heroism sown among our people and in our spirits by such giants of our country's history as Martí, Maceo, Gómez, Agramonte, and Céspedes. That is how the real revolution was made in Cuba, based on its unique characteristics, its own traditions of struggle, and the consistent application of universal principles."[5]

NOTES

1. V.I. Lenin. "A Caricature of Marxism and Imperialist Economism" in Lenin, *Collected Works* (Moscow: Progress Publishers, 1974), vol. 23, p. 36.

2. *Programmatic Platform of the Communist Party of Cuba* (Havana: Department of Revolutionary Orientation of the Central Committee of the Communist Party of Cuba, 1976), p. 47.

3. Fidel Castro, "Report of the Central Committee of the Communist Party of Cuba to the First Congress" in *First Congress of the Communist Party of Cuba* (Moscow: Progress Publishers, 1976), p. 47.

4. Lenin, "'Left-Wing' Communism—An Infantile Disorder" in *Collected Works,* vol. 31, pp. 70–71.

5. Fidel Castro, *Fidel Castro Speeches: Cuba's Internationalist Foreign Policy 1975–80* (New York: Pathfinder Press, 1981), p. 40.

THE COMMUNIST INTERNATIONAL IN LENIN'S TIME

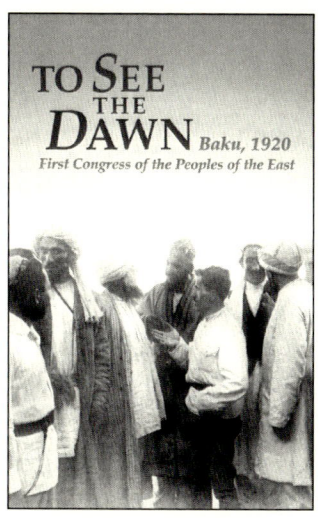

To See the Dawn
Baku, 1920—First Congress of the Peoples of the East

How can peasants and workers in the colonial world achieve freedom from imperialist exploitation? By what means can working people overcome divisions incited by their national ruling classes and act together for their common class interests? These questions were addressed by 2,000 delegates to the 1920 Congress of the Peoples of the East. $17

Workers of the World and Oppressed Peoples, Unite!
Proceedings and Documents of the Second Congress, 1920

The debate among delegates from 37 countries takes up key questions of working-class strategy and program and offers a vivid portrait of social struggles in the era of the October revolution. 2 vol. set. $45

Lenin's Struggle for a Revolutionary International
Documents, 1907–1916; The Preparatory Years

The debate among revolutionary working-class leaders, including V.I. Lenin and Leon Trotsky, on a socialist response to World War I. $30

Other volumes in the series:

The German Revolution and the Debate on Soviet Power (1918–1919). $27

Founding the Communist International (March 1919). $25

WWW.PATHFINDERPRESS.COM

CUBA'S SOCIALIST REVOLUTION AND THE WORLD

Cuba and Angola: The War for Freedom
HARRY VILLEGAS ("POMBO")

The story of Cuba's unparalleled contribution to the fight to free Africa from the scourge of apartheid. And how, in the doing, Cuba's socialist revolution was strengthened. $10. Also in Spanish, Farsi, and Greek.

Our History Is Still Being Written
The Story of Three Chinese Cuban Generals in the Cuban Revolution
ARMANDO CHOY, GUSTAVO CHUI, MOISÉS SÍO WONG, MARY-ALICE WATERS

"What was the key measure to uproot discrimination against Chinese and blacks in Cuba? It was the socialist revolution itself." New edition sheds light on Chinese Cubans' involvement in Cuba's internationalist course, including in Africa and Latin America. $15. Also in Spanish, French, Farsi, Greek, and Chinese.

How Far We Slaves Have Come!
South Africa and Cuba in Today's World
NELSON MANDELA, FIDEL CASTRO

Speaking together in Cuba in 1991, Mandela and Castro discuss the role of Cuba in the history of Africa and Angola's victory over the invading US-backed South African army. That victory accelerated the fight to bring down the racist apartheid system. $7. Also in Spanish and Farsi.

Red Zone

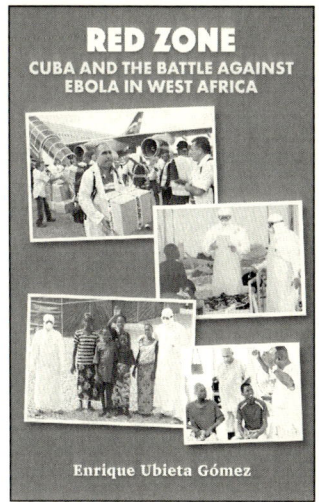

Cuba and the Battle against Ebola in West Africa

ENRIQUE UBIETA GÓMEZ

When three African countries were hit in 2014–15 by the Ebola epidemic, Cuba's revolutionary government sent what no other country even pretended to provide: more than 250 volunteer doctors, nurses, and other medical workers. This firsthand account of their actions shows the kind of men and women only a socialist revolution can produce. $17. Also in Spanish and French.

The First and Second Declarations of Havana

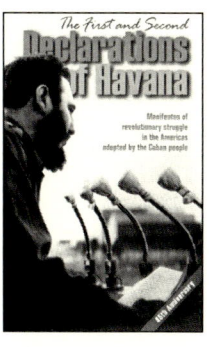

Nowhere are the questions of revolutionary strategy that today confront men and women on the front lines of struggles in the Americas addressed with greater truthfulness and clarity than in these uncompromising indictments of imperialist plunder and "the exploitation of man by man." Adopted by million-strong assemblies of the Cuban people in 1960 and 1962. $10. Also in Spanish, French, Farsi, Arabic, and Greek.

Playa Girón/Bay of Pigs

Washington's First Military Defeat in the Americas

FIDEL CASTRO, JOSÉ RAMÓN FERNÁNDEZ

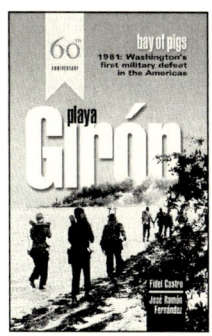

In fewer than 72 hours of combat in April 1961, Cuba's revolutionary armed forces defeated a US-organized invasion by 1,500 mercenaries. In the process, the Cuban people set an example for workers, farmers, and youth the world over that with political consciousness, class solidarity, courage, and revolutionary leadership, we can stand up to enormous might and seemingly insurmountable odds—and win. $17. Also in Spanish.

WWW.PATHFINDERPRESS.COM

'A NOSE FOR POWER':
PREPARING THE
NICARAGUAN REVOLUTION

by Tomás Borge

W E HAVE AGREED to make some comments on the history of the Sandinista Front. They will at least serve as a basis for us to reflect more seriously and finally to make some notes toward a modest contribution to the glorious history of our organization.

Those who killed Sandino believed they had killed the revolution.[1] They believed they had killed even the possibility of a revolution. Such superstition is akin to fetishism, which affects everybody in some way. It has something to do with the way individuals tend to be presented either as standing outside of history or as the exclusive architects of history.

This speech by Commander Tomás Borge, a member of the National Directorate of the Sandinista National Liberation Front (FSLN) and Nicaragua's minister of the interior, was presented at the "Commander Iván Montenegro Báez" Second National Seminar of Political Education in Nicaragua, May 20, 1983. It has been translated by Fred Murphy from the Spanish text printed in the August 1983 issue of Cuadernos del Tercer Mundo, *published in Mexico.*

ENDNOTES BEGIN ON PAGE 247

The other side of this coin involves denying, in a rather scholastic way, the role of individuals in history. Nonetheless, history (which is not just "noise," as [the eighteenth-century French Enlightenment philosopher] Montesquieu asserted) takes place under certain conditions, and it is regulated by laws that operate independently of the will of individuals. So, in this concrete case, those who sought to wipe out the memory of the man who became even more than the architect of the Nicaraguan people were mistaken once again. The material conditions that had led Sandino to point out the road of popular struggle remained in force after his death as a result of the economic and political domination of Nicaragua by the United States. The commonplace egotism of the domestic exploiting classes remained, as did, of course, the existence of an instrument of coercion—the so-called national army. Hence the bullets that killed Sandino did not mark the end but rather the prologue to a new beginning, to a leap forward with a will to persist, to the future founding of the Sandinista National Liberation Front. Meanwhile, the objective strength of the National Guard, the instrument of Yankee domination, provided life insurance for the superexploitation of the Nicaraguan people.

D<small>UE TO THE DEATH</small> of Sandino and domination by a brutal instrument of repression, the period from 1934 to 1956 was to be a dark and sad interlude. The practical expression of this—as we have said on other occasions although perhaps in different ways—was a downturn in the revolutionary movement. The people went on struggling stubbornly, but they were weak and undernourished in terms of ideology and organization.

What was lacking in that period was undoubtedly a revolutionary leadership. Throughout that period, the opposition bourgeoisie dominated the struggle against Somozaism. They went through a lengthy process of bargaining in which the astute and cruel godfather of the Somoza dynasty always came out ahead. The objective conditions—and all of us have already become familiar with this notion—were dramatic and evident: hunger, poverty, malnutrition, social insecurity, and a ridiculous culture, sugary and imported like Adams Chiclets. But the subjective conditions of organization and consciousness were invisible at that time, which is to say virtually nonexistent. This contradiction between the objective and subjective conditions eventually served to shed enough light on the situation so that the people could discover that without a vanguard it was impossible to defeat the Somozaist dictatorship.

The cultivation of cotton in Nicaragua dates from the 1950s. With cotton came the dust storms as well as the imported pesticide toxins that were added to the meager, indigenous fare of our agricultural workers. Capitalist development was thereby concretized historically in Nicaragua in accord with the narrow pattern of single-export agriculture, with its productive structure bound up with demand on the world capitalist market.

Cotton was the determining factor in the agro-export character of the Nicaraguan economy. It was a key symptom of the development of capitalist relations of production in agriculture. The surpluses accumulated were applied either to expansion of the area allotted to cotton cultivation; to the construction, in bad taste, of some new residential areas such as you can see in León and other Nicaraguan cities; to periodic visits by the cotton-growers to the Louvre museum in Paris, or to the formation of one part of the private financial system.

This process contributed to the consolidation of the state and to the development of certain industrial and commercial activities having to do with the dazzling but unstable market for cotton. The necessary result—which couldn't be added up the same way cotton bales were at the Banco de América—was a greater class polarization within the framework of a historical reality (a reality that is generally denied from the pulpits and banquet tables of the bourgeoisie). A polarization between the exploiting and exploited classes in our country placed at one extreme the agro-exporting bourgeoisie and the commercial and industrial groups, and at the other extreme the agricultural workers. This represented the deepening of a process that had begun with the cultivation of coffee at the end of the nineteenth century and had led to a greater concentration of landed property and finally to the technological development of cotton production. Reflected through the Somozaist government and its laws, this process had as its consequence the sharpening of the class struggle between exploiters and exploited.

The 1956 economic crisis began, of course, on the world capitalist markets. It subjected the Nicaraguan economy to the effects of a cyclical fluctuation in external demand (a fall in prices for coffee and cotton and a drop in the volume of exports). This crisis of the agro-export model dealt blows to profit rates, and it increased popular discontent. But the agricultural proletariat and semiproletariat that had been born along with the cotton seeds, as well as the incipient urban proletariat, were not yet able to respond collectively to the repression and poverty.

That explains why there was no political organization with the strategic clarity necessary to overcome the silence, stagnation, and inactivity. The bringing to justice of Somoza García took place in this framework. On September 21, 1956, Rigoberto López Pérez marked the beginning of the end of the dictatorship. To do so was the hero's express aim, as lucidly explained by Carlos Fonseca and further discussed by José Benito Escobar.[2] Twenty different armed movements took place one after the other following Rigoberto's action. This crisis put an end to the dark interlude.

AT THE BEGINNING of the 1960s, the plan for Central American economic integration began to take shape. This plan, a product of the developmentalist strategy, was presented with a smile far broader than the resources allotted to it. Its aim was to slow the wave of popular uprisings. In that regard, however, the errors committed by enthusiastic Latin American revolutionaries who had mechanical conceptions about the victory of the Cuban revolution proved more effective.

The Alliance for Progress [launched by U.S. President John F. Kennedy] was part of a new period of expansion in U.S. foreign investment, now primarily directed at the industrial sector. The idea of the Central American Common Market originated from the United Nations Economic Commission for Latin America, which held developmentalist notions of how to overcome economic backwardness. The initial plans called for a gradual process of import-substitutions and balanced industrial development. This abstract project was soon distorted by the conditions imposed by those who financed it. The Central American Common Market served as the institutional and political framework for the transfer of local and foreign capital into the industrial sector, with the aim of consolidating the basis for capital accumulation. But the effort was distorted, since land reform and income redistribution—preconditions for industrial development—were not contemplated in this integrationist strategy.

Rigoberto's action, as has been said many times, was not a terrorist act. But we cannot resign ourselves to saying that and nothing more. It is necessary to say also that it corresponded to the conditions of underdevelopment and economic and cultural backwardness that prevailed at the time. Under such conditions, there is a tendency to individualize social conflicts. The dramatic individual phenomenon of Somoza found its parallel at that moment in a response of similar character. This also helps explain why a personal military dictatorship was an adequate instrument for guaranteeing foreign and oligarchic domination.

Rigoberto's action showed that the dictator was not physically invulnerable. This constituted the first step in making the people conscious of the social forces that were hidden behind Somoza's apparently personal power. Rigoberto's action was the first in a cascade of popular actions and armed movements through which our people answered the thoughtless and cannibalistic leaders of the bourgeois opposition. It marked a new beginning for the popular movement—the first stirrings around Sandino's enormous sepulcher before his resurrection.

THE CUBAN REVOLUTION, as Carlos Fonseca observed, had an impact on Nicaragua even before its victorious culmination. As we pointed out in the pamphlet, *Carlos, el amanecer ya no es una tentación* [Carlos, the dawn is no longer a temptation], "The victory of the armed struggle in Cuba, more than a joy, was the drawing back of innumerable curtains, a powder flash that shed light from afar on the naive and tiresome dogmas of the moment. The Cuban revolution certainly sent a shiver of terror through the ruling classes of Latin America. It was also a violent assault on the suddenly forlorn relics with which we had first adorned our altars. Fidel was for us the resurrection of Sandino, the answer to our reservations, the justification of the dreams and heresies of some hours before."[3]

The repressive actions of the dictatorship were only the political expression of one of the sides of the contradiction. The popular classes sought political expression through the Patriotic Youth, the teachers' and workers' strikes, student demonstrations, land seizures, and the creation of trade unions and labor and peasant federations.

This popular agitation involved sectors that had never before demonstrated openly against the Somozaist regime. The ferment pointed up the congenital helplessness of the Nicaraguan bourgeoisie, or, more precisely, the absence of a national bourgeoisie able to assume leadership of the anti-Somozaist movement.

The armed opposition movements repeatedly covered Nicaraguan territory with blood, but at no time did they manage to involve the entire people in the armed struggle. We can seek the explanation for this in the diversity of social composition, ideologies, and political programs of those guerrilla groups. At that time, there was still no theory that could make it possible to determine the character of the social forces in conflict, and to guide their strategic and tactical priorities.

All the spontaneous actions with which the masses illuminated this opening phase of revolutionary ascent serve to show us the revolutionary potential of the Nicaraguan people. They also highlight the lack of a revolutionary organization and leadership. Without a vanguard, this revolutionary potential could not be converted into a powerful popular fist capable of bringing down the Somozaist dictatorship.

Such a vanguard is necessary to give organized expression to the sweat, rage, and intuition of the people. I repeat that in this phase of ascent the economic conditions for the emergence of a revolutionary vanguard did exist. On the basis of these objective conditions, certain subjective conditions had also been forged. But these forces still lacked an ideology or a theory that could put them in order and give them coherence.

The Sandinista National Liberation Front was founded in July 1961. This historic event signified the people's alternative, as opposed to the bourgeois reformist alternative, in the struggle against Somozaism.

We cannot speak of a vanguard without a vanguard theory. In referring to the creation of the vanguard, we must emphasize the way Carlos Fonseca rehabilitated Sandino and his revolutionary ideas. Carlos saw in Sandino and his ideas not an ethereal symbol, not an abstraction, but rather a guide for understanding Nicaraguan reality and transforming it in a revolutionary way.

We could say that Sandino's thought can be summed up in two great ideas retrieved by Carlos Fonseca:

Only the workers and peasants are capable of struggling to the end against imperialism and its local political representatives. With this notion, Sandino's intuition grasped above all the class character of the revolutionary movement, the class struggle as the motor of history.

Besides pointing to the workers and peasants as the fundamental subjects of this struggle, Sandino also grasped the form the popular revolutionary movement in Nicaragua had to take. In the economic, social, and political conditions of Nicaragua, the armed struggle was the only road that could lead to the revolutionary transformation of society. Stated from our current perspective this seems like all too obvious a notion. But at the time, when contradictory notions were playing a role, it was very important to retrieve this essential idea of Sandino: "Freedom is not conquered with flowers but with bullets," the general said. This became for us a beautiful saying, an axiom in the formation of a people's army, a guerrilla army to begin with, for the conquest of national liberation.

This was the sufficient foundation, from the standpoint of consciousness, for the defense of national sovereignty. In these two great ideas is summed up the strategy that led us to victory—the combination of guerrilla struggle with the mass movement, through a dialectic in which the guerrillas became the people and the people became an army.

THESE INEXORABLE ideas were rooted in Nicaraguan soil. They were brought together with the revolutionary theory that synthesizes the experiences of all revolutions. And it was the application of this notion, without dogmatism, that led a handful of revolutionaries to found the Sandinista National Liberation Front in 1961.

The founding of the Sandinista Front confirmed the truth of Sandino's words: "We will go toward the sun of liberty or toward death, and if we die it doesn't matter, our cause will go on living, others will follow us."

Sandino's cause had indeed gone on living, and the Sandinista Front did no more than take it up again under different material conditions and with the guidance of a revolutionary theory. Sandino's cause defied dangers and betrayals and turned the vacillators into pillars of salt. Sandino's cause lives and will go on living.

THE FSLN'S FIRST DECADE

THE ARMED STRUGGLE was initiated with the Río Coco and Bocay guerrilla front in 1963. This was the first armed action prepared by a revolutionary group that was more or less homogeneous from the military and political-ideological standpoint. That is, the inevitable contradictions that arise in any revolutionary movement were not ones of principle in this case. The men involved were united first of all by ideological conceptions; later by the terrible privations they underwent in the bitter moments of the first armed actions; and, finally, by the bouts of pessimism that often harden men at difficult moments and by the basic initial optimism that our brother Carlos knew how to instill.

It must be taken into account that at that time in Latin America a schematic interpretation of the Cuban revolution had been propagated, one that isolated the guerrilla warfare from the mass movement. We have already referred to the different basis on which the Sandinista Front had begun. (This question ought to be studied someday, in order to analyze further the struggle of the peoples of Latin America, their difficulties, failures, and achievements.)

Nonetheless, unity between theory and practice is not something that is established once and for all at the outset. Rather, it is something that must be achieved in the course of the struggle itself. The vanguard itself needed to grasp this principle at that first moment, in that initial armed experience.

Around Río Coco and Bocay a minimal infrastructure at the level of the masses had been prepared to support the guerrillas, but not within the zone where the guerrilla struggle was initiated. The efforts that had been made there had broken down owing to the persistence of certain mechanical conceptions, even though some of us had managed to grasp the need for adequate conditions before initiating the guerrilla movement in the areas along the Río Coco. One such effort had indeed been made in the area around Wiwilí. It was not possible to take advantage of that because of other factors, so the guerrillas began operating in an area that had not been previously explored, where no political work had been done with the local population. This tactical error became for us a makeshift and difficult source of lessons that both reaffirmed the correctness of our overall conception and revealed from the outset the importance of work among and with the masses.

The Río Coco and Bocay experience constituted a defeat—not precisely from the military standpoint, since the main problems did not arise from armed engagements but rather from the absence of the minimal conditions on the ground necessary for the guerrillas' survival. There were no supply lines. Even food, clothing, and weapons were lacking. This led to a decision to return to the original base.

The vanguard turned the military defeat of 1963 into a source of lessons. The correction of its errors had allowed it to survive and put together a clandestine apparatus in the cities. It managed to carry out certain armed propaganda actions, economic blows, and the distribution of Sandinista materials. These were always beautiful—some of them were ingenuous, but they never lacked that special profundity that Carlos Fonseca knew how to impart.

Small training schools were set up.

The experiences of Río Coco (or Wankí, as the Miskitos call it) and Bocay constituted a defeat that coincided with the temporary decline of the anti-Somozaist movement. Nonetheless, between 1963 and 1966 the FSLN managed to establish certain contacts with the masses in the barrios, workplaces, student milieus, and rural unions. This work among the masses was carried out not only by the intermediate organizations of the FSLN, such as the People's Civic Committees and the well-known Revolutionary Student Front [FER], but also through temporary alliances with the Republican Mobilization Party (which ceased to exist a little while later) and with the Nicaraguan Socialist Party (which still exists).

The military defeat of 1963 coincided with, and contributed to, a temporary downturn in the anti-Somozaist movement. A period of economic upswing was under way (Somozaism's best period in that sense). The most dynamic sectors of the bourgeoisie took full advantage of this. They were able to combine their agro-export and commercial interests with the new phase of industrialization spurred by the government's economic policy.

IMPERIALISM's new development strategy for Latin America, the so-called Alliance for Progress, which some of you may not even recall, was Kennedy's political response to the Cuban revolution. This famous alliance received a great deal of publicity, and it had an effect in altering the facade of many Latin American countries. In Nicaragua, it gave a certain cover to the Somozaist dictatorship.

As a variant of the dictatorship's form of political domination there arose the cosmetic civilian regime of René Schick.[4] More than anything else, his period in office made possible the reorganization of bourgeois politics in the framework of a strictly electoral struggle. This engendered a certain pessimism regarding the possibility of continuing with the armed struggle.

But the FSLN was already in existence. It had the will to struggle and had organized in a way that went beyond guerrilla characteristics. This made it different from other, exclusively guerrilla, organizations that had disappeared completely once guerrilla warfare came to an end. We expanded beyond a guerrilla conception. We overcame that limitation, and when the guerrilla movement temporarily disappeared, the Sandinista National Liberation Front continued to exist.

The civic maneuvers could not succeed, given the economic process they were supposed to structure politically. In fact, the growing decomposition of the system and the revolutionary ascent that had begun with the 1956 assassination of Anastasio Somoza García had as their consequence the failure of these maneuvers ten years later. The dictatorship then opted for the military alternative, with Anastasio Somoza Debayle himself at the head. This process, whereby the repressive character of the Somozaist dictatorship was thoroughly unmasked, culminated in the massacre of January 22, 1967—the year that Don Fernando Agüero went around passing out smiles and false promises.[5]

The bourgeois opposition led the people into a massacre on January 22. That opened the final chapter in the bourgeoisie's hegemony as the social sector guiding the anti-Somozaist struggle in our country. Along with the peasants who died that day, the possibility that the Nicaraguan bourgeoisie would lead the anti-Somozaist struggle was also buried. Not only because of what occurred there, but also because after that massacre of hundreds of Nicaraguans, the bourgeois opposition withdrew comfortably and made a pact with the regime—the so-called Kupia Kumi Pact that Fernando Agüero signed with Somoza in 1971. Its fundamental proposition was not the restoration of peace in Nicaragua, which from the bourgeoisie's standpoint was not endangered anyway, but rather the smashing of the Nicaraguan revolutionary movement. From 1967 on, the FSLN established direct contact with the people, making use for this purpose of its own basic clandestine apparatus, out of which an open apparatus arose.

In the course of the year 1967, the FSLN also went about preparing the Pancasán front. A communiqué signed by leaders of the FSLN was issued; among the signers was Compañera Doris Tijerino, who used the pseudonym Conchita Alday.[6] The guerrilla movement now managed for the first time to rid itself of its earlier preference for invasions from outside Nicaragua. At Pancasán the armed actions were organized not from Honduras but rather in the mountains in the central part of our own country. The work of preparing the guerrilla campaign was centered at Pancasán and Fila Grande, with the support of the peasants of the area. Compañeros such as Oscar Turcios and Rigoberto Cruz began to stand out in this work; Cruz had already been involved in the armed incursion of 1963.

In the Pancasán campaign the vanguard suffered a military defeat that Ricardo Morales would later analyze quite correctly.[7] When we begin to study this history more carefully we will have to take into account the whole bibliography that has arisen on those events.

Despite the military defeat, Pancasán had immense significance for the revolutionary movement. The armed struggle was reaffirmed, while the impossibility of overthrowing the military dictatorship through peaceful methods was demonstrated. When I say this, I mean that the Nicaraguan people became conscious that only armed struggle was capable of defeating the Somozaist dictatorship. This involved a total discrediting of the so-called civic methods of struggle. Despite everything, such methods became famous later in the pulpits of our Catholic churches, from which certain members of the hierarchy always insisted on the need for civic struggle, right down to the last moments of the Somozaist dictatorship. Such a position was nonetheless discredited in the consciousness of the people. The need for armed struggle became powerfully felt.

Despite the military defeat at Pancasán and Fila Grande, that struggle had immense significance for the Sandinista Front, because it managed to consolidate the FSLN's influence among the Nicaraguan people. It convinced the people that ours was the only organization truly able to represent the people's interests, the only force capable of seriously confronting the Somozaist dictatorship. This elevated the moral authority and the political standing of the Sandinista National Liberation Front.

By then the Sandinista Front had managed to create a vanguard detachment that survived despite the serious blows we suffered. You will recall that near Pancasán they massacred a group of compañeros, among them Silvio Mayorga. There were no survivors from that guerrilla column Silvio led; it included a series of extraordinarily valuable cadres—Rigoberto Cruz, Chelito Moreno, and so many others. We already had a clandestine apparatus in the cities, which allowed us to carry out certain armed propaganda actions and actions to secure funds, which

helped us overcome our great scarcity of resources.
There were days when the clandestine fighters didn't even have their daily bread. We lacked tortillas. We had no transportation to get supplies to the mountains. There were no resources to maintain the guerrillas. The extraordinary spirit of sacrifice certain compañeros showed at that time, as in 1963, is worthy of being recalled in the pages of the history of our organization.

Sandinista propaganda by then had reached a certain level of circulation. We had set up a few tiny training schools. We had already put to the test the incipient mechanisms of contact with the masses through what we began to call around that time, I believe, the intermediate organizations: the People's Civic Committees and the Revolutionary Student Front (FER), which played an extraordinarily important role.

IN 1967 WE DREW UP the outline of a program and some statutes, as well as notes on the strategic line of the Sandinista Front. These later served as the basis for further development of the program and statutes. By then we were also involved in internationalist activity; it was around that time that Compañero Patricio Argüello died heroically in defense of the interests of the Palestinian people.[8] Another expression of internationalism was that Compañero Víctor Tirado had joined our ranks.[9]

We had already made a critical analysis of the notion of the guerrilla foco. The foco had aroused great enthusiasm among fighters for national liberation in Latin America, but Carlos Fonseca and all the rest of us viewed it with something more than distrust. Our critical analysis of this notion was of great value in finding an adequate strategic road.

After Pancasán the Sandinista Front again took up the guerrilla struggle by establishing a front in the mountains of Matagalpa and Zelaya. While there was a certain reassessment in our ranks, the idea of guerrilla combat was not abandoned. We began to prepare the conditions in the mountains.

Within this framework, we also managed to set up some tactical combat units in the cities. Moreover, supply lines to those guerrilla columns and their very survival called for close ties to the barrios and the trade unions. The Sandinista Front thus began to make efforts to penetrate certain cities of the country, especially León but also Managua, Masaya, Matagalpa, and Chinandega.

The immediate aim of this work was to organize the barrios to struggle for better living conditions, raising immediate demands such as drinkable water, electricity, medical services, and so on, but without falling into making these demands ends in themselves. We differed from other groups that made immediate demands their final aims. For us, they were instead a means for seeking out the best individuals among the people and instilling in them the notion that they must organize for the taking of power.

This is very important. From the beginning, we had always had a nose for power, and we went on developing that instinct and transmitting it to our cadres even when we recruited them through struggles around immediate demands.

In sum, the key question was achieving a close link between the work in the barrios and the work in the mountains. The latter received the most attention at that time.

Our link to the masses was maintained through intermediate organizations like the FER and through mass mobilizations for the release of political prisoners. In the struggle to free the prisoners, we made contact with the most conscious and combative groups of Christians in the student movement.

We were well aware that the banners of the Sandinista Front had to be upheld, and it was in that spirit that the character of the struggle was taking shape. This was expressed throughout our history in extraordinarily heroic acts, such as that of Julio Buitrago.[10]

Julio Buitrago was not just an anecdote, not an isolated instance. Julio Buitrago was the product of an entire philosophy and an entire attitude toward life. Julio Buitrago did not do what he did solely out of personal courage—which of course he had—but rather because he was the expression of an entire conception, an overall attitude toward the revolutionary struggle. Just as those who went on hunger strikes did not yield to the temptation of eating, those who were putting up resistance to the enemy also did not yield in face of danger. Like Julio, they were capable of giving their lives without the slightest vacillation. A style was being forged that was finally transmitted to the entire people.

Those mobilizations I referred to were the product of broad mass work the vanguard carried out between 1970 and 1975. They made it possible to save the lives of many compañeros who had been taken prisoner. In that period the vanguard functioned in such a way as to deliberately avoid combat with the Somozaist troops. Tactically, we evaded combat. This corresponded to the military strategy we adopted in those years, which consisted in accumulating forces but not appearing publicly, and engaging in combat openly when this was unavoidable. It was a question of fighting not when the enemy wanted to, but when the vanguard considered it appropriate. That period is today generally referred to as the "silent accumulation of forces."

This silent accumulation of forces was ended on December 27, 1974, by the Juan José Quezada Command, led by Commander Eduardo Contreras, a member of the National Directorate. This action dealt a severe blow to the Somozaist military dictatorship.[11] I emphasize the role of Commander Eduardo Contreras, because I have seen it written in several places that this action was led by both Germán Pomares and Eduardo Contreras.[12] We ought to be faithful to historical truth—Germán Pomares has merit enough without receiving credit for actions for which he was not responsible. Germán Pomares was a thousand times a hero, but it was Commander Eduardo Contreras who had the merit of having led that action. We ought to have the decency to rise above any sectarian hangovers, such as giving to others the honor of having led an action that they did not lead. I say this because it is something that could be repeated in other cases.

In leading that action, Eduardo Contreras had a particular virtue—he did not take off his mask. He remained anonymous until the enemy discovered through its own resources who he was. This was different from certain others who—as soon as they could, as soon as they had the slightest opportunity—pulled off their mask, so that everyone could see them as the great heroes of the movie.[13]

BY TAKING OVER THE HOUSE of a Somozaist on December 27, 1974, the vanguard broke through the stage of accumulation of forces. This action accelerated the decomposition of the regime and the development of the Sandinista Front. In fact, it brought to light the fragility of the dictatorship, which was forced to free the prisoners and broadcast a revolutionary statement on radio and television and even publish it in the newspapers. The regime also had to hand over a million dollars and provide a plane to take the victorious command and the released prisoners to Cuba.

These achievements by the FSLN attest that our organization was the only vanguard force our people had. They were also important because they had big international repercussions, contributing in a certain way to the isolation of the dictatorship and also helping to make the FSLN known worldwide and to enhance its prestige. Men like [Panamanian leader Omar] Torrijos began to pay more attention to us and lend us some assistance. Even our strategic allies began to take us more seriously.

F‍ROM 1975 ON, despite the Somozaist repression, the popular struggle not only continued but became more and more intense. The repression did not permit the launching of large-scale military actions by the vanguard, however. It was an unfortunate period for us, in that extremely valuable militants of the Sandinista Front fell in action, among them no less than Carlos Fonseca. Eduardo Contreras fell the day after Fonseca. Later, we also lost that great fighter named Carlos Agüero; the peasant Jacinto Hernández; Pedro Aráuz, Carlos Roberto Huembes, Filemón Rivera, Mauricio Duarte, René Tejada; the young Compañera Arlen Siu; Edgard Munguía, Crescencio Rosales, Augusto César Salinas, Bonifacio Montoya, and many others.

The death of Carlos, of course, was interpreted as a victory by the reaction and the dictatorship. They assumed his death would effectively put a stop to the Sandinista struggle. The phenomenon was repeated once again:

when Sandino died, they thought it was all over for Nicaragua, that Nicaragua was going to be the perpetual colony of the United States. When Carlos Fonseca died, they thought that now the Sandinista Front would be liquidated once and for all.

I remember how triumphantly they came to tell me when I was in jail—they thought we were crazy, because we insisted that victory would still be ours. When we said in jail, "Carlos Fonseca is among the dead who never die," we meant that the revolutionary classes never die, the workers and peasants are as immortal as their historic task. That is what we meant. Carlos could not die because he represented a synthesis, an idea that was not only comprehensible but ready to be put into practice. Carlos died, but he did not die—that is what our enemies did not understand. Carlos did not die because it is the peoples who make revolutions. Revolutions are nothing but the resurrection of the heroes.

At first sight, nonetheless, the results of the repression justified the illusions held by the National Guard and the reactionaries. The exigencies of an organized struggle had given rise to a sort of division of labor in the FSLN, in which militants were distributed among complementary activities in the mountains, in the cities, and in tasks related to mass work. The blows of the dictatorship turned this division of labor into the isolation of the various elements one from the other. Various perceptions of reality emerged, based on different experiences, conditioned by this division of labor and their isolation. This led, along with other factors, to the formation of three tendencies inside the Sandinista National Liberation Front.

As I understand it, no one today wants to mention these tendencies. It's as if they had been a mortal sin. But I think that this forms part of our history, and we must make the effort to analyze it. I have seen some of our documents where the history of our organization is analyzed, and it would seem from those documents that there never were internal tendencies in the Sandinista Front.

And of course there were! Besides, everyone knows it.

It is necessary to analyze this experience. We think that isolation is one of the factors that contributed to the formation of those tendencies. The existence of tendencies does not harm the image of the revolution. The great thing about this revolution is that we have been able to unite despite the tendencies. We have provided the peoples of Latin America with the example of what maturity means among Nicaraguan revolutionaries. That is the great thing, the important thing, about our experiences. To emphasize that greatness, we have to say that we were divided at a certain point in our history, but that we were mature enough to unite.

Only those who are ignorant of the fact that the movement of history unfolds through contradictions, only those who do not grasp the fact that a political organization is nothing more than an instrument in the class struggle, could have concluded that as a result of the tendencies the Front would dissolve into factions and would disperse the popular struggles in isolated actions without any major impact on the dictatorship. In fact, the three tendencies continued to uphold the name of the Sandinista Front. The people always recognized but a single Sandinista Front, and all the compañeros know that fighters from the three tendencies all shouted "Free Homeland or Death!" They fought in the same trenches and shed their blood together. So why should it be strange that we united?[14]

Unity on a higher level was required in order to synthesize the different experiences. The first stone was laid toward this end with the continuation of the popular movement. In the cities, hunger strikes continued for the political prisoners. Labor conflicts became more acute owing to the stepped-up selling off of our economy and the voracity of foreign capital. Protest movements demanding human rights continued. Land seizures were carried out in Tonalá, Sirama, and San José de Obraje, in response to the massive expropriation of the western peasants. Sandinista militants carried out literacy campaigns, neighborhood improvement projects, youth and cultural movements.

OUR AIM in all this work was to project ourselves into the various sectors of society. Committees of solidarity with the Nicaraguan people were set up in a number of countries at the initiative of members of the vanguard. In response to the popular upsurge, reaction and imperialism activated the Central American Defense Council (CONDECA). In Somoza's time military advisers from Brazil, Colombia, Central America, and Vietnam (from the reactionary Vietnam of those days), and of course Yankees from the United States as well, came to Nicaragua to smash the armed struggle of the people.

The relative downturn that affected the vanguard on the military level after 1974 was brought to an end in October 1977 with a Sandinista offensive that began with the seizure of the San Carlos barracks and continued with the taking of the village of Mozonte, the attack on the main barracks in Masaya, and the seizure of the San Fernando barracks.

October 1977 was the result of a shift to an offensive mode of operations in the armed struggle at a moment when the crisis of Somozaism was becoming acute. This crisis began after the 1972 earthquake and deepened after 1974.

The Somozas' corruption, while it had its worst effects on the masses, also harmed the interests of the small and middle bourgeoisie. This led to broadening the base of opposition to the dictatorship. To this must be added the fact that the big-business sectors themselves began to lose confidence in Somoza's abilities. Somoza came to be an obstacle to capitalist development, and even to the preservation of the bourgeois order in Nicaragua.

More and more, the regime was being called into question internationally for its stupid and repressive policies. In the particular conditions of our country, the Somoza family and its cronies had a tremendous appetite for wealth and power and began to utilize the state apparatus to satisfy their own needs.

THE GROWTH of the Somozaist dictatorship and all its ramifications began to harm a broad sector of the bourgeoisie. Somoza refused to share the wealth of the country equally among the bourgeoisie as a whole. The use of exemptions from taxation, easy bank credit, loans, and even smuggling to benefit a minority provoked conflicts between the Somozaists and a sector of the bourgeoisie. That sector, in turn, tended to modernize in order to offset its lack of opportunities.

This economic contradiction was later expressed in political terms. We wrote a letter from jail saying, "A party of the bourgeoisie is about to appear." But it was already too late for that. Somewhat later such a party did arise, known as the MDN [Nicaraguan Democratic Movement], but it was too late.

The bourgeoisie really did not have a party of their

own. The Liberal Party belonged to the Somozas and upheld the interests of an oligarchy that was highly centralized around a single family. The Conservative Party was the party of the landowners, a rather anachronistic party. No modern party of the bourgeoisie had appeared in this country. The MDN was born at the moment when the bourgeois regime was in total agony—it did not even manage to be a premature infant. In the end it could only survive artificially through the umbilical cord that tied it to imperialism.

The bourgeoisie was thus trapped by the voracity of imperialism, which under the circumstances of crisis was reducing the bourgeoisie's rate of profit: by the loss of economic activities to groups of Somoza's cronies (construction, insurance, urban development, banks, finance corporations, and so on); and by the rise of the popular movement. It had no other alternative than to desperately change its clothing and try to gain the leadership of the anti-Somozaist struggle.

But what could a premature infant do at such a moment? The Robelos and the other gentlemen of the COSEP[15] were obliged by the course of events to function within the framework of the developing popular movement, which for them was a sort of straitjacket. While the dictatorship was losing ground both nationally and internationally, the guerrillas were carrying out a tenacious struggle with the aim of regaining the military initiative we had lost to the Somozaists at the end of 1975. Guerrilla activity was combined with the FSLN's day-to-day work. At the national level, the enemy's plans aimed at liquidating the vanguard had failed.

Faced with the acute crisis of the Somoza dictatorship, imperialism and reaction maneuvered to provide the regime with a way out. With this end in view, they sought to make certain adjustments in the Somozaist system without touching in any way the system's fundamental bases: its economic might and the National Guard. Somoza was forced to lift the state of siege and martial law and to call municipal elections. With these measures, the regime sought to improve its discredited image before public opinion and play along with the imperialists' maneuvers.

Of course, these maneuvers were carried out at a time when the imperialist enemy and the local enemy both assumed that they had managed to reduce the FSLN's capacity for struggle, if not to liquidate it. They thought we had been very hard hit.

So, when we decided to go on the offensive in October 1977, our aim was to cause these maneuvers by the enemy to fail. After we regained the initiative in October, we were not to lose it again.

October was a historic achievement, because it disrupted the enemy's plans, strengthened the vanguard's hegemony among the masses, and fortified the masses' self-confidence. All this led the Somozaists to commit one of their gravest errors: they murdered Pedro Joaquín Chamorro [on January 10, 1978]. Chamorro had become the leader of the incipient national bourgeoisie. Through journalistic activity over many years, he had also managed to gain the sympathy of broad sectors in our country. The crime caused the masses to take to the streets—you saw this better than I did, since I was still a prisoner. They expressed their repudiation with revolutionary violence. In those demonstrations the masses openly identified with the Sandinista National Liberation Front. The people reiterated that the Sandinista Front was the only possibility for confronting the Somoza dictatorship.

The October actions, as well as the armed actions the

vanguard launched in February 1978 (at Granada and Rivas, and the taking of the counterinsurgency base at Santa Clara, Nueva Segovia), had the aim of keeping alive the people's spirit of struggle. This was achieved; the masses' willingness to fight multiplied like manna in the desert.

The overall impact of these actions had its highest expression in the Monimbó insurrection. While the Monimbó events were not planned by the vanguard, they were a response to the encouragement the FSLN had provided by taking over several towns a few days earlier. Still, the FSLN managed to put itself at the head of the Monimbó insurrection. This spurred the morale and the efforts of the people as a whole. They were encouraged by the mounting activities of FSLN combat units in the cities and countryside. Everything was ready for the insurrection.

ANOTHER SIGNIFICANT event that helped to raise the fighting spirit of the people and that demonstrated the Somoza regime's inability to halt the advance of the popular struggle was the taking of the National Palace on August 22, 1978, by the Rigoberto López Pérez Sandinista Command. This operation was entitled "Commander Carlos Fonseca Amador—Death to Somozaism." It was led by Edén Pastora, the traitor. As Humberto Ortega has pointed out in his interesting and thorough analysis of Pastora's activities, Germán Pomares was originally designated to lead the action at the palace. But for health reasons Pomares couldn't take on that responsibility.

The seizure of the palace had a great impact, not only among the people but also on international public opinion. But something happened there that is not too well known or that has not been sufficiently explained; Pastora revealed his lack of political and ideological consistency at that moment.

When we arrived from the Tipitapa jail, we found him and realized that there were a number of our compañeros who were not included on the lists of freed prisoners—not because they were deliberately omitted, but as a result of certain slip-ups. We told Pastora that having the hostages there meant we had the real possibility of getting those other compañeros out of jail as well. He refused; we insisted. Afterwards, it was said that we had had our first falling out. That is true, we had quite a serious discussion. We insisted that the freedom of those compañeros omitted from the list be demanded as well. But he had already achieved his objective—becoming what Reagan would now call "a paladin."

The rest of the story you already know—he's still there under the bright lights filming the movie he dreamed of acting in as the leading man, allied with imperialism and locked in a fraternal, tight, and amorous embrace with the murderous Somozaist Guardsmen. He had already achieved his aims.

THERE IS A SHARP contrast between what Pastora did, smilingly posed on the stairs of the airplane, and what Eduardo Contreras did, or what all the other compañeros who participated in the taking of the palace did—Hugo Torres, Walter Ferreti, and Dora María Téllez. They all kept their masks on. The error was not his alone; rather, it was our fault for not having had the instinct, the foresight we sometimes lack for detecting traitors that skulk inside our shirts like scorpions. We ought to have enough sense to realize who they are. I don't think anyone should be startled when I say this—only those with something to hide could think I was alluding to them.

The dictator Somoza—with his image tarnished and feeling pressure for change from a halfhearted human-rights policy that U.S. President Carter was trying to implement—found it necessary to utilize more and more brute force against the people. This led to events like those of September 1978, which opened the road to victory. There were insurrections in Estelí, Masaya, León, and Chinandega, and popular uprisings in certain barrios of Managua. Through these struggles, the people began to lose their fear of the National Guard. So the people began to move forward and take the offensive. While September did not bring the overthrow of the dictatorship, it was, in a certain way, a strategic victory for us. It was a historic achievement, because the vanguard emerged from it fortified. Our ability to recruit was extended to the entire people; we gained in weaponry and, more importantly, in decisiveness and confidence.

The rising struggle was headed by a revolutionary organization, and imperialism and the reaction began to view this with fear. They saw that their interests were in danger. So they cooked up the "mediation" scheme, which involved removing the dictator and leaving in place Somozaism without Somoza. Somoza, being arrogant, would not accept this. He proposed holding a plebiscite that never took place. Mediation was to reconcile, through shady deals, the interests of the corrupt party of Somoza, the genocidal National Guard, the bourgeois opposition political parties, and private capital. It sought to unite all the oppressive and exploitative forces that were dispersed or in opposition to Somoza. In this way, they sought to isolate and destroy the popular revolutionary movement.

These mediation maneuvers were shattered by the unity of the vanguard; by the political alliance of the revolutionary parties and organizations of the country in the FSLN-led United People's Movement (MPU); and by the broad alliance of the MPU with the anti-imperialist and antidictatorial parties and organizations that made up the National Patriotic Front (FPN). The mediation scheme ran up against the unity of the entire nation that was taking shape around the FSLN, which kept on fighting with arms in hand down to the end. Whatever vacillations arose were neutralized by the FSLN's will to carry the fight to a higher level.

Plans for insurrection were drawn up on the basis of the people's experience in struggle; military actions by armed detachments were combined with popular uprisings and the general strike, which played a complementary and very important role. The final insurrection began in May 1979. The general strike called by the FSLN combined with the uprising of the masses to give to the people the historically inevitable victory that rightly belonged to them. All the factors had been brought together exactly at the opportune moment and in the opportune places.

The July 19, 1979, victory was possible because of the years-long struggle our people had carried out against the Somozaist military dictatorship. It was possible owing to the emergence of a revolutionary vanguard, whose founder, Carlos Fonseca, has been quite justly placed where only the saints, heroes, and immortals belong.

July 19 was possible because at a crucial moment of historical maturity we set aside the search for personal power in the spirit of revolutionary unity, putting the interests of the nation above all. July 19 was only the beginning. Great dangers still await us along the road. The powerful imperialists are trying to invent a machine to turn back the course of history and, meanwhile, scratching and biting us with the ferocity of a tiger.

We have confidence in the toilers, in this people that was born to make history and is expert at forging new victories.

Free homeland or death!

NOTES

1. Augusto César Sandino led an army of workers and peasants in an anti-imperialist war against the U.S. military occupation of Nicaragua between 1927 and 1933. Before withdrawing, U.S. imperialism set up a Nicaraguan military force called the National Guard; its first Nicaraguan commander was Anastasio Somoza García. In February 1934 Somoza invited Sandino to the capital, Managua, ostensibly for political negotiations. National Guardsmen acting on Somoza's orders murdered Sandino and several of his top lieutenants on February 21, 1934. Massacres of Sandino's followers in northern Nicaragua were launched during the next several months and what remained of his movement was wiped out.

2. Rigoberto López Pérez, a young poet, assassinated Anastasio Somoza García on September 21, 1956, in the city of León. In a letter to his mother earlier the same month, López wrote that the action he was planning would be "the beginning of the end" of the dictatorship. The political ramifications of López's deed were analyzed by FSLN founder Carlos Fonseca in a 1972 essay entitled "Notes on Rigoberto López Pérez's Letter-Testament" (*Obras*, Tomo 1, pp. 393–406), and by FSLN leader José Benito Escobar in a 1976 pamphlet entitled *El principio del fin* (The beginning of the end) (Managua: SENAPEP, 1979).

3. An abridged English translation of Borge's homage to

Carlos Fonseca was published in the July 1980 *International Socialist Review* (supplement to the July 11, 1980, *Militant*).

4. In 1963 the Somozas engineered the election of a civilian lawyer, René Schick, to the presidency. He replaced Luis Somoza Debayle, who had ruled since his father's assassination in 1956. Despite a certain relaxation of the repression in the 1963–67 period, the apparatus of the dictatorship remained firmly in place, with Anastasio Somoza Debayle holding the reins as chief of the National Guard. His brother, Luis, continued to head the Liberal Party.

5. Conservative Party leader Fernando Agüero was the candidate of a coalition called the National Opposition Union (UNO) in the 1967 elections against Anastasio Somoza Debayle. The circle of bourgeois oppositionists around Agüero secretly planned to turn a mass UNO demonstration on January 22 into an armed uprising against the dictatorship. The result was a tragic fiasco in which hundreds were massacred by the National Guard.

6. Doris Tijerino, a leading fighter in the FSLN, was imprisoned and tortured by the dictatorship. She became well known internationally for her book *Inside the Nicaraguan Revolution*. She currently serves in the Nicaraguan Ministry of the Interior. Conchita Alday fought in Sandino's army.

7. See the poem *Pancasán* in Ricardo Morales Avilés, *Obras: no pararemos de andar jamás* (Managua, 1983), pp. 58–68.

8. Patricio Argüello was killed by an Israeli guard in the September 6, 1970, attempted hijacking of an El Al airliner by the Popular Front for the Liberation of Palestine.

9. Commander Víctor Tirado López, now a member of the FSLN National Directorate, was born in Mexico. He traveled to Nicaragua in the early 1960s to join the struggle against the dictatorship. After the victory of the revolution, he was declared a "natural-born citizen of Nicaragua" by the Junta of the Government of National Reconstruction.

10. Julio Buitrago, a member of the FSLN National Directorate, was killed on July 15, 1969, in a Managua battle that

pitted Buitrago and a handful of other Sandinistas against hundreds of National Guardsmen backed up by artillery, aircraft, and a Sherman tank.

11. On December 27, 1974, a squad of Sandinistas seized the house of top Somoza crony José María Castillo during a reception being held there for the U.S. ambassador. The ambassador had left, but more than thirty top cabinet ministers and Somoza cronies were taken hostage. After a three-day standoff, Somoza was forced to back down and grant a series of FSLN demands.

12. Germán Pomares and Eduardo Contreras were central leaders of the FSLN. Both died in action against the dictatorship—Contreras in November 1976 and Pomares in May 1979.

13. A reference to publicity stunts by FSLN traitor Edén Pastora, who took off his mask and posed for photographs after leading the August 1978 seizure of the National Palace in Managua.

14. The FSLN tendencies began a process of reunification in June 1978 with a series of agreements on unity in action. The process culminated in March 1979 with the establishment of the nine-member Joint National Directorate (three representatives from each tendency). Dissolution of the three separate tendencies followed. In late 1979 the word "Joint" was removed from the name of the leading body to symbolize the completion of reunification.

15. MDN leader Alfonso Robelo Callejas, a wealthy industrialist, was a member of the first Junta of the Government of National Reconstruction after the revolutionary victory. He resigned in April 1980 in protest against the Junta's decision to allocate a large majority of seats in the Council of State, the top legislative body, to representatives of the workers and peasants. Robelo currently heads an armed counterrevolutionary organization operating from Costa Rica.

COSEP is the Superior Council of Private Enterprise.

The Militant

Socialist newsweekly published in the interests of working people

- Covers labor battles and workers fights for jobs, safety, and to organize the unorganized around the world.

- Reports on fights against cop brutality and frame-ups, against attacks on women's right to choose abortion, and for amnesty for workers who are foreign born.

- Explains the roots of the worldwide crisis of the capitalist system, and the never-ending imperialist interventions and wars in the Mideast and elsewhere as the old order unravels.

- Defends the socialist revolution in Cuba. Champions the fight to end Washington's economic embargo against Cuba and to demand US out of Guantánamo. Supports the fight against US colonial rule in Puerto Rico.

- Reports weekly campaigning by Socialist Workers Party members on workers' doorsteps and the road forward they explain for the working class to take political power out of the hands of the capitalist rulers.

The Militant • 306 West 37th Street, 13th floor • New York, NY 10018

Subscribe today!
New readers 12 weeks for $5
6 months $20   1 year $35   2 years $65

WWW.THEMILITANT.COM

REVOLUTION IN CENTRAL AMERICA AND THE CARIBBEAN

The Second Assassination of Maurice Bishop
STEVE CLARK

The lead article in *New International* no. 6 reviews the accomplishments of the 1979–83 revolution in the Caribbean island of Grenada. Explains the roots of the 1983 coup that led to the murder of revolutionary leader Maurice Bishop, and to the destruction of the workers and farmers government by a Stalinist political faction within the governing New Jewel Movement. $14. Also in Spanish and French.

The Rise and Fall of the Nicaraguan Revolution

Based on ten years of socialist journalism from inside Nicaragua, this special issue of *New International* recounts the achievements and worldwide impact of the 1979 Nicaraguan revolution. It traces the political retreat of the Sandinista National Liberation Front leadership that led to the downfall of the workers and farmers government in the closing years of the 1980s. Documents of the Socialist Workers Party by Jack Barnes, Steve Clark, and Larry Seigle. In *New International* no. 9. $14. Also in Spanish.

War and Crisis in the Americas
Speeches, vol. 3, 1984–85
FIDEL CASTRO

The stakes in the looming showdown with Washington in Central America and the Caribbean, and the explosive social consequences of the foreign debt in Latin America. $17

WWW.PATHFINDERPRESS.COM

IMPERIALISM, HIGHEST STAGE OF CAPITALISM

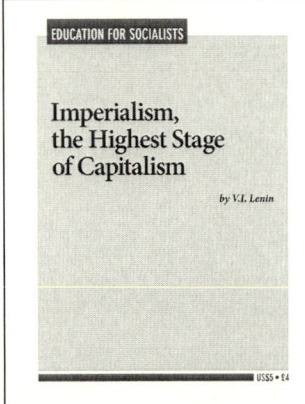

Imperialism, the Highest Stage of Capitalism
V.I. LENIN

"I trust that this pamphlet will help the reader to understand the fundamental economic question, that of the economic essence of imperialism," Lenin wrote in 1917. "For unless this is studied, it will be impossible to understand and appraise modern war and modern politics." $5. Also in Spanish, Farsi, and Greek.

To Speak the Truth
Why Washington's 'Cold War' against Cuba Doesn't End

FIDEL CASTRO, ERNESTO CHE GUEVARA

In historic speeches before the United Nations and UN bodies, Guevara and Castro address the peoples of the world, explaining why the US government so fears the example set by the socialist revolution in Cuba and why Washington's effort to destroy it will fail. $15

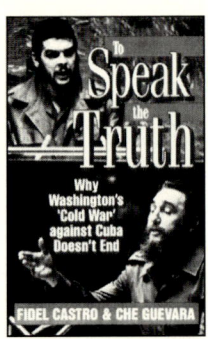

By Any Means Necessary
MALCOLM X

"The imperialists know the only way you will voluntarily turn to the fox is to show you a wolf." In eleven speeches and interviews, Malcolm X presents a revolutionary alternative to this reformist trap, taking up political alliances, women's rights, US intervention in the Congo and Vietnam, capitalism and socialism, and more. $15

INDEX

A
Agramonte, Ignacio, 212
Agüero, Fernando, 229, 230, 236, 248
Alday, Conchita, 248
Algeria, 147
Alliance for Progress, 221, 228
Anarchists, 72; in Spain, 90–91, 93
April Theses (Lenin), 110
Aráuz, Pedro, 236
Argüello, Patricio, 232, 248
Australian Labour Party, 134, 135–36

B
Bakuninists, 90–91
Bauer, Heinrich, 152
Bavarian revolution (1919), 134
Bishop, Maurice, 6, 27
Blanc, Louis, 51
Blanquists, 70–71, 100
Bolsheviks: factional crisis of (1921), 122; in 1917, 99, 100–101, 107, 110; party-building accomplishments of, 103; perspectives on coming Russian revolution, 78–79, 87, 93, 96, 110–11. *See also* Lenin, V.I.
Bonaparte, Louis, 60, 155
Borge, Tomás, 5, 12–13, 145, 217–47; on FSLN "nose for power," 3, 31, 233; jailing of, 237, 242
Born, Stephan, 50, 51–52
Britain, 55, 132, 134. *See also* English revolution
Buitrago, Julio, 234, 248

C
Camphausen, Ludolf, 43
Capitalism: in Latin America, 172–73, 175, 176, 179, 180, 182, 183, 185–88, 187, 220; in nineteenth century, 54, 55, 76, 169, 170–71; peasantry under, 57; state monopoly, 177, 180; world crisis of, 170, 174–75, 181, 183
Capitalist class: in 1848 revolutions, 39–40, 42–47; in Latin America, 8, 176, 179, 185–88; in Nicaragua, 218, 219, 220, 223, 229–30, 240, 241; and Paris Commune, 64, 69, 71, 76; and peasants, 57; and reforms, 128; in Russia, 79, 95
Carpio, Salvador Cayetano, 17
Carter, James, 245
Castillo, José María, 249
Castro, Fidel, 26–27, 130, 205, 206, 223; on Cuban revolution, 174, 212; on revolutionary strategy, 3, 14–15, 200
Catholic hierarchy, 206

253

Céspedes, Carlos Manuel de, 212
Chamorro, Pedro Joaquín, 242
Chile, 6, 176, 184, 203
Christian Democracy, 205–6
Civil War in France, The (Marx), 61, 62–63, 65, 67, 71, 73, 74
Class Struggles in France, 1848 to 1852, The (Marx), 55, 57, 76
Coard, Bernard, 27
Cologne Workers Society, 50–51
Communism, 37; as movement, not sect, 28, 34, 38–39, 49
Communist International, 5, 20; need for new, 149; on NEP, 126–27, 129–32; revolutionary legacy of, 29, 132–33, 143, 144, 147; on workers and peasants governments, 133–43, 144, 148; world perspective of, 133, 144
Communist League, 33–34, 50, 53
Communist Manifesto (Marx and Engels), 19–20, 25–26, 33–36, 39, 51, 53, 61, 144; on communists' tasks, 40–41
Communist Parties of Latin America, 9, 10, 17–19, 201
Communist Party of Cuba, 4, 8–9, 169; Programmatic Platform of, 172
Communist Party of Russia. *See* Bolsheviks
Communist Party of Venezuela, 10–11
Conservative Party (Nicaragua), 241
Contreras, Eduardo, 235, 236, 244, 249
COSEP (Superior Council of Private Enterprise, Nicaragua), 241, 249
Critique of the Gotha Programme (Marx), 112

Cruz, Rigoberto, 230, 231
Cuban revolution, 4; as example, 8, 147, 181–82, 184, 222–23; as "exception," 5–6, 18; expropriation of capitalists by, 28–29, 174; and Latin America, 10–11, 147, 181–82, 184, 222–23; lessons, 6–8, 19, 28–29, 173–74, 194, 208, 211; mechanical imitation of, 15–16, 221, 226, 227; and Soviet workers state, 147; and U.S. imperialism, 28, 199, 228

D

Democracy, 32, 66
Democratic dictatorship of workers and peasants, 83, 109, 111; and October revolution, 105–6, 118; and socialism, 80, 81; and soviets, 87–89, 95; working-class participation in, 82, 83–86, 88–89, 91–92
Democratic Party, 13–14
Democratic rights, 32, 84, 201
Dictatorship, revolutionary: nature of, 72–73; need for, 31, 42, 47
Dictatorship of proletariat, 31–32; as "cudgel," 114–15, 127; defined, 150–52; Marx on, 37, 112; and Paris Commune, 73–74; and Russian revolution, 59, 78, 80, 87, 105, 122; withering away of, 36, 37; and worker-peasant alliance, 128–30; and workers and farmers government, 32, 105, 136, 137, 138–39
Dual power, 95–96, 101, 105
Duarte, Mauricio, 236
Dutch revolution, 45

E

Eighteenth Brumaire of Louis Bonaparte, The (Marx), 57, 61

Electoralism, 3, 6, 10–15, 210
El Salvador, 181, 193, 202; revolutionary strategy in, 17, 18–19, 194, 211
Engels, Frederick, 5, 19, 211, 212; on Bakuninists in Spain, 90–91; on communism as movement, 28, 37–38; and Communist League, 33–34, 152; and Communist Manifesto, 33, 34–36, 37, 41; on dictatorship of proletariat, 73–74, 112; and 1848 revolutions, 39, 41–55, 80–81; on Paris Commune, 60–61, 65, 70–72, 73–74, 76, 77; on worker-peasant alliance, 56–59
English revolution (1640–60), 40, 45
Escobar, José Benito, 221
Estonia, 113

F

Farabundo Martí National Liberation Front (FMLN, El Salvador), 9, 17–18
Ferreti, Walter, 244
First International, 60
Fonseca, Carlos, 221, 226, 227, 232, 236–37, 246; on Cuba, 222; on Sandino, 224
Franco-Prussian War (1871), 60, 68
French revolution: of 1789, 40, 45, 46; of 1848, 33, 39, 54, 55, 56–57, 59–60, 76. See also Paris Commune

G

Gairy, Eric, 26
Galliffet, Gaston, 89
Germany, 57, 94; 1848 revolution in, 39–40, 42–54; feudal relations in, 42, 44, 46–47; workers and peasants in, 39–40, 42, 46, 47–48, 57
Gómez, Máximo, 212
González, Andrea, 14
Gottschalk, Andreas, 50–51
Grenadian revolution: accomplishments, 26; and Cuban road, 6, 181, 184; historic significance, 4, 6, 26–27; lessons, 6–8, 194, 208, 211; overthrow of, 27, 146, 147
Guatemala, 181, 193, 194, 202
Guevara, Ernesto Che, 10

H

Handal, Schafik Jorge, 17–19
Hernández, Jacinto, 236
Honduras, 202, 232
Huembes, Carlos Roberto, 236
Hungarian revolution (1919), 134

I

Imperialism, 171, 176. See also U.S. imperialism
International Monetary Fund, 179

K

Kamenev, Leon, 109
Kennedy, John F., 221, 228
Kornilov, Lavr G., 102
Kronstadt uprising (1921), 123

L

Land reform, 187, 192, 222; in Russian revolution, 98, 104, 105, 120
Latin America: agrarian relations in, 178, 182, 186–87, 191–92; armed struggle in, 9–11, 183–84, 209–11; bourgeoisie in, 8, 176, 179, 185–88; bourgeois reformism in, 6, 10, 180–81, 183;

capitalism in, 172–73, 175, 176, 179, 180, 182, 183, 185–88, 187, 220; class structure in, 179–81, 185–93; continent-wide struggle in, 203–4; guerrilla warfare debate in, 6, 9–11, 15–16, 226, 227, 232; imperialist domination of, 178–79, 182, 185, 198–200, 221, 228; indigenous population in, 191, 193; industrialization in, 168–70, 176, 190; left forces in, 9, 195, 200–201, 202, 203; liberation theology in, 184, 206; military dictatorships in, 177, 181, 184, 192, 201, 221–22; military nationalist movements in, 184, 206–7; peasantry in, 173, 191–92, 193; socialist character of revolution in, 7, 171, 173–74, 175, 180, 183; working class in, 173, 176–77, 183, 190–91, 193, 202

Lenin, V.I., 19, 145, 176, 211, 212; on bourgeois-democratic revolutions, 52, 79, 81, 169; on democratic dictatorship, 79, 81, 82–84, 89, 93, 95–96, 111; on dictatorship of proletariat, 31–32, 105, 114–15, 121; on fight for soviet power, 95–103; on Marxism, 37–38; on NEP, 122–23, 124–26, 130–31; on Paris Commune, 62, 65–67, 72–73, 76–77, 89–90, 96; on participation in provisional revolutionary government, 82, 83–86, 91–92; on peasantry, 101–2, 107, 119–22; on people's revolutions, 30, 97; on Russia's transition to socialism, 105, 115–17; on soviets, 86, 87–88, 96, 99, 100, 109, 144; on strategy and tactics, 204, 207–8; on transition to socialism, 104, 108, 111–14; on worker-peasant alliance, 79, 88, 93, 104, 107, 109–10, 122, 129–30, 131–32

Liberal Party (Nicaragua), 241
López Pérez, Rigoberto, 221, 222, 247
Lumpen-proletariat, 192

M

Maceo, Antonio, 212
Manifesto of the Communist Party. See Communist Manifesto
Martí, José, 212
Marx, Karl, 5, 19, 211, 212; and Communist Manifesto, 33–36, 37, 38; on dictatorship of proletariat, 36–37, 112; and 1848 revolutions, 39, 41–55, 80–81; on Paris Commune, 60–64, 67–70, 71, 73, 74–75; on worker-peasant alliance, 56–57, 59, 102
Mason, Mel, 14
Mayorga, Silvio, 231
MDN (Nicaraguan Democratic Movement), 240, 241
Mensheviks: on coming Russian revolution, 78–79, 80, 82, 83, 86, 87, 88, 89, 91, 92–93; during 1917, 95, 98, 99, 102
Middle classes: in Latin America, 8, 188–90; Paris Commune and, 67–68; in Russian revolution, 97–98, 102, 113; workers and farmers government stance toward, 33
Millerand, Alexandre, 89
Moll, Joseph, 152
Monimbó, 243
Montesquieu (Charles-Louis de Secondat), 218
Montoya, Bonifacio, 236
Morales, Ricardo, 230

Moreno, Chelito, 231
Munguía, Edgard, 236

N

National Patriotic Front (FPN, Nicaragua), 246
Neue Rheinische Zeitung, 39, 43, 48, 50, 52
New Economic Policy (NEP, Russia), 124–27, 129–31; as stage in proletarian revolutions, 130, 137–38, 141–42
New Jewel Movement (Grenada), 6
Nicaragua, 217–49: assassination of Somoza, 221, 222, 247; bourgeois opposition in, 12–13, 219, 222, 224, 229–30, 240–41; capitalist class in, 218, 219, 220, 223, 229–30, 240, 241; economy of under Somoza, 219–20, 228; Sandino-led struggle in, 224–25, 247; Somocista repression in, 218, 220, 236, 237, 248; and U.S. imperialism, 27, 145, 199, 218, 245; working class in, 219, 220, 239. *See also* Sandinista National Liberation Front (FSLN)
Nicaraguan revolution: and armed struggle, 211, 226–28, 230–31, 233, 235–36, 239–40, 242–43; and Cuba, 147, 148, 184, 222–23; historic significance, 4, 6, 26–27, 181; lessons, 6–8, 18–19, 194, 208; 1978 uprising, 242–43, 245; 1979 insurrection, 246; taking of National Palace (1978), 243–44; and workers and farmers government, 26, 144–47. *See also* Sandinista National Liberation Front (FSLN)
Nicaraguan Socialist Party, 228

O

OLAS conference (1967), 9–11, 14–15
Ortega, Humberto, 243

P

Pancasán, 230–31
Paris Commune, 55, 60–77, 75–76, 155; and dictatorship of proletariat, 73–74; errors, 64, 70–72; legacy and lessons, 20, 38, 77, 89–90; measures, 63, 64–65, 66–67, 69–70, 73, 74–75; as new type of state, 63, 65–67, 73, 96; and peasantry and middle classes, 67, 68–69; as revolutionary dictatorship, 63–64, 72–73, 74, 77; slaughter following, 64; and socialism, 67, 71, 73, 74; and working-class organization, 69–70, 76–77
Party, proletarian vanguard: in bourgeois-democratic revolution, 81, 82, 85–86, 92; need for in fight for power, 8, 107, 149; need for in workers and farmers government, 33, 70, 77, 81; not a two-class party, 141; orientation of toward taking power, 31, 34–35, 138. *See also* Bolsheviks; Revolutionary vanguard
Pastora, Edén, 235, 243, 244, 249
Peasants: against forced expropriation of, 58–59; class divisions within, 115–16, 118–22; craft prejudices toward, 139; in 1848 revolutions, 46, 49–50, 51, 53, 56–57; exploitation by capital, 57; in Latin America, 173, 191–92, 193; and Russian revolution, 101–2, 104, 110, 121–22, 123–24, 127. *See also* Worker-peasant alliance

Peasant war, 57, 59, 102
Petty bourgeoisie. *See* Middle classes
Piñeiro, Manuel, 3, 4, 6–8, 15, 169–212
Pinochet, Augusto, 6
Pomares, Germán, 235, 243, 249
Proudhon, Pierre-Joseph, 51, 70–71, 72

R

Reagan, Ronald, 13–14, 244
Reformism, 134, 138, 208; in Latin America, 180–81, 183
Reforms, 128
Revolutionary Student Front (FER, Nicaragua), 232
Revolutionary vanguard, 177, 193, 197, 224; and fight for power, 184–85, 194, 195–96; strategy and tactics of, 195–98, 210–11, 225, 233–34. *See also* Party, proletarian vanguard
Revolution, bourgeois-democratic, 44–45, 55, 169–70; need for popular revolutionary dictatorship in, 31, 42, 47; working class and, 40–41, 108. *See also* Revolution of 1848
Revolution of 1848, 33, 39–55; bourgeoisie in, 42–44, 45–47; communists in, 41, 49–51, 54; Engels balance sheet on, 54, 55; in France, 33, 39, 54, 55, 56–57, 59–60; and Marx-Engels anticipation of imminent proletarian revolution, 41, 52, 53–54, 55, 80–81; Marx-Engels participation in, 39, 41, 43, 47, 48–51, 52–53; and peasantry, 46, 49–50, 51, 53, 56–57; proletariat and, 42, 45, 47–49, 50, 51, 52

Revolution, proletarian socialist: anti-imperialist tasks in, 7–8, 10, 18–19, 171, 173–84, 199–200, 209; in colonial and semicolonial countries, 8, 18–19, 171–72, 173, 175, 181–82; as people's revolution, 7–8, 30, 97, 201–2; smashes bourgeois state apparatus, 6–7, 61–62, 65, 104, 107, 194–95. *See also* Transition to socialism
Rivera, Filemón, 236
Robelo, Alfonso, 241, 249
Rosales, Crescencio, 236
Russian revolution: bourgeois-democratic tasks of, 78, 79, 80, 93, 108, 109; bourgeoisie and, 79, 93–94, 113; capitalist Provisional Government in, 95, 96, 98–99, 119; class alliances in, 79–80, 88, 93; and democratic dictatorship of workers and peasants, 81, 105–6, 111; dual power in, 95–97, 101, 105; of 1905, 20, 78, 86–88; of February 1917, 94–95; of October 1917, 101–2, 103–5, 111; peasants in, 101–2, 104, 110, 119–20; soviets in, 86–88, 94–95, 96, 99, 100, 109; worker-peasant alliance and, 79, 88, 102–3, 104, 107, 109, 110, 122, 127, 129–30, 131; working class in, 80, 82–83, 93–94, 97–98, 107, 110–11, 119; world impact of, 4, 20, 144, 172
Russian Social Democratic Labor Party, 84. *See also* Bolsheviks; Mensheviks
Russian Soviet republic: characterization of, 105–6; and class divisions in countryside, 115–16, 118–22; measures, 104, 105, 108; New Economic

Policy of, 124–27, 129–31; as revolutionary dictatorship, 59, 107, 116; and Russian civil war, 117–18, 121–22, 125, 126; and transition to socialism, 108, 111–12, 113–14, 117, 125–26; utilizes bourgeois technicians, 116–17; and War Communism, 118, 119, 122, 123, 124, 125–26; worker-peasant alliance and, 103–4, 111, 119–20, 129–30, 131; as workers and peasants government, 105, 110, 136–37

S

Salinas, Augusto César, 236
Sandinista National Liberation Front (FSLN), 6, 9; and armed struggle, 226–28, 230–31, 233, 235–36, 239–40, 241, 242–44; and bourgeois opposition, 12–13, 224, 229–30; and Cuban revolution, 15–16, 222–23, 226; division into tendencies, 237–38; fills leadership vacuum, 219, 223–24; founding of, 224, 225; guerrillaism in, 15–16, 226–27, 229, 232; influence of among masses, 146, 231, 236, 243, 245; leads workers and peasants government, 144–45; mass work by, 16, 228, 230, 232, 233–34, 239, 241; "nose for power" by, 3, 31, 233; recruitment to, 3, 16, 31, 233, 245; strategy of, 16–17, 225, 232, 233, 234; unity of, 202–3, 238–39, 246; as vanguard, 16, 146, 224, 231, 236, 245, 246. See also Nicaragua
Sandino, Augusto César, 217, 218, 222, 223, 247; on workers and peasants, 3, 224–25
Schapper, Karl, 152

Schick, René, 228–29, 248
Second International, 134, 138, 139. See also Social Democracy
Siu, Arlen, 236
Social Democracy, 134; in Latin America, 205. See also Second International
Social Democratic Party (Germany), 73–74, 134, 135–36
Socialist Revolutionary Party (Russia), 95, 98, 99, 102
Socialist Workers Party (SWP), 14, 27, 150
Somoza Debayle, Anastasio, 26, 229, 241, 242, 245, 248
Somoza García, Anastasio, 219, 220–21, 222, 229, 247
Somozaism, 12, 219, 239–40; and imperialism, 220, 228
Soviet Union, 147, 151. See also Russian Soviet republic
Spain, 90–91
State and Revolution (Lenin), 37–38, 62–65
State apparatus, bourgeois: nature of, 14, 32, 194–95; need to replace, 6–7, 61–62, 65, 104, 107, 194–95
Strategy and tactics, 15, 193–200; and armed struggle, 209–11, 225, 234; electoralist, 3, 6, 10–15, 210; in El Salvador, 17, 18–19, 194, 211; of FSLN, 16–17, 225, 232, 233, 234; Marx and Engels on, 37, 41–42, 51, 58–59, 62, 112; and mass action, 16, 17, 196, 200, 207–9, 225, 233; and Russian revolution, 78, 79–80; and seizure of power, 3, 4, 7, 10, 15, 17, 62, 78, 112, 133, 194, 210

T

Tejada, René, 236
Téllez, Dora María, 244

Thiers, Adolphe, 64, 155
Tijerino, Doris, 230, 248
Tirado, Víctor, 232, 248
Torres, Hugo, 244
Torrijos, Omar, 236
Trade unions, 69–70, 118, 139
Transition to socialism, 131, 151, 171; and Cuban revolution, 28–29; Marx and Engels on, 35, 37, 63, 66, 67, 74, 112–13; pace of, 66, 114; and Russian revolution, 84, 104, 106–9, 111, 113–14, 117–18, 123, 125–26, 131–32, 137; workers and farmers government and, 26, 29, 32–33, 74, 130, 136, 147
Trotsky, Leon, 126–27, 128, 136–37
Turcios, Oscar, 230

U

Ultraleftism, 10, 17, 127, 134, 142
Underdeveloped countries, 171–72, 176–77; fight for soviet power in, 133, 144; socialist revolution in, 8, 18–19, 171–72, 173, 175, 181–82. *See also* Latin America
Unemployed, 172, 178, 192
United front: anti-imperialist, 8, 199–200; working-class, 134–35, 139, 190
United People's Movement (MPU, Nicaragua), 246
United States, 13–14, 45, 140; revolutionary prospects for, 148–49. *See also* U.S. imperialism
Unity, 200–204; of Bolsheviks, 122; and FSLN, 202–3, 238–39, 246. *See also* United front
U.S. imperialism: attacks on Cuba by, 28, 228; and Latin America, 6, 172–73, 198–99, 218, 221, 228; and Nicaragua, 6, 27, 145, 218, 239, 245

V

Varlin, Louise-Eugène, 89
Venezuela, 10–11
Vietnam, 239

W

Wage Labour and Capital (Marx), 52–53
War Communism, 118, 119, 122, 123, 124, 125–26
Wedemeyer, Joseph, 37
Worker-peasant alliance: centrality of, 7, 56–59, 132, 137, 139, 140–41, 142; and 1848 revolutions, 51, 53; in Latin America, 146, 191–92; no coercion in, 58–59, 142; and Paris Commune, 68–69; in Russian revolution, 79, 88, 102–3, 104, 107, 122, 127, 129–30, 131. *See also* Peasants
Workers and peasants government: in Algeria, 147; Comintern resolutions on, 133–43; in Cuba, 28–29; and dictatorship of proletariat, 105, 136, 137, 138–39; in Hungary and Bavaria, 134; in Nicaragua and Grenada, 26, 144–47; in Russia, 103–5; tasks of, 25, 32–33, 135; as transitional slogan, 138–39, 140, 141–42; as world perspective, 148–49. *See also* Russian Soviet government
Workers Brotherhood, 50, 51–52
Working class: agricultural, 190–91, 219, 220; in Cuban revolution, 29; and 1848 revolutions, 42, 45, 47–49, 50, 51, 52; growth of, 54, 55–56, 93–94; in Latin America, 173, 176–77, 183,

190–91, 193, 202; in Nicaragua, 219, 220, 239; and Paris Commune, 69–70, 76–77; revolutionary potential of, 25, 34–36, 149; in Russian revolution, 80, 82–83, 93–94, 97–98, 102, 107, 110–11, 114, 117, 119, 123, 129, 149; as vanguard of oppressed and exploited, 7, 102, 140, 149, 194

World Marxist Review, 4, 169

World War I, 94, 97, 98; Bolshevik position on, 99, 104, 105

Z

Zinoviev, Gregory, 136, 140–41, 142–43

FROM PATHFINDER

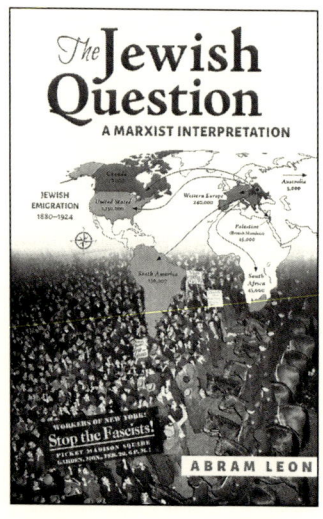

The Jewish Question
A Marxist Interpretation
ABRAM LEON

Why is Jew-hatred still raising its ugly head? What are its class roots—from antiquity through feudalism, to capitalism's rise and current crises? Why is there no solution under capitalism? The author, Abram Leon, was killed in the Nazi gas chambers. Revised translation, new introduction, and 40 pages of illustrations and maps. $17. Also in Spanish and French.

Is Socialist Revolution in the US Possible?
A Necessary Debate among Working People
MARY-ALICE WATERS

Fighting for a society only working people can create, it is our own capacities we will discover. And along that course we will answer the question posed here with a resounding "Yes." Possible but not inevitable. That depends on us. $7. Also in Spanish, French, and Farsi.

The Clintons' Anti-Working-Class Record
Why Washington Fears Working People
JACK BARNES

What working people need to know about the profit-driven course of Democrats and Republicans alike over the last three decades. And the political awakening of workers seeking to understand and resist the capitalist rulers' assaults. $10. Also in Spanish, French, Farsi, and Greek.

The Teamster Series
FARRELL DOBBS

"The principal lesson from the Teamster experience is not that, under an adverse relationship of forces, the workers can be overcome, but that, with proper leadership, they can overcome." —*Farrell Dobbs*

Four books on the strikes, organizing drives, and political campaigns that transformed the Teamsters across the Midwest in the 1930s into a militant industrial union movement. Written by the general organizer of these Teamster battles and leader of the Socialist Workers Party.

A tool for workers seeking to use union power in every workplace and advance the fight for an independent labor party.

$16 each, series $50. Also in Spanish. *Teamster Rebellion* is available in French, Farsi, and Greek.

Are They Rich Because They're Smart?
Class, Privilege, and Learning under Capitalism

JACK BARNES

In battles forced on us by the capitalists, workers will begin to transform our attitudes toward life, work, and each other. We'll discover our worth, denied by the rulers and upper middle classes who insist they're rich because they're smart. We'll learn in struggle what we're capable of becoming. $10. Also in Spanish, French, Farsi, and Arabic.

"It's the Poor Who Face the Savagery of the US 'Justice' System"
The Cuban Five Talk about Their Lives within the US Working Class

How US cops, courts, and prisons work as "an enormous machine for grinding people up." Five Cuban revolutionaries framed up and held in US jails for 16 years explain the human devastation of capitalist "justice"—and how socialist Cuba is different. $10. Also in Spanish, Farsi, and Greek.

WWW.PATHFINDERPRESS.COM

WOMEN'S LIBERATION AND SOCIALISM

Cosmetics, Fashions, and the Exploitation of Women
Joseph Hansen, Evelyn Reed, Mary-Alice Waters

How big business reinforces women's second-class status and uses it to rake in profits. Where does women's oppression come from? How has the entry of millions of women into the workforce strengthened the battle for emancipation, still to be won? $12. Also in Spanish, Farsi, and Greek.

Woman's Evolution
From Matriarchal Clan to Patriarchal Family
Evelyn Reed

An expedition from prehistory to class society that reveals women's still largely unknown contributions to civilization. Pinpointing the historical factors that led to the subordination of women as a sex, Reed offers fresh insights on the struggle against their oppression and for the liberation of humanity. $25. Also in Farsi and Indonesian.

Feminism and the Marxist Movement
Mary-Alice Waters

Since the founding of the modern workers movement 150 years ago, Marxists have championed the struggle for women's rights and explained the economic roots in class society of women's oppression. $5. Also in Farsi.

Communist Continuity and the Fight for Women's Liberation
How did the oppression of women begin? Who benefits? What social forces have the power to end women's second-class status? 3 volumes, edited with preface by Mary-Alice Waters. $12

THE CLASS STRUGGLE IN THE UNITED STATES

Malcolm X Talks to Young People

"The young generation of whites, Blacks, browns, whatever else—you're living at a time of revolution," said Malcolm in 1964. "And I for one will join with anyone, I don't care what color you are, as long as you want to change this miserable condition that exists on this earth." Four talks and an interview in the last months of Malcolm's life. $12. Also in Spanish, French, Farsi, and Greek.

50 Years of Covert Operations in the US

Washington's Political Police and the American Working Class

LARRY SEIGLE, FARRELL DOBBS, STEVE CLARK

How class-conscious workers have fought against the drive to build the "national security" state essential to maintaining capitalist rule. $10. Also in Spanish and Farsi.

Puerto Rico: Independence Is a Necessity

RAFAEL CANCEL MIRANDA

One of the five Puerto Rican Nationalists imprisoned by Washington for more than 25 years and released in 1979 speaks out on the brutal reality of US colonial domination, the example of Cuba's socialist revolution, and the ongoing struggle for independence. $5. Also in Spanish and Farsi.

WWW.PATHFINDERPRESS.COM

New International
A MAGAZINE OF MARXIST POLITICS AND THEORY

NEW INTERNATIONAL NO. 12
Capitalism's Long Hot Winter Has Begun
JACK BARNES

Today's global capitalist crisis is but the opening stage of decades of economic, financial, and social convulsions and class battles. Class-conscious workers confront this historic turning point for imperialism with confidence, Jack Barnes writes, drawing satisfaction from being "in their face" as we chart a revolutionary course to take power. $14. Also in Spanish, French, Farsi, Arabic, and Greek.

NEW INTERNATIONAL NO. 14
Setting the Record Straight on Fascism and World War II
STEVE CLARK

World War II was not "a popular war against Fascism." It was several wars in one. It was a massacre by imperialism in order to redivide the world. It was a war to defend the Soviet Union against attempts by the capitalist powers to undo the world's first socialist revolution. It gave impetus to struggles for national liberation throughout the world. The book sets apart myths from reality concerning the causes and the results of these wars, and shows how communists in the United States charted a revolutionary course of class struggle as they were unfolding. $14. Also in Spanish and French.

NEW INTERNATIONAL NO. 13
Our Politics Start with the World
JACK BARNES

The huge economic and cultural inequalities between imperialist and semicolonial countries, and among classes within them, are accentuated by the workings of capitalism. To build parties able to lead a successful revolutionary struggle for power in our own countries, vanguard workers must be guided by a strategy to close this gap. $14. Also in Spanish, French, Farsi, and Greek.

NEW INTERNATIONAL NO. 10
Imperialism's March toward Fascism and War

JACK BARNES

"There will be new Hitlers, new Mussolinis. That is inevitable. What is not inevitable is that they will triumph. The working-class vanguard will organize our class to fight back against the devastating toll we are made to pay for the capitalist crisis. The future of humanity will be decided in the contest between these contending class forces." $14. Also in Spanish, French, Farsi, and Greek.

NEW INTERNATIONAL NO. 11
U.S. Imperialism Has Lost the Cold War

JACK BARNES

The collapse of regimes across Eastern Europe and the USSR claiming to be communist did not mean workers and farmers there had been crushed. In today's sharpening capitalist conflicts and wars, these toilers are joining working people the world over in the class struggle against exploitation. $14. Also in Spanish, French, Farsi, and Greek.

NEW INTERNATIONAL NO. 7
Opening Guns of World War III: Washington's Assault on Iraq

JACK BARNES

Washington's murderous 1991 war on Iraq heralded conflicts among imperialist powers, growing capitalist crisis, and spreading wars. Working people in the region—from the Kurds, to Palestine and Israel, to Iran, Iraq, and Syria—are fighting for space to defend national rights and class interests. $14. Also in Spanish, French, and Farsi.

WWW.PATHFINDERPRESS.COM

PATHFINDER AROUND THE WORLD

UNITED STATES
(and Caribbean, Latin America, and East Asia)
*Pathfinder Books, 306 W. 37th St., 13th Floor
New York, NY 10018*

CANADA
*Pathfinder Books, 7107 St. Denis, Suite 204
Montreal, QC H2S 2S5*

UNITED KINGDOM
(and Europe, Africa, Middle East, and South Asia)
*Pathfinder Books, 5 Norman Rd.
Seven Sisters, London N15 4ND*

AUSTRALIA
(and Southeast Asia and the Pacific)
*Pathfinder Books, Suite 103, 124-128 Beamish St.
Campsie, Sydney
Postal address: P.O. Box 73, Campsie, NSW 2194*

NEW ZEALAND
*Pathfinder Books, 188a Onehunga Mall Rd.
Onehunga, Auckland 1061
Postal address: P.O. Box 13857, Auckland 1643*

JOIN THE PATHFINDER READERS CLUB
BUILD YOUR LIBRARY!

$10 / YEAR
25% DISCOUNT ON ALL PATHFINDER TITLES
30% OFF BOOKS OF THE MONTH

Valid at pathfinderpress.com and local Pathfinder book centers

Go to: www.pathfinderpress.com/
products/pathfinder-readers-club